THE TROUBLED RELATIONSHIP BETWEEN RELIGIONS AND THE STATE

ANDRÁS KOLTAY has been a lecturer at the Pázmány Péter Catholic University Faculty of Law and Political Sciences in Budapest, Hungary since 2002. In 2012, he was appointed Associate Professor and in 2017, Head of Department of Private Law. He was conferred the LL.M. degree in Public Law by University College London in 2006, and the PhD degree in law at the Pázmány Péter Catholic University in 2008. His principal research has been concerned with freedom of speech, personality rights and media regulation, but he also deals with other constitutional questions. He is the author of more than 200 publications, and three monographs on freedom of speech (in English: *Freedom of Speech – the Unreachable Mirage*, Wolters Kluwer, 2013).

OXFORD LEGAL PUBLISHING
HUMAN RIGHTS SERIES

THE TROUBLED RELATIONSHIP BETWEEN RELIGIONS AND THE STATE

Freedom of Expression and Freedom of Religion

ANDRÁS KOLTAY

OXFORD LEGAL PUBLISHING

OXFORD

Published by
OXFORD LEGAL PUBLISHING LIMITED
www.oxfordlegalpublishing.com
contact@oxfordlegalpublishing.com

Oxford Legal Publishing Limited,
Clarendon House 52 Cornmarket Street Oxford OX1 3HJ United Kingdom
Published in the United Kingdom by Oxford Legal Publishing Limited

First published in 2017 by Whitelocke Publications Limited
This edition 2021 by Oxford Legal Publishing Limited

British Library Cataloguing in Publication Data
Data Available

ISBN: 978-1-912142-37-8

The painting on the cover is
Louis-Jacques-Mandé Daguerre's
Ruins of Holyrood Chapel (c. 1824).

To the memory of Tamás Lábady,
judge, teacher, and Christian

Contents

Table of Cases

European Commission of Human Rights

European Court of Human Rights

European Court of Justice

Germany

United Kingdom

United States of America

Johanns v Livestock Marketing Association 544 US 550, 562 (2005)...35
Joseph Burstyn, Inc. v Wilson 343 US 495, 505 (1952)...[illegible]
Kitzmiller v Dover Area School District 400 F Supp 2d 707 (M D Pa [illegible])...38
Lee v Weisman [illegible] US 577 (1992)...[illegible]
Lemon v Kurtzman 403 US 602 (1971)...[illegible]
Lynch v Donnelly 465 US 668 (1984)...[illegible]
Marsh v Chambers 463 US 783 (1983)...[illegible]
McCreary County v ACLU 545 US 844 (2005)...[illegible]
[illegible]
[illegible]
Pleasant Grove City v Summum 555 US 460 (2009)...[illegible]
[illegible]
[illegible]
Rust v Sullivan 500 US 173 (1991)...[illegible]
Salazar v Buono 559 US 700 (2010)...37, 44–45, 47, 48
Santa Fe Independent School District v Doe 530 US 290 (2000)...104–105
[illegible]
Spence v Washington 418 US 405 (1974)...[illegible]
Stone v Graham 449 US 39 (1980)...[illegible]
Texas v Johnson [illegible]
Town of Greece v Galloway 572 US (2014)...[illegible]
Van Orden v Perry 545 US 677 (2005)...37, 40, 44–45
Virginia v Black 538 US 343 (2003)...131
Wallace v Jaffree 472 US 38 (1985)...102–103
Walz v Tax Commission of City of New York 397 US 664 (1970)...44
West Virginia State Board of Education v Barnette
319 US 624 (1943)...[illegible]

Table of Legislation

THE TROUBLED RELATIONSHIP BETWEEN RELIGIONS AND THE STATE

Introduction

1. On Freedom of Religion, Conscience and Thought

Both the European Convention on Human Rights (hereinafter: ECHR, Article 9) and the International Covenant on Civil and Political Rights (Article 18) contain provisions on the freedom of thought, conscience and religion, as do individual national constitutions. Freedom of religion is inseparable from the right to freedom of expression and it includes the freedom to manifest one's belief, while recognising religious beliefs as an inherent part of one's personality. The right to freedom of conscience is more extensive than freedom of religion, and protects not only religious but all types of convictions, including ideological, political and others. Notwithstanding this difference, both freedom of conscience and freedom of religion guarantee the right to refrain from accepting or following *any* conviction.[1]

However, according to certain interpretations, freedom of conscience and freedom of religion are not among the 'communication rights'. In this interpretation, these freedoms are not closely linked to freedom of expression, because they primarily belong to the private sphere of the individual, and their external manifestation is not a necessity in the course of practising them.[2] In our judgement, this interpretation significantly narrows the coverage of these rights particularly the public manifestation of these freedoms. The expression of one's belief and conviction is an integral part of freedom of religion and conscience. Institutionalised religious conviction (represented by recognised communities and churches) is not purely a private matter, and its

1 David Harris, Michael O'Boyle, Ed Bates, Carla Buckley, *Law of the European Convention on Human Rights* (Oxford University Press 2014, 3rd edn) 594–7.

2 Norman Wirzba, 'Is Christian Faith a Private Matter?', *Huffington Post*, 22 February 2016, http://www.huffingtonpost.com/norman-wirzba/is-christian-faith-a-priv_b_9284910.html.

freedom is simultaneously an individual and a collective right.[3] Not allowing such convictions to be represented or manifested in the public sphere would narrow opportunities for individual fulfilment and thereby violate human dignity. Additionally, it would also endanger the diversity of social life and public debate on important issues. If there were no collective manifestation of freedom of religion and conscience, then, in the absence of legal and constitutional recognition of institutional churches, it would be unjustified to select freedom of religion from the constellation of other forms of manifesting freedom of expression. Its external manifestation would be properly safeguarded by the right to freedom of expression, whereas its internal expression would be guarded by the protection of privacy.[4]

One element of practising freedom of religion which generally prevails, is the manifestation of religious conviction *within* the religious community and communication of it *outside* this community (after all, most religions strive to attract as many people as possible to join them). However, freedom of conscience and freedom of religion include much more than just the right of individuals to communicate the manifestation of their religion. They also encompass the free choice of conviction, the freedom to change it, and the right to practise someone's conviction, or teach it to others, through religious activities or in any other way.[5] While these freedoms overlap in several respects with freedom of expression, they are clearly independent fundamental rights, and should thus be treated separately.

The freedom of religion and conscience entails that everybody has the right to attempt to convince others of their own convictions and to persuade others to follow them. Religious believers and churches therefore have the recognised individual and collective right to convince others of their rectitude.[6] Consequently, churches

3 Harris et al (n 1) 594, 604–5.

4 Mine Yildirim, *The Collective Dimension of Freedom of Religion or Belief in International Law* (Åbo Akademi University Press 2015) 18–22.

5 Harris et al (n 1) 602–5.

6 *Kokkinakis v Greece*, App no 14307/88, judgment of 25 May 1993, para 31.

cannot be deprived of the right to participate in public life and questions of belief, and religious conviction cannot be considered as a purely private matter. Of course, the subjects of such attempts have the right to reject those convictions, and they also have the right to not be targeted by those attempting to convince them in a burdensome, harassing or violent way.[7] Freedom of religion and conscience cannot serve as a reason for forcing somebody to pay attention to such attempts. Individuals who practise their freedom of religion and conscience can also expect that the state and other members of society will respect their convictions. For example, conscientious objectors, whose convictions do not allow them to perform armed military service, cannot be obliged to engage in such activities.[8] Employers also have to respect religious rules to a certain degree. The celebration of religious feasts have to be allowed to the extent it is possible, in addition to toleration of employees refusing to carry out certain obligations due to religious convictions (e.g., physicians might refuse to carry out abortions for religious reasons).[9] However, respect for one's conviction is not an absolute right—religious conviction is not necessarily a good enough excuse for somebody refusing to work on Sundays or for a functionary refusing to administer the marriage of same-sex couples.[10] Although the obligation to respect other people's convictions does not extend to prohibiting criticism of those convictions, instigation of hatred, incitement to hatred and violence against those pursuing certain convictions are not allowed.[11]

7 *Ibid*, para 48.

8 *Bayatyan v Armenia*, App no 23459/03, judgment of 7 July 2011 [GC].

9 'Seven in 10 Italian gynaecologists refuse to carry out abortions', *The Guardian*, 11 March 2016, https://www.theguardian.com/world/2016/mar/11/italian-gynaecologists-refuse-abortions-miscarriages.

10 *Stedman v the United Kingdom*, App no 29107/95, admissibility decision of 9 April 1997; *Eweida and Others v the United Kingdom*, App nos 48420/10, 59842/10, 51671/10 and 36516/10, judgment of 15 January 2013.

11 *Blasphemy, insult and hatred: finding answers in a democratic society* (Council of Europe Publishing 2010), http://www.venice.coe.int/webforms/documents/?pdf=CDL-STD(2010)047-e.

The state has multifaceted and complex tasks relating to granting freedom of religion and conscience. The separation of church and state and the religious neutrality of the state, is one of the indisputable achievements of modern societies. (Although its theoretical basis is generally thought to be rooted in the ideology of Enlightenment,[12] some argue that they were already laid down in the New Testament.[13]) A society which has frequently experienced, the burdens of living in an ideologically-driven state in various ways might greatly appreciate state neutrality.[14] The religious neutrality of the state prevails even in European states where the state and churches are not formally separated (e.g., the United Kingdom, Greece, Denmark, and Finland).[15]

The state is required to meet both negative obligations (obliging it to refrain from acting) and positive obligations (prescribing an active, proactive conduct) with respect to the freedom of religion and conscience. After establishing the conditions of religious practice, ensuring that churches can obtain legal personality and are recognised as legal subjects, establishing places of worship, providing for religious education, and making it possible to practise one's religion in institutions of health care, social care and within the armed forces, the state should step back and refrain from interfering with the practice of this right. Furthermore, it must protect the rights of its citizens by prohibiting the violation of freedom of conscience and religion.

Churches in several European countries receive financial support in the form of state subsidies. According to some justifications of this arrangement, churches assume several public duties from

12 Kate A Tunstall (ed), *Self-Evident Truths?: Human Rights and the Enlightenment. The Oxford Amnesty Lectures* (Bloomsbury Academic 2012).

13 Larry Siedentop, *Inventing the Individual: The Origins of Western Liberalism* (Allen Lane 2014).

14 For example, the post-communist countries around Central and Eastern Europe.

15 Jeroen Temperman, *State-Religion Relationships and Human Rights Law. Towards a Right to Religiously Neutral Governance* (Brill 2010) 31–48.

the state, including operating schools, hospitals and institutions of social care. The entirety of religious life might deserve support because, according to the *status quo* of the relation between churches and the state, churches represent and pass on values that enrich society as a whole, including those who reject the conviction of the church. Examples of such enrichment include increasing respect for individuals, families and other communities, and promoting honesty and the fundamental values of human dignity. According to this interpretation, if the state subsidises culture or mass sports out of the recognition that by doing so it promotes the public good, then churches also have the right to state subsidy on a similar basis.[16]

2. On the Principle of State Neutrality

The religious neutrality of the state is undoubtedly an important achievement of constitutional development in modern history, whereby the public sphere and churches function separately from one another. The state does not prefer any religion or creed but provides equal status for churches and enables individuals to practise their religion freely, thus respecting various convictions and the freedom of its citizens and the communities established by them. This is a natural characteristic of modern democracies, built upon granting fundamental human rights.

No consensus exists on the exact content of the concept of state neutrality. According to the most extreme interpretation, religion does not have the right to be present in the public sphere (in the course of the functioning of the individual organs of the various branches of government and in public space, in general). On the one hand, this implies that 'constitutionality can only exist where society does not take transcendent considerations into account'.[17] Excluding religions from all areas of societal life is considered desirable, while

16 See generally: Leni Franken, *Liberal Neutrality and State Support for Religion* (Springer International 2016).

17 András Sajó, 'Preliminaries to a Concept of Constitutional Secularism', (2008) 6(3–4) *International Journal of Constitutional Law* 605, 618.

on the other hand, neutrality ensures that even indirect state subsidy is not allowed, thus the state cannot finance ecclesiastical schools. In this interpretation, neutrality means freedom *from* the negative aspect of religions and nothing more, with the freedom to accept religions relegated entirely to the private sphere.[18] Religious neutrality is thus identical to extreme secularisation, the complete exclusion and separation of religion from public life. (Secularisation is the consequence of the principle of the state's religious neutrality, and more moderate interpretations define it as the separation of the state and religion—individual interpretations of this concept might differ in terms of the degree and levels of this separation.)

Such extreme interpretations of secularisation have been criticised as being incompatible with the multifaceted nature of a society and for imposing a restriction on the freedom of religious (and consequently cultural) communities. The state thereby imposes the values of a certain ideology (extreme secularisation) on its citizens, whereas instead it should ensure general freedom which allows everybody to live in accordance with their own cultural and social norms, as long as they do not abuse this freedom, or as long as they do not clash with others pursuing similar choices.[19] While the justification of a piece of law or a court decision cannot be based on religious grounds, this does not require the complete exclusion of religion from public life.[20] Despite this, if we still go down this road, we diminish the choices available to the individual, because the individual will not encounter certain convictions, arguments and opinions in the public sphere.

According to a more moderate view of religious neutrality and secularism, the state and various churches function separately, but when overlap between the areas they cover occurs, they take note of each other's presence and cooperate. In Jeroen Temperman's typology, certain European states follow a model of religious tolerance, whereas in other states, a 'joint venture' model operates,

18 *Ibid*, 622.

19 Lorenzo Zucca, 'The Crisis of the Secular State: A Reply to Professor Sajó', (2009) 7(3) *International Journal of Constitutional Law* 494, 502.

20 *Ibid*, 505–6.

while a third category of states have opted for the model of separation. In all three approaches, the state reconciles with the functioning of churches, and to some extent, adapts to the religious convictions existing in society. At least, the state promotes a socio-political environment in which various religious convictions can exist without discrimination against any convictions.[21] In this reading, state neutrality is not a stringent liberal doctrine, and the decisive feature of the state is that it refrains from promoting or strengthening certain values. State neutrality means no discrimination in matters of religion; it means the exclusion of partiality, bias or taking sides.[22]

State neutrality does not imply indifference, because the neutral state is not a state without values. The positive and negative freedoms of religion are partial rights of the same value, which should be granted by the state. If, in accordance with the extreme interpretation of secularism, we attributed greater value to negative freedoms, we would diminish the content of the right to freedom of religion. The religious neutrality of the state is an approach which helps people with different creeds to coexist peacefully. This means that the state exists separately from the churches, but cooperates with them, recognising that churches represent, create and preserve values, which may be useful and important for the state, and which, in many cases, pursue the same objectives. Neutrality does not exclude firm choices of values, neither in state church law, nor family law, nor taxation policy.

The state cannot be completely and generally neutral in terms of values. When subsidising culture, maintaining and running public service media, prescribing the celebration of certain historical events, organising public education or deciding upon the curriculum, it is driven by certain well-defined values. Taking decisions on such actions, irrespective of their religious content, does not happen due to 'neutrality'. If we completely eliminate

21 Jeroen Temperman, 'The Neutral State: Optional or Necessary? A Triangular Analysis of State-Religion Relationships, Democratisation, and Human Rights Compliance', (2006) 1(3) *Religion & Human Rights* 269; Temperman (n 15) 111–37.

22 Temperman (n 21) 302.

religion-based considerations from the values taken into account by the state, as 'allowed' by secularisation, essentially and finally we reduce the pluralism and diversity of values represented in the public sphere, and thereby narrow the range of options available to the individual.

Even if it were desirable, it would not be possible to exclude religious convictions from the entirety of the public sphere and it would seriously damage the fundaments of modern constitutionality. Some authors argue that fundamental human rights are rooted in Christianity.[23] Larry Siedentop goes so far as to assert that the idea of human rights and the individual as a value are derived from Christianity, and that it is not by accident that the respect for these is widespread only in the Western world, which is traditionally Christian.[24] Ronald Dworkin, a declared atheist and 'perhaps the most influential law philosopher of the past half a century',[25] elaborated in his last posthumous book his idea that religiousness can exist without a belief in God. The acceptance of the fundamental values of religious conviction, in this view, is independent of what we think of God,[26] and independent of what we think of these convictions. We may conclude that the permanent clash between religious conviction-based arguments and secular arguments is not a necessity. Moreover, modern secular democracy and related views on fundamental rights in most cases overlap with arguments rooted in Christianity. For example, the acceptance of the idea, and all its consequences, that all people are equal, is a fundamental element of both ideologies even though, on other important issues (such as abortion or same-sex marriage) they might clash very fiercely. If representing the religious and secular convictions in many cases does not lead to contradictory outcomes, it is not plausible to argue for the complete religious neutrality of the state, which completely excludes churches from the public sphere.

23 Michael J Perry, *Toward a Theory of Human Rights: Religion, Law, Courts* (Cambridge University Press 2006).

24 Siedentop (n 13).

25 Stanley Fish, 'Deeper than God: Ronald Dworkin's Religious Atheism', *New York Times*, 23 September 2013.

26 Ronald Dworkin, *Religion without God* (Harvard University Press 2013).

3. On the Subject Matter of the Book

The issues discussed in this book all stand at the crossroads of freedom of speech and freedom of religion. In some cases, the two rights clash when somebody practising their right to freedom of speech affects others' rights to freedom of religion, as in instances of blasphemy and hate speech. In other cases, the two rights, reinforcing one another, together provide protection for the individual. Not even this joint protection, however, is always sufficient to prevent state intervention, for example, the restriction of rights in wearing religious symbols or religious advertising rules. A question of a third type is when the state, or a state body, enters the public space and becomes the 'speaker' on matters of religion, in which case the state might be subject to special restrictions.

Although their ideological and constitutional foundations seem stable, the extent of freedom of religion and freedom of speech have repeatedly been the subject of public debates because of social and political changes in a dynamically transforming Europe. Identifying the precise demarcation lines between these rights by means of the law is not a task that has been accomplished completely or for all time. The increasing rate of immigration, with a resulting involuntary cohabitation of various religious cultures, as well as the continual weakening of the Christian character of the continent make it critical to find the right responses to the questions discussed in this book, both in the individual European legal systems and at the level of the European community of states and of the European system of protecting human rights.

Everybody is afraid of something nowadays. Some are afraid of Europe's Christian roots being forgotten, others are afraid of increasing religious hatred (which has a historical presence in Europe), some are afraid of the failure of multiculturalism, others fear diminishing populations, others are concerned by the gradual 'closing' of open democracies and societies and the increasing influence of churches, and for others the management of the resulting difficulties or the unavoidable social and cultural changes emerging as the consequence of immigration are of concern. In public discourse, we often offend each other or attempt to exclude certain opinions from the public domain, even if those do not go beyond the limits of freedom of speech. Some people feel offended if their religious beliefs are criticised, while others believe that the foundations of the secular democratic state are at risk if somebody is concerned about Europe's historically developed present being jeopardised by increasing migration.

Europe today is not the same as it was in our childhood, and a few decades from now it might look completely different again. The considerations raised regarding freedom of speech and religion cannot respond to the broad questions of immigration, social integration and the survival and future of the European Union and European culture, which obviously cause serious headaches to even the most developed European states. However, this topic is of outstanding significance. On the one hand, the respect and protection of fundamental rights is an underlying feature of Europe and Western civilisation, which—if lost or significantly diminished—will also mean the loss of our civilisation or a huge loss to our civilisation. On the other hand, the way the questions (which, in chronological terms, always follow social and political changes) relating to these rights are managed is an excellent indicator of the nature of those changes. The attitude to fundamental rights is also indicative of how a state and its constitutional system, and its most important decision-making bodies view Europe's Christian heritage, the problem of immigration and the role of the state.

The first and second chapters of the book discuss the appearance of religions in the public sphere and in public education. Traditionally, the state is not a subject of fundamental rights, and yet it takes a position on questions relating to religion, which—no matter how we explain it—is a type of 'speech'. This raises the question of how such speech can be restricted, or 'where are the limits on the "freedom of speech" of the state'? The role of the state might be to defend or even shape the community identity of its citizens. A clear example of a pan-European discussion of this was the debate on the recitals of the European Constitutional Treaty which aimed to lay down the foundations of the functioning of the European Union.[27] This proved abortive as no consensus emerged amongst the Member States of the European Union on the question of whether it is necessary or

27 See JHH Weiler, *Un'Europa Cristiana* (BUR Saggi 2003).

justified to refer to the Christian traditions of the Continent in the document. The majority decision was that the idea of the unity of Europe is better served by leaving out such a reference with no binding consequences, i.e., on this question, 'Europe' opted to avoid an expression of opinion—unless we take silence as an opinion.

The use of religious symbols in schools can be interpreted as a constitutional problem if the state makes it mandatory to display them in state schools. In several European states, Christian crucifixes and crosses are displayed mandatorily in classrooms. In a wider sense, the appropriateness of religious education in state schools can also be questioned. Essentially, by making religious education mandatory or supporting it (e.g., in several states of the United States even common prayer is prescribed for students), even if students can be exempted from religious education on request, the state 'expresses an opinion' in a specific way on the importance and social role of religion and its impact. Religion in education could be approached solely in terms of culture, as religions and religious or religiously inspired texts are unavoidable when teaching history or literature. In this vein, the Bible is not only the Holy Book of Christianity but it is also a literary work. It would also be a shame to exclude religious poems from the curriculum in the spirit of secularisation, and it might be noted that Jesus Christ was a historical figure in addition to the Christian saviour. However, any explicit religious education, even if it is denomination-neutral, raises the question of the limits of the state's religious neutrality. Crucifixes on the walls of classrooms are easier to think of as an 'expression' or 'opinion' because non-verbal, symbolic acts of communication are generally accepted as falling under the scope of freedom of speech. Even with all these considered, religious education, which raises similar questions, can be regarded as the manifestation of 'the freedom of speech of the state', even if we do not consider this state policy as a 'speech act'. The American doctrine of *government speech*, in which state organisations and stare bodies enjoy freedom of speech, is not a generally used or accepted doctrine in Europe.[28]

28 Mark G Yudof, *When Government Speaks: Politics, Law, and Government Expression in America* (University of California Press 1983); Frederick Schauer, 'Is Government Speech a Problem?', (1983) 35 *Stanford Law Review* 373.

Nevertheless, the state also communicates and, considering what it says and how, we can raise the question of why and in what cases it is necessary to adopt rules imposing restrictions on this freedom of the state.

Chapters 3 and 4 discuss the restriction of opinions with religious content. Chapter 3 analyses the restrictions on wearing symbols and clothing imposed by both the state and private entities, whereas Chapter 4 discusses the regulation of publishing religious advertisements in the media. Unlike the issues related predominantly to Christianity discussed in the first two chapters, the questions of wearing symbols and clothing also involve the restrictions of opinions expressed by followers of Islam. While it is primarily the ban imposed in certain states on wearing the Muslim headscarf covering the entire face which is raised in public fora, there is evidence that intolerance and discrimination against Christians is also gaining strength all over Europe.[29] We might also be left with the impression that the reaction against Islam, which public discourse considers to be a threat to Europe, might also be an excuse to try and restrict Christianity. Since the argument against the latter cannot draw on contemporary violent acts as validation, it typically refers to either the historical sins of Christian churches, or an interpretation of state neutrality and secularisation. Thus, in this very specific way Christianity and Islam are lumped together. We also discuss this question, namely whether, by recognising all religions and convictions equally and to the same degree, and providing freedom of religion for all of them, it is still possible for the state to display different attitudes to individual religions and churches (a question raised in Chapter 1 as well).

Chapter 5 of the book is dedicated to questions relating to defamation of religions and blasphemy. The topicality and significance of these issues became obvious after the tragic events in Paris on January 2015, where many were killed in an attack against the editorial offices of the magazine *Charlie Hebdo*. It will become

29 So much so that the Parliamentary Assembly of the Council of Europe adopted a resolution urging action against that, see Tackling intolerance and discrimination in Europe with a special focus on Christians. Resolution 2036 (2015) of the Parliamentary Assembly.

apparent how complex an issue blasphemy is, and the variety of ways there are to tackle the question in the legal systems of European states.

The book does not, however, deal with questions whose legal judgement enjoys broad public consensus, or which are far removed from the scope of the right to freedom of speech. An example of the former is the question of 'proselytism', for which a generally recognised rule in Europe is that while everybody has the right to try and convince others of the rectitude of their own convictions, this cannot be done in a violent, harassing way, intruding upon the other person's private sphere. The European Court of Human Rights (hereinafter: ECtHR) clarified this matter in a case when they established that Greece was in breach of the law because the relevant criminal law provisions of the state prohibited convincing Orthodox believers to change their convictions. The ECtHR states that this general restriction is not necessary in a democratic society, providing that the attempt to convince is not carried out by 'improper' means. Therefore, to convince others of their rightness is a recognised individual and collective right of believers and churches, but, because of freedom of religion, nobody can be requested to take heed of this attempt.[30]

Whether the state should allow the construction of buildings for religious ceremonies is an example of a question far from the question of freedom of speech. Although, even a building has an *expressive* character and expresses something, we do not deal with, for example, the freedom of speech element of the Swiss ban on constructing minarets.[31] Neither do we include in this book the restriction of freedom of speech through other means than legislation or law enforcement. A relevant example is the case of the former coach of the English national football team, Glenn Hoddle. In an interview Hoddle expressed his conviction that those born with physical disabilities are being punished for sins they committed in their former lives. After the resulting public scandal, the Football Association promptly terminated the contract of the

30 *Kokkinakis* (n 6).

31 See Todd Green, 'The Resistance to Minarets in Europe', (2010) 52 *Journal of Church and State* 619.

coach. Therefore Hoddle suffered a disadvantageous consequence of practising his right to freedom of speech and freedom of religion. No matter what we think of his statement, a restriction of his fundamental rights was imposed by a public body.[32] It is possible that Hoddle might have won the case in a labour court, but in this instance, his freedom was not restricted on the basis of legislation. Moreover, it is an interesting question whether a fundamental right can ever be restricted in a civil law agreement even if it can be assumed that there was no clause restricting Hoddle's freedom of speech in his contract.[33]

Certain types of conduct are rooted in religious conviction and may have legal consequences, but which, in the absence of an *expressive* content, do not belong to the sphere of freedom of speech. Examples of this include doctors refusing to carry out an abortion, or registrars unwilling to administer the marriage of same-sex couples. Since we do not regard such types of conduct as relating to the freedom of speech, they are not discussed in this book.

***

A few of the texts that appear in this book have previously been published elsewhere. Parts of Chapter 1 were published under the title 'Europe and the Sign of the Crucifix: On the Fundamental Questions of the *Lautsi and Others v Italy* case' in the collected volume *The Lautsi Papers: Multidisciplinary Reflections on Religious Symbols in the Public School Classroom* edited by Jeroen Temperman (Martinus Nijhoff, 2012) and in a separate article titled 'Religious Neutrality and the Government's Freedom of Speech in the Jurisprudence of the US Supreme Court' in the journal *Religion & Human Rights* (2015), vol. 10, issue 1.

I would like to thank the valuable comments and suggestions of my colleagues at the Pázmány Péter Catholic University, Budapest,

32 Patrick Elias & Jason Coppel, 'Freedom of Expression and Freedom of Religion: Some Thoughts on the *Glenn Hoddle* Case' in Jack Beatson & Yvonne Cripps (eds), *Freedom of Expression and Freedom of Information. Essays in Honour of Sir David Williams* (Oxford University Press 2000).

33 *Ibid*, 59–60.

and also of the participants of the 2015 Free Speech Discussion Forum in Louisville, Kentucky which were necessary to correct the mistakes of the original manuscript. Thanks are also due to my colleagues who helped with the publication of the book, especially to Édua Reményi, who did a devoted job editing it and to Szabolcs Nagy and Stephen Patrick, who helped with the English adaptation of my original drafts. I am also grateful for the enormous support of the publisher. Without them this work would never have been born.

The research for this book was carried out with the support of the Hungarian Ministry of Justice's lawyer's education enhancement programs.

Budapest, 15 January 2017

András Koltay

Chapter 1

The Use of Religious Symbols in Public Places and Schools

1. Introduction

The debate on the use of religious symbols by the state has flared up on several occasions, both in Europe and the United States. Most of these debates have focused on Christian symbols, and sometimes these debates ended up in court proceedings, meaning that the courts had to take a position on the permissibility of the use of these symbols in public life. The issues in Europe relate to crucifixes being mandatorily displayed in classrooms, whereas, in the United States, legal proceedings involved memorials and festive installations with religious content erected in public places. In this chapter, we will first discuss the decision of the German Federal Constitutional Court handed down in the 1990s. This will be followed by an analysis of the jurisprudence of the US Supreme Court. Finally, we will review the *Lautsi* case deliberated upon by the European Court of Human Rights (hereinafter: ECtHR), and will discuss theoretical questions raised but left unanswered by the court. After this, we will attempt to draw certain conclusions from the experience reflected in jurisprudence.

2. The Bavarian Crucifix Case

In 1973, a lawyer of Jewish origin submitted a complaint concerning the crucifix placed on the table in his courtroom. In its decision, the German Federal Constitutional Court established that the fundamental right to freedom of religion of a person involved in the proceedings might be violated by having to appear and participate in courtroom proceedings where a crucifix is displayed, a symbol not compatible with the lawyer's religious conviction and creed.[1] Displaying the crucifix was not unconstitutional in itself; it did not expect anybody to identify with the dogmas or institutions of Christianity, nor did it have any coercive effect, but the concrete circumstances of the case were of concern. The way the crucifix was displayed in the courtroom, with one crucifix on the bench where parties to the proceedings present themselves, made the symbol 'obtrusive'. It created the impression that the oath taken by those involved in the proceedings and the whole proceedings were 'under the Cross'. The crucifix had to be removed from the courtroom if required by the party concerned for religious reasons. However, this statement applied only to parties who are involved in the proceedings and not to other people present in the courtroom.

The 'crucifix-decision' (*Kruzifix-Beschluss*) handed down on 16 May 1995 has been one of the most disputed decisions in the history of the German Federal Constitutional Court.[2] As an antecedent of the constitutional complaint submitted to the Constitutional Court, the Bavarian Ministry of Education and Culture adopted a regulation promulgated on 21 June 1983 on the state's public schools (*Volksschule*).[3] According to the third sentence in Article 13(1) of the regulation, crucifixes shall be fixed to the walls of classrooms in public schools. The legal basis of the regulation was the Act on Bavarian Education and Teaching and the Act on public schools (*Volksschulgesetz*).[4] It is important to note that state schools in Bavaria are both public and Christian schools. In Bavaria, public education is the responsibility of the state with the Christian spirit of public education being enshrined in the state's Constitution. The Federal Constitutional Court ruled that the above regulation is unconstitutional, as it violates the fundamental right to freedom of religion.

Earlier, the administrative court of first instance in Regensburg rejected the claim of the complainant parents.[5] The Court's position

1 BVerfGE, 1 BvR 308/69.

2 BVerfGE, 1 BvR 1087/91.

3 Volksschulordnung, 21 June 1983 (GVBl 597).

4 Bayerische Gesetz über das Erziehungs- und Unterrichtswesen (BayEUG), 9 March 1960.

5 VG Regensburg, 01.03.1991 – RN 1 E 91.167.

was that displaying crucifixes in classrooms violated neither the right of the parents to bring up their children, nor the fundamental rights of children. The Bavarian state regulation did not stipulate that the crucifix is an integral part of education, or that it is part of the school curriculum. Therefore, it does not go beyond the constitutional limit of religious and ideological references. The claimant cannot demand that their negative freedom of religion (refraining from religion) should enjoy an absolute priority over the positive freedom of religion of students who receive a religious upbringing; as opposed to this, they (the claimant) can be expected to show tolerance and respect.

The court of second instance, the Bavarian administrative court, also rejected the claim.[6] In the reasoning, it mentioned that, although the disputed situation had existed since 1986, the parents turned to the court only in 1991. Furthermore, the submission of the claim was preceded by a long negotiation with the school, during which the school showed signs of willingness to compromise. Based on the circumstances, the complainant could have been expected to accept an interim solution that was suitable for everybody. The court called the sight of the crucifix 'an insignificant inconvenience', which is not the only one children encounter in different places. The very presence of the crucifix in classrooms does not require anybody to identify with the dogma or religious conviction it represents. The court did not find sufficient grounds for the claim that the children of the claimant suffered severe emotional harm due to the sight of the crucifix displayed in the classroom.

The Federal Constitutional Court, contrary to previous decisions, declared that the Bavarian regulation was in breach of the Federal Constitution (*Grundgesetz*). The starting point of the decision is Article 4(1) of the *Grundgesetz*, which ensures freedom of religion and freedom of religious belief. On this basis, the individual is free to choose their belief or decide to refrain from becoming religious and using religious symbols. It also follows from the freedom of religion that in society, there are space and opportunity for convictions and beliefs of different kinds. However, situations that are created by the state and unavoidable for the individual (for

6 VGH Bayern, 03.06.1991 – 7 CE 91.1014.

instance, participation in public education is mandatory) are to undergo a specific judgment. In such cases, the neutrality of the state must prevail, because this is the only way to maintain the peaceful coexistence of different religions and beliefs. The right of parents to convey a message they think is appropriate for their children in questions of beliefs and ideology is also derived from the *Grundgesetz*. The right to keep them away from views that they deem inappropriate or harmful (section II. 1 of the resolution) is also rooted in the Constitution.

As the crucifixes were ordered by the state to be fixed onto the walls of classrooms, it was the state that forced children to study 'under the cross' (II. 2). From this perspective, the crucifix in the classroom is different from when it is erected in other public places. The crucifix in the classroom is there based on the will of the state, whereas in other cases, the presence of the crucifixes is the consequence of the presence of a religious community in society. The possibility of avoiding the encounter with this religious symbol is not equivalent in both situations. Related to this, the court remarked that the opportunity enshrined in Article 7(4) of the *Grundgesetz* concerning the establishment of private schools does not solve the problem of the unavoidability of encountering the crucifix because, due to stringent criteria, it is extremely difficult to have access to such schools, and the obligation to pay a tuition fee further restricts access.

According to the court, the crucifix is the symbol of one specific religious conviction, embodying the sacrifice of Christ's death and symbolising the Christian belief itself. The Cross is the subject of veneration for a practising Christian, and decorating a building or a place with the crucifix embodies the confession of this belief.

It would be a profanation of the Cross, running counter to the self-perception of Christianity and the Christian churches, to regard it, as the decisions challenged do, as a mere expression of Western tradition or cult token without a specific reference to faith. (II. 2b).

Although hanging a crucifix in a classroom does not require identification with or paying predefined respect to something, or showing a certain conduct, it is not true that the crucifix will determine the way various secular subjects are taught. Nevertheless, the crucifix has an indisputable effect on students. Education at schools not only serves the purpose of acquiring fundamental cultural techniques and developing cognitive skills, it should also provide an opportunity for students to develop their emotional and expressive skills.

Public education serves the purpose of providing comprehensive support for personal development, and especially influences one's behaviour in a community. The crucifix hanging in the classroom acquires its meaning in this context. It has an inviting, appealing character, and shows the content symbolised by it as a model that is exemplary and worth following. In addition, all this affects people who, due to their young age, have not yet developed stable ideological convictions, and are at an age when they should learn how to be critical and formulate their individual positions, therefore, they are extremely vulnerable to being mentally influenced (II. 2c).

The crucifix cannot be deprived of its specific content, which refers to the content of the Christian belief, neither can it be reduced to being a simple symbol of Western cultural traditions. It symbolises the very essence of Christian belief, which might have influenced the Western world in various ways, though this is not accepted universally, by each and every member of society, who can reject it by way of exercising their fundamental rights enshrined in Article 4(1) of the *Grundgesetz* (II. 3a).

Not even the positive freedom of religion of Christian parents and students renders the display of the crucifix legal. Positive freedom of religion is the right granted to every parent and student, not only to Christians. The conflict emerging from this cannot be solved through the majority principle, because the fundamental right to the freedom of religion is largely aimed at protecting the minority. Those pursuing different views cannot detach themselves from the presence and influence of the crucifix (II. 3b).

The decision of the Constitutional Court was not unanimous. It also included three dissenting opinions. Judges Haas, Seidl, and Söllner argued that the mere presence of the crucifix in classrooms does not embody any coercion or constraint for students. It is not appropriate to base the decision on the negative freedom of religion, because nobody has the personal, universal right to avoid a sight which is unpleasant to them. Per their reasoning, the Bavarian Constitution enshrines that public education is based on fundamental Christian principles. The crucifixes displayed in classrooms do not violate the ideological and religious neutrality of the state; they only express support for churches and the cooperation with them. All this will not make schools 'proselytising' institutions, and does not exclude the possibility of taking other religious content into account.[7]

Winfried Brugger, an acknowledged expert in constitutional law, also elaborated on the decision.[8] According to Brugger, the disputed provision is not unconstitutional as the Act prescribes tolerance *vis-à-vis* all views and prohibits discrimination on the grounds of religion or ideology. At school, there are religious and non-religious students, and religious students also belong to various denominations. There is no regulation that would be equally acceptable to all. The positive and negative freedoms of religion are entitled to the same constitutional protection, and efforts have to be made to ensure that the given regulation contains the smallest possible degree of coercion. Accordingly, in the present case, the interests of the Christian majority should have been considered because this is the one that carries the smallest degree of coercion, and affects the smallest number of students and parents.

7 It is remarkable to note that the Austrian Constitutional Court (in its decision G 287/09) came to the opposite decision in a similar case. The complainant objected to the requirements set forth in the Act adopted in Lower Austria on kindergartens (*Niederösterreichischen Kindergartengesetz* 2006 – *Nö KindergartenG*), on the basis of which crucifixes were hung on the walls of kindergartens. According to the Austrian Constitutional Court, if the majority of the children belong to the Christian denomination, hanging a crucifix on the wall does not violate the Constitution. The court also declared that displaying the crucifix does not in any way mean that the state gives preference to any religion over the others. The crucifix is also the symbol of Western cultural history; the consistent enforcement of the law in line with the Constitution does not provide any benefits for Christian denominations.

8 Winfried Brugger, 'Zum Verhältnis von Neutralitätsliberalismus und liberalem Kommunitarismus – Dargestellt am Streit über das Kreuz in der Schule' in Winfried Brugger & Stefan Huster (eds), *Der Streit um das Kreuz in der Schule* (Nomos 1998) 109–54.

Brugger's second argument is that the crucifix is more of a cultural than a religious symbol; it expresses values generally accepted in European and Western cultures, such as tolerance and solidarity, with its religious message being only of secondary importance.

Brugger's third argument is that the state might support important community values, provided that by doing so it does not violate others' rights. In the disputed case, the support provided by the state is only of minor importance; the practice it prescribed, namely displaying the crucifix in classrooms, did not result in intolerance against those pursuing other religious convictions.

Opposing this, Stefan Huster agreed with the decision of the Constitutional Court.[9] On the basis of state neutrality, it cannot be disputed that the state has the right to prescribe norms that are mandatory for everyone. However, the state, in this context, has some limitations to observe. It is not entitled to take a position or express preferences concerning the views of its citizens living a 'good' life, and cannot prefer any of these views on the grounds that they are more valuable or superior to other views or beliefs. Based on the requirement of neutrality, the state cannot adopt a regulation that gives preference to a certain religious symbol over others. The legitimacy of the disputed regulation cannot be explained or justified by reference to the positive freedom of religion of parents and students, because the regulation did not take real demands into account, since it prescribed the obligation to display the crucifix irrespective of whether students and/or their parents required it, or whether most students are Christian at all. The requirement of neutrality does not exclude the possibility to integrate the expressions of religious convictions into everyday life at school. However, this cannot be implemented in a way which, even if only symbolically, excludes students who, in terms of their religious convictions, do not belong to the majority.

According to Josef Isensse, the Court's statement that displaying the crucifix in classrooms violates freedom of religion is erroneous.[10]

9 Stefan Huster, 'Die religiös-weltanschauliche Neutraliät des Staates – Das Kreuz in der Schule aus liberalem Sicht' in Brugger & Huster (n 8) 69–108.

10 Balázs Schanda, 'A "feszület-döntésről"', (1996) 7 *Vigilia* 548–52.

In this view, expressed by others, nobody has the personal right to avoid a sight which is unpleasant to them. Citizens are obliged to tolerate the expression of others' religious convictions in the spirit of tolerance, for example, the chiming of church bells. A question to be answered in the context of the case is what the crucifix on the wall of the state school means. The symbol also belongs to the identity of the state, and through prescribing its mandatory display, the state presents 'its own self'. This is not an interference with the freedom of religion, not even if the symbol might also carry some religious content. If the existence of Christian people's schools (state schools) is constitutional due to a previous decision of the Constitutional Court, then the crucifix decision would be in contradiction with the previous decision. The 'content' (education in the spirit of Christianity) is constitutional, whereas the 'symbol' (crucifix) is not.

In Joseph Listl's view, the greatest mistake of the decision is that it provides absolute advantages for the minority and, by doing so, it attaches priority to the negative freedom of religion as opposed to the positive one.[11] The crucifix does not violate students' freedom of religion to such an extent that would provide grounds for requests to remove them. The Constitutional Court, in its decision, rightly said that the display of the crucifix in classrooms does not force anybody to identify with or pay predefined respect to it, and yet later it comes to the opposite conclusion, in which having the crucifix on the wall orientates students towards identification with Christianity.

The decision of the Constitutional Court was received with significant public outrage in traditionally Catholic Bavaria. The Bavarian Prime Minister, Edmund Stoiber, said that in his view, the decision of the Constitutional Court had related only to the *obligation* to display the crucifix prescribed by the state. However, this did not mean that in future, it would become impossible to display a crucifix in the classroom if this is in line with the wishes of parents. Accordingly, crucifixes will stay where they are if there are no protests against them. Stoiber believed that the judgment was intolerant because it did not respect the sentiments of the majority,

11 *Ibid.*

and it gave an erroneous interpretation to the content of the crucifix as the symbol of Christianity.[12]

As a result of the Constitutional Court decision, the Bavarian Act on Education was amended on 23 December 1995.[13] Article 7(3) of the Act now reads as follows:

> Taking into account the historical and cultural character of Bavaria, a crucifix shall be fixed onto the wall of every classroom. This serves the implementation of the educational objectives specified in the Constitution, the promotion of the values of Christianity and Western civilisation in line with freedom of conscience. Should those having the right to education object to the display of the crucifix for serious and acceptable reasons of religious or ideological conviction, the director of the school shall make efforts to come to an equitable, reasonable agreement with them. Should such an agreement fail to be reached, the educational authority, after being notified, shall apply a solution to the unique case, which duly respects the freedom of religion of the person objecting, and establishes a fair balance between the ideological conviction of all students of the class concerned; in the course of this activity, the will of the majority should be taken into account to the greatest possible extent.

Based on the new regulations, only very few complaints were submitted by parents or teachers affected by the regulations. In these cases, courts always carry out a case-by-case analysis, and so the judicial decision requiring the removal of the crucifix in line with the regulations is not automatic.

12 Die Kreuze bleiben. Interview with Edmund Stoiber, Prime Minister of Bavaria. *Der Spiegel*, 14 August 1995, 32–34.

13 Bayerische Gesetz über das Erziehungs- und Unterrichtswesen.

3. Religious Neutrality and the Government's Freedom of Speech in the Jurisprudence of the United States' Supreme Court

The First Amendment to the United States Constitution states that, 'Congress shall make no law respecting an establishment of religion, or prohibiting the free exercise thereof'. In this respect, it is primarily the task of the Supreme Court of the United States to provide for the constitutional interpretation of 'establishment' of religion and the determination of the latitude of the government. Several decisions of the US Supreme Court deal with the separation of the government and the churches and/or religions. However, the issue of the 'official' use of religious symbols (i.e., by the state, the government, the municipalities, Courts, etc.) has emerged as a practical constitutional problem only during the last 25 years. Contradictory examples of Supreme Court jurisprudence prove that this issue belongs among the 'hard cases'. At the same time, the relatively recent appearance of the problem clearly indicates the ways in which American social conditions have changed and the transformation of US society's attitude to religion.

Several lower court decisions have been passed regarding these issues, but I did not have the opportunity to review these. In any case, the jurisprudence of the Supreme Court is also binding for the lower courts, which makes Supreme Court decisions of key significance. A separate survey of these decisions would provide a more comprehensive picture of the US constitutional approach.[14] At the same time, considering the cultural similarities between the United States and Europe, as well as the dialogue between them regarding the interpretation of fundamental rights, the findings of

14 When referring to action 'attributable' to the State, I uniformly mention the Government as the subject of the given action, regardless whether the given symbol has been used by the Federal Government, a federal state, or any state governments, courts or municipalities. The reason for this is that, in these matters, the government, the municipalities and the courts all act on behalf of the state, which is bound by the First Amendment.

the present chapter may prove useful beyond simply satisfying an interest in legal curiosities.

3.1. Symbols Used by the Government

3.1.1. Symbols Used during Holidays

3.1.1.1. *Lynch v Donnelly* (1984)[15]

The city of Pawtucket (Rhode Island), annually puts on a Christmas display in a park owned by a non-profit organisation located in the heart of the city's shopping district. The display includes, among other things, a *crèche* or Nativity scene, which has been part of this annual display for 40 years or more. An action was brought in the Federal District Court, challenging the inclusion of the *crèche* in the display.

According to the Supreme Court, the Constitution does not require complete separation of church and state; it affirmatively mandates accommodation, not merely tolerance, of all religions, and forbids hostility toward any. Anything less would require the 'callous indifference' that was never intended by the Establishment Clause. This interpretation of the Establishment Clause comports with the contemporaneous understanding of the Framers' intent. That neither the draftsmen of the Constitution, who were Members of the First Congress, nor the First Congress itself saw any establishment related problem in employing Chaplains to offer daily prayers in the Congress is a striking example of the accommodation of religious beliefs intended by the Framers.[16]

Here, the focus of the inquiry must be on the *crèche* in the context of the Christmas season. The Court ruled that, based on the record in this case, the city has a secular purpose for including the *crèche* in its Christmas display, and has not impermissibly advanced religion or created an excessive entanglement between religion and government. The display is sponsored by the city to celebrate the Holiday recognised

15 *Lynch v Donnelly* 465 US 668 (1984).
16 *Ibid*, 673.

by Congress and national tradition, and to depict the origins of that Holiday, and these are legitimate secular purposes.[17]

Justice Brennan protested the majority decision in a dissenting opinion, believing that all valid secular purposes (i.e., the celebration of the holiday) could be attained without erecting the *crèche*. However, the display of the Nativity scene set the state's *imprimatur* on the Christian creed. Historical traditions in themselves do not justify the city's conduct. The main question is whether the practices challenged here 'threaten those consequences which the framers deeply feared'.[18]

3.1.1.2. *County of Allegheny v ACLU* (1989)[19]

This litigation concerns the constitutionality of two recurring holiday displays located on public property in downtown Pittsburgh. The first, a *crèche* depicting the Christian Nativity scene was placed on the Grand Staircase of the Allegheny County Courthouse. The *crèche* was donated by a Catholic group, and bore a sign declaring this. The second of the holiday displays in question was an 18-foot Chanukah menorah or candelabrum, which was placed outside the City-County Building next to the city's 45-foot decorated Christmas tree. At the foot of the tree was a sign bearing the mayor's name and containing text declaring the city's 'salute to liberty'. The menorah is owned by Chabad, a Jewish group, but is stored, erected, and removed each year by the city. The Greater Pittsburgh Chapter of the American Civil Liberties Union and seven local residents filed suit seeking permanently to enjoin the county from displaying the *crèche* and the city from displaying the menorah.

The majority decision of the Supreme Court banned the display of the *crèche* while approving that of the menorah. The majority ruled that the *crèche* display violated the Establishment Clause. The *crèche* angel's words endorse a patently Christian message: Glory to God for the birth of Jesus Christ. Moreover, in contrast to *Lynch*, nothing

17 *Ibid*, 683.

18 *Ibid*, 719.

19 *County of Allegheny v ACLU* 492 US 573 (1989).

in the *crèche*'s setting detracted from that message.[20] Although the government may acknowledge Christmas as a cultural phenomenon, it may not observe it as a Christian holy day by suggesting that people praise God for the birth of Jesus.

The majority concluded that, unlike the *crèche*, the menorah display did not have the prohibited effect of endorsing religion, given its 'particular physical setting'. Its combined display with a Christmas tree and a sign saluting liberty did not impermissibly endorse both the Christian and Jewish faiths, but simply recognised that both Christmas and Chanukah are part of the same winter-holiday season, which has attained a secular status in our society.[21] The tree was clearly the predominant element in the holiday display, and the placement of the menorah beside it was readily understood as simply recognition that Christmas is not the only traditional way of celebrating the season.[22]

According to Justice Brennan, Chanukah, as opposed to Christmas, does not have a secular dimension; hence, the erection of the menorah represented favouritism towards the Jewish religion.[23] The City expressed its 'respect for freedom' message through religious symbols; however, this message is not religious but patriotic, and hence could violate those citizens whose attitude to the nation is not linked to any religious beliefs.[24]

Justice Kennedy's opinion (shared by Chief Justice Rehnquist and Justice White and Justice Scalia) was that both displays were constitutionally permissible, and the majority decision demonstrated a partly unjustified hostility towards religions. The First Amendment permits some latitude to the government to recognise religion's role in society. Justices should also consider the old and impeccably applied practices and previous court decisions which showed due respect to historically evolved traditions.[25]

20 *Ibid*, 598.

21 *Ibid*, 611.

22 *Ibid*, 614.

23 *Ibid*, 644.

24 *Ibid*, 644–5.

25 *Ibid*, 669.

3.1.2. Permanent Symbols

3.1.2.1. *Stone v Graham* (1980)[26]

A Statute passed by the Commonwealth of Kentucky required the posting of the Ten Commandments in every public schoolroom. A sign indicated at the bottom of each display of the Ten Commandments that it is clearly seen by Western civilization and the common law of the United States as the fundamental legal code; in other words, it has a secular significance. Plaintiffs sought temporary and permanent injunctive relief to prevent the Commonwealth of Kentucky from enforcing the Statute.

In connection with the certiorari, the Supreme Court of the United States concluded (by a unanimous and jointly worded *per curiam* decision) that the Statute thus challenged without doubt attempted to attain a religious purpose, and therefore it was contrary to the Establishment Clause. An 'avowed' secular purpose was not sufficient to avoid conflict with the First Amendment, and conflict was not avoided by the provision, in the statute, that there be included, in small print at bottom of each display, a notation indicating the secular nature of the text. This conflict with the constitution was not mitigated by the provision that the copies be financed by voluntary private contributions or by fact that Bible verses involved were merely posted on the wall rather than read aloud. The certiorari was granted and the judgment was reversed.

3.1.2.2. *McCreary County v ACLU* (2005)[27]

After the petitioners, two Kentucky Counties, each posted large, readily visible copies of the Ten Commandments in their courthouses, the respondents, the American Civil Liberties Union et al., sued to enjoin the displays. The Counties then adopted resolutions calling for a more extensive exhibit, meant to show that the Commandments are Kentucky's 'precedent legal code'. The displays around the Commandments were modified to

26 *Stone v Graham* 449 US 39 (1980).

27 *McCreary County v ACLU* 545 US 844 (2005).

include eight smaller, historical documents containing religious references as their sole common element. Later, the two Counties modified the displayed objects. These new exhibits, however, were not authorized by a new resolution, nor did the Counties repeal the resolutions that preceded the second one. The new display, entitled 'The Foundations of American Law and Government Display', consists of nine framed documents of equal size. One sets out the Commandments, explicitly identified as the 'King James Version', quotes them at greater length, and explains that they have profoundly influenced the formation of Western legal thought and this Nation.

According to the majority decision, there are two obvious similarities between the display Stone rejected and the first one here. Both set out the Commandments' text as distinct from any traditionally symbolic representation like blank tablets, and each stood alone, not as part of an arguably secular display. Stone stressed the significance of integrating the Commandments into a secular scheme to forestall the expression of an otherwise clearly religious message, as the Commandments are a central point of reference in the religious and moral history of Jews and Christians. Where the text is set out, the intent of the religious message is clear in the absence of a context plausibly suggesting a message going beyond an excuse to promote the religious point of view. The display in Stone had no such context, and the Counties' solo exhibit here did nothing more to counter the religious implication than the posting in Stone had.

The Counties' second display, unlike the first, did not present the Commandments in isolation, but included the statement of the government's purpose expressly set out in the county resolutions, and underscored it by juxtaposing the Commandments with other documents, highlighting that the references to God in them were their sole element in common. The display's unstinting focus was on religious passages, showing that the Counties posted the Commandments precisely because of their sectarian content. Together, the display and resolution presented an indisputable and undisputed showing of an impermissible purpose.

According to the majority view of the Court, no legitimising secular purpose prompted the Counties' third display, the

'Foundations of American Law and Government' exhibit. That display placed the Commandments in the company of other documents the Counties deemed especially significant to the historical foundation of the US government. In trying to persuade the District Court to lift the preliminary injunction, the Counties cited several new purposes for the third version, including a desire to educate County citizens as to the significance of the documents displayed. The selection of posted material did not, according to the Court, suggest a clear theme that might prevail over evidence of the continuing religious object.[28]

Justice Scalia voiced a long and strongly dissenting opinion. Scalia accused the majority of having demonstrated an unprincipled application of previous jurisprudence. He cited those cases when the state subsidy provided to churches had been approved by the court as being constitutional, for example in the form of tax reliefs,[29] or in the form of exceptions from the discrimination rule granted in favour of religious associations,[30] or when the practice that state legislatures open public sessions with common prayers had been held to be constitutional by the court.[31] According to Justice Scalia, the only circumstance which separates the interpretation of the neutrality principle appearing in these decisions from the present case is the 'age' of the challenged practice, or in other words, its duration.[32] While the court found old practices constitutional, it rejected the erecting of a new monument as being unconstitutional. In Justice Scalia's view, the court cannot go too far down the road of an enforced neutrality that contradicts both historical fact and current practice.[33]

28 *Ibid*, 872.

29 *Walz v Tax Commission of City of New York* 397 US 664 (1970).

30 *Corporation of Presiding Bishop of Church of Jesus Christ of Latter-day Saints v Amos* 483 US 327 (1987).

31 *Marsh v Chambers* 463 US 783 (1983).

32 545 US 844, 892 (2005).

33 *Ibid*, 903.

3.1.2.3. *Van Orden v Perry* (2005)[34]

Among the 21 historical markers and 17 monuments surrounding the Texas State Capitol is a six-foot-high monolith inscribed with the Ten Commandments. The legislative record illustrates that, after accepting the monument from a national social and patriotic organisation, the state selected a site for it based on the recommendation of the state organisation that maintains the capitol grounds. The petitioner, an Austin resident who encounters the monument during his frequent visits to the grounds, brought this suit seeking a declaration that the monument's placement violates the First Amendment's Establishment Clause, and seeking an injunction requiring its removal.

By majority decision, the monument remained in place. Four of the Justices constituting the majority in *McCreary* were a minority, whereas the Justices who were in a minority in *McCreary*, plus Justice Breyer, represented the majority. This resulted in the two decisions, passed on the same day, being in contradiction at first sight.

The majority concluded that the monument did not violate the Establishment Clause. From at least 1789, there has been an unbroken history of official acknowledgement by all three branches of government of religion's role in American life.[35] The display of the Commandments on government property in Texas is typical of such acknowledgements. Representations of the Commandments appear throughout the Court and its grounds, as well as in the Capital of this Federal State. Moreover, the Court's opinions, like its building which also displays the Commandments, have recognised the role the Decalogue plays in America's heritage.[36] While according to the majority opinion, the Commandments are religious in nature, they also have an undeniable historical meaning. The fact that they have religious content or promote a message consistent with a religious doctrine does not run afoul of the Establishment Clause.[37]

34 *Van Orden v Perry* 545 US 677 (2005).

35 *Ibid*, 686.

36 *Ibid*, 688–90.

37 *Ibid*, 690–1.

All of the Justices adhered to the opinions they expressed in *McCreary*, and maintained that the facts of both cases were analogous, except for Justice Breyer, whose vote finally decided the case. According to Breyer, an inquiry into the context in which the text of the Commandments is used demonstrates that the Commandments also convey a secular moral message about proper standards of social conduct, and a message about the historic relationship between those standards and the law. The circumstances surrounding the monument's placement on the capitol grounds and its physical setting provided a strong, but not conclusive, indication that the Commandments' text as used on this monument conveyed a predominantly secular message.[38] However, the determinative factor, according to Breyer, is that 40 years passed in which the monument's presence was legally unchallenged. Those 40 years suggest more strongly than can any set of formulaic tests that few individuals, whatever their belief systems, are likely to have understood the monument as amounting to a government effort to establish religion.[39]

3.1.2.4. *Pleasant Grove City v Summum* (2009)[40]

Pioneer Park, a public park in Pleasant Grove City (Utah), has several permanent, privately donated displays, including a Ten Commandments monument. Respondent Summum, a religious organisation, filed a request to erect a monument containing the Seven Aphorisms of Summum. The Municipality of the City rejected the request, and the organisation brought the case to court.

The case is somewhat different from the previous cases as the court did not examine the case on the grounds of the Establishment Clause but from the perspective of freedom of speech. The question to be decided in the procedure was not whether the government's granting of permission to a private party to display a religious symbol while simultaneously prohibiting other parties from doing the same qualifies as governmental endorsement, but whether free

38 *Ibid*, 701.

39 *Ibid*.

40 *Pleasant Grove City v Summum* 555 US 460 (2009).

governmental speech can be restricted upon judging such requests. In other words, whether the government is obliged to reject such requests (since permission would mean endorsement of some religion or church) or to permit the erection of monuments on public property to every applicant on equal terms.

According to the Supreme Court decision, a government entity 'is entitled to say what it wishes',[41] and is entitled to choose what views it wishes to express.[42] It may exercise this same freedom when it receives private assistance for the purpose of delivering a government-controlled message.[43] This does not mean that there are no restraints on government speech. For example, government speech must comport with the Establishment Clause. Permanent monuments displayed on public property typically represent government speech.[44] Governments have long used monuments to speak to the public. Thus, a government-commissioned and government-financed monument placed on public land constitutes government speech. So, too, are privately financed and donated monuments that the government accepts for public display on government land. Although many were donated in completed form by private entities, the City has 'effectively controlled' their messages by exercising 'final approval authority' over their selection.[45]

Respondent's legitimate concern that the government speech doctrine not be used as a subterfuge for favouring certain viewpoints does not mean that a government entity should be required to publicly embrace a privately donated monument's 'message' in order to escape Free Speech Clause restrictions. A city engages in expressive conduct by accepting and displaying a privately donated monument, but it does not necessarily endorse the specific meaning that any particular donor sees in the monument.[46]

41 Having reference to judgment *Rosenberger v Rector and Visitors of University of Virginia* 515 US 819, 833 (1995).

42 See *Rust v Sullivan* 500 US 173 (1991).

43 *Johanns v Livestock Marketing Association* 544 US 550, 562 (2005).

44 *Pleasant Grove City v Summum* (n 40) 464.

45 *Ibid*, 471.

46 *Ibid*, 473–4.

3.1.2.5. *Salazar v Buono* (2010)[47]

In 1934, members of the Veterans of Foreign Wars (VFW) placed a Latin cross on federal land in the Mojave National Preserve to honour American soldiers who died in World War I. Claiming to be offended by a religious symbol's presence on federal land, respondent Frank Buono, a regular visitor to the Preserve, filed a suit alleging a violation of the First Amendment's Establishment Clause, seeking an injunction requiring the government to remove the cross. In the litigation's first stage, the District Court found that the presence of the cross on federal land conveyed an impression of governmental endorsement of religion, and hence it granted the requested injunctive relief in 2002. Subsequently, while the Government's appeal was pending, Congress passed the Department of Defense Appropriations Act 2004, which directed the Secretary of the Interior to transfer the cross and the land on which it stands to the civil society organisation erecting the cross, in exchange for privately owned land elsewhere in the Preserve. Buono then returned to the District Court seeking injunctive relief against the land transfer, either through enforcement or modification of the 2002 injunction. The court rejected the government's claim, concluding that it was instead an invalid attempt to keep the cross on display. The court granted Buono's motion to enforce the 2002 injunction, denied as moot his motion to amend it, and permanently enjoined the government from implementing the land transfer statute.

The majority decision of the Supreme Court reversed the judgments, and the case was remanded. According to the judgement, by dismissing as illicit the motives of Congress in passing it, the District Court took insufficient account of the context in which the statute was enacted and the reasons for its passage.[48] Placement of the cross on federal land by private persons was not an attempt to set the state's imprimatur on a particular creed. Rather, the intent was simply to honour fallen soldiers.[49] Moreover, the cross stood for nearly seven decades before the statute was enacted, by

47 *Salazar v Buono* 559 US 700 (2010).

48 *Ibid*, 715.

49 *Ibid*.

which time the cross and the cause it commemorated had become entwined in the public consciousness.[50] The 2002 injunction thus presented the government with a dilemma. It could not maintain the cross without violating the injunction, but it could not remove the cross without conveying disrespect for those whom the cross was intended to honour. Deeming neither alternative satisfactory, Congress enacted the land-transfer statute. The statute embodied a legislative judgment that this dispute is best resolved through a framework and policy of accommodation. The statute should not have been dismissed as an evasion, for it brought about a change of law and a congressional statement of policy applicable to the case.[51]

According to the dissenting opinion of Justice Stevens, the decision should have approved the decisions of lower courts. On the one hand, the land transfer statute's unequivocal purpose was to preserve the cross at its original site, and this qualifies as an impermissible governmental endorsement of religion. On the other hand, even if the land transfer was implemented, the existence of the cross could be understood as governmental endorsement of religion, because, among other factors, the fact that the land concerned became private property would not change the circumstance that the cross was originally erected by the government as its own monument, thereby proclaiming its own message. Hence, the monument's character and its connection to the government would not have changed.[52]

3.1.3. Symbols Erected on Public Property by Private Initiative

3.1.3.1. *Capitol Square Review Board v Pinnette* (1995)[53]

Ohio law made Capitol Square, the Statehouse plaza in Columbus (the capital of Ohio), a public forum for discussion of public ques-

50 *Ibid*, 716.
51 *Ibid*, 717.
52 *Ibid*, 740.
53 *Capitol Square Review Board v Pinnette* 515 US 753 (1995).

tions and for public activities, and gave the petitioner, the Capitol Square Review and Advisory Board responsibility for regulating access to the square. After the Board denied the application of the respondent (the local branch of the Ku-Klux-Klan) to place a cross on the square during the 1993 Christmas season, the respondent filed a suit.

According to the Supreme Court decision, the erection of the cross would have been permissible under the Constitution. According to the majority of the Justices, the object the respondent wished to erect qualified as a private religious expression, enjoying constitutional protection of freedom of speech.[54] Because Capitol Square is a traditional public forum, the Board could regulate the content of the respondent's expression there only if such a restriction was necessary, and narrowly drawn, to serve a compelling state interest.[55]

The court's majority opinion rejected the petitioner's argument that the forum's proximity to the seat of government may be misconstrued as the state's approval for the cross, and that their content based restriction was thus constitutional under the so called 'endorsement test'.[56] Where the court has tested for endorsement, the subject of the test was either expression by the government itself (see *Lynch*), or else government action alleged to discriminate in favour of private religious expression or activity (see *County of Allegheny*). There is a difference between forbidding government speech endorsing religion and protecting private speech. Given that it was a public forum open to all on equal terms, as well as a purely private sponsorship of religious expression, the previous court decisions of state endorsement could not be considered in this case.[57]

According to Justice Stevens's dissenting opinion, serious reasons should be present to declare an unattended religious symbol standing on public property, not linked to a particular event, as unconstitutional. The display of the symbol is not permissible if it

54 *Ibid*, 759.
55 *Ibid*, 761.
56 *Ibid*, 766.
57 *Ibid*, 767.

suggests governmental endorsement of religion. The sign indicating the private nature of the display is of no avail here, since the approval granted by the owner of the public property to the erection of the symbol constituted the same kind of governmental endorsement as if the given symbol was erected by the government itself.[58]

3.2. Overview of the Tests Used for the Judgments

No unambiguous test can be deduced from the Supreme Court's diverse, sometimes apparently contradictory jurisprudence, which could provide a predictable and clear basis for deciding similar cases in the future. However, it is still worth summarising the tests used in the different cases.

We must start with a case quite different from the subject matter of this paper, which nevertheless provides a good starting point for judging the above-mentioned cases. The test determined in *Lemon v Kurtzman* served as the basis for later decisions passed concerning the public usage of symbols.[59] In *Lemon*, the court had to decide on the constitutionality of two Acts which regulated the government's reimbursement obligation regarding the costs of private schools. The government had to reimburse the salaries of teachers and the price of the textbooks and other instructional materials, regardless of whether the given institution was secular or religious. The Supreme Court ruled that these Acts qualified as a subsidy to religious schools and thus violated the Establishment Clause. The court established a three-pronged test, and ruled that the government must meet all three conditions of the test in order to ensure that its conduct is not considered unconstitutional. These conditions are: (1) the government's action must have a secular purpose; (2) the government's action must not have the primary effect of either advancing or inhibiting religion; (3) the government's action must not result in an 'excessive government entanglement' with religion.

The 'endorsement test' (which can be viewed as a modification of the *Lemon* test) was already expressed by Justice O'Connor in her concurrent opinion to the *Lynch* case, but it was only embraced

58 *Ibid*, 802.

59 *Lemon v Kurtzman* 403 US 602 (1971).

by the majority in *County of Allegheny*.[60] This test combines the individual elements of the above-mentioned three prongs and elaborates on the possible interpretations of the test connected with symbol-related cases. The requirement of 'secular purpose' and the prohibition of 'primary effect' are mixed in the test. According to the test, when considering constitutionality, in addition to the purpose prong, both the message the government intends to convey and the message actually conveyed must be examined. This twofold test is crucial since the perceived opinion is not necessarily identical to the opinion intended to be expressed. Of the two, the perceived opinion is more important according to O'Connor. Based on this, later the court examined in *County of Allegheny* how a reasonable observer might interpret the display, also taking into account the environment of the symbols on display.

Another element that was used as one of the bases of subsequent decisions was the 'historical approach'.[61] Though it cannot be viewed as an independent test, it nevertheless had a dominant role in judgment of the cases. A consideration that first appeared in *Lynch* and which has assumed decisive importance is that a practice can be considered constitutional if it has been conducted for a long time, undisturbed, and has become a tradition. Based on this, the Christmas *crèche* erected in Pawtucket was allowed to remain in its place since the court acknowledged the City's forty-year tradition, and hence took into account history, the roots of the tradition and the position of the community. Similarly, Justice Rehnquist's majority opinion in *Van Orden* emphasised that the Ten Commandments monument involved in the case proclaimed the historic significance of the displayed text.

It was not this approach, but the 'predominant purpose' test which was used in *McCreary*.[62] This test, similarly to the 'endorsement

60 Adam Linkner, 'How *Salazar v Buono* Synthesizes the Supreme Court's Establishment Clause Precedent into a Single Test', (2011) 25 *Emory International Law Review* 57, 73.

61 *Ibid*, 75–78; Elizabeth A Murphy, 'Courts Mistakenly Cross-Out Memorials: Why the Establishment Clause is not Violated by Roadside Crosses', (2011) 39 *Hofstra Law Review* 723, 732.

62 Linkner (n 60) 78–81.

test', can be viewed as a modification of the *Lemon* test, taking the first prong to a more stringent level. According to the decision the 'secular purpose' requirement must be assessed based on all facts and circumstances of the case, including the history and developments of the case, in order to determine whether the secular purpose cited by the government really exists or is just being used as a pretext for displaying a religious symbol. Based on the complex history of *McCreary*, the court drew the conclusion that the government had displayed a religious expression under the guise of a secular purpose.

3.3. Governmental Endorsement of Religious Symbols

3.3.1. Prohibition of Government Endorsement

The prohibition laid down in the First Amendment of the Constitution, forbidding the Congress to establish a religion, in practice also involves the prohibition of government endorsement of religion. Simply expressed, this non-endorsement principle means that the government must refrain from any conduct which may create the perception in the mind of its citizens that the government is either endorsing a specific religion or church or that the government would welcome it if its citizens would favour, accept or follow the religion or church endorsed by the government.

However, there is only a small difference between endorsement and acknowledgement. If the government's right and obligation to acknowledge is restricted to merely acknowledging the existence of religions and ensuring undisturbed religious practices, the government would be denied the opportunity to acknowledge the importance of religions and their role in the historical development of America. Obviously, the dispute between the Supreme Court justices did not concern the minimum meaning of the First Amendment (i.e., the prohibition of active endorsement) but the levels of acknowledgement and their constitutionally permissible options. Certain justices considered a particular religious symbol as constitutional and thereby also approved the 'passive acknowledgement' of the historical importance of the religions concerned, as long as it could be proven that the government did not have any religious motivation for using the symbol. In certain cases these justices were in the majority.

It was probably Justice Scalia and Justice Thomas who went the furthest in this regard. The former held that the government was allowed to prefer religion against irreligion, but even the acceptance of this would not lead to preferential treatment of a specific religion or religions.[63] Justice Thomas held that we should return to the original meaning of the First Amendment and that the word 'establishment' should be interpreted as a certain constraint on the citizens to accept the religion established by the government, which would thus represent an inevitably forbidden act.[64] According to Justice Kennedy, the First Amendment leaves some latitude for the government to recognise and express its agreement regarding the central role of religion in society.[65]

In general, not even the justices voting against the usage of symbols disputed the permissibility of government acknowledgement. At the same time, they required certain other conditions for the constitutionality of this usage of symbols, such as an obvious secular motivation, as the description of the cases has demonstrated. It is certain that it is impossible to draw a clear and distinct line between (permitted) government acknowledgement and (prohibited) endorsement. At least, the successive court decisions have failed to draw such a line.

In *Lynch*, Justice Brennan argued that a strict distinction between the obviously totally formal religious government expressions and what is not truly secular usage of religious symbols should have been made. For him and for the other justices, the most important question of these cases was whether the government usage of the symbol had a genuine and overwhelmingly secular purpose. If not, the usage was constitutionally impermissible.

3.3.2. The Divisive Nature of Religious Symbols

Another important factor used by the American justices when judging the symbol cases was the divisive nature of the symbol

63 Justice Scalia's dissent, *McCreary* (n 27).
64 *Van Orden* (n 34), J Thomas' concurring opinion.
65 *County of Allegheny* (n 19), J Kennedy's dissenting opinion.

concerned. In other words, they examined how much the 'official' usage of the symbol contributed to the divisiveness of society. Some believe that if the government usage of the symbol creates the perception in the mind of those citizens who do not identify with the symbol concerned that they are second-class citizens, or at least that their belief or disbelief is less preferred by the government, then social cohesion is undermined. However, the court emphasized already in *Lynch* that respondents cannot create the appearance of divisiveness simply by starting the procedure, and then later use this as a proof of divisiveness.[66] The divisive nature of the symbols is not to be assessed on the basis of individual sensitivity.

Justice Breyer, whose vote in *Van Orden* was decisive, took into account the absence of dispute surrounding the symbol.[67] Symbols whose erection is disputed and which thereby receive a significant amount of media attention are in a more difficult situation in this respect. Similarly, a tolerant atmosphere surrounding a symbol and an environment respecting social pluralism are both reasons in favour of the constitutionality of usage of the given symbol.[68] According to Kent Greenawalt, Breyer was afraid that if the erection of the symbol examined in *Van Order* (the Ten Commandments monument in a public park) qualified as unconstitutional, and hence a debate was started regarding similar symbols as well (of which there are many in the United States), this unfortunate debate itself would create the very divisiveness which the Establishment Clause is designed to prevent.[69]

Richard Garnett highlights that disagreement between members of society and a dispute regarding the usage of a symbol cannot

66 *Lynch* (n 15), majority opinion. See Stephanie Barclay, 'Passive Acknowledgement or Active Promotion of Religion? Neutrality and the Ten Commandments in *Green v Haskell*', (2010) *Brigham Young University Law Review* 3, 13–15.

67 *Van Orden* (n 34), J Breyer's concurring opinion.

68 Greg Abbott, 'Upholding the Unbroken Tradition: Constitutional Acknowledgement of the Ten Commandments in the Public Square', (2005–06) 14 *William & Mary Bill of Rights Law Journal* 51, 69.

69 Kent Greenawalt, *Religion and the Constitution*. Vol 2, 'Establishment and Fairness' (Princeton University Press 2008) 86–87.

serve as a ground for establishment of unconstitutionality. Religious issues are important and disputed elements of social life, but there are other similarly disputed issues too, regarding which no-one would ever argue that the government cannot take a stand. The 'establishment prohibition' stipulated in the First Amendment may not lead to a situation where one cannot use religiously founded arguments during public debates or where public policy and government decisions supported by such arguments are banned.[70] Lack of agreement and a state of disunity are inherent features of all democracies. These are necessary and concomitant phenomena and not to be eliminated.[71]

3.3.3. The Role of Time Elapsed

The history of the symbol or monument examined and the time elapsed since its erection have played a crucial role in the court decisions. They similarly have affected not only the symbol-related cases but also other freedom of religion-related issues.[72] It is indisputable that long-displayed or long-used symbols (see *Lynch*, *Van Orden*, *Buono*) enjoy a degree of advantage over newer symbols, although this distinction is not always decisive.[73] It is certain that so far no Supreme Court decision has banned the usage of any 'long-used' (that is, at least for several decades) symbol.

At the same time, Greenawalt stresses that even long-used, undisturbed practices can become problematic as a result of changing social circumstances. An issue formerly generally accepted and

70 Richard W Garnett, 'Religion, Division, and the First Amendment', (2005–06) 94 *Georgetown Law Journal* 1667, 1718.

71 *Ibid*, 1724.

72 In the *Walz v Tax Commission* (n 29) case, the Supreme Court concluded that the property tax benefits granted to churches, introduced in 1802, were constitutional; moreover, in *Marsh v Chambers* (n 31), the Supreme Court did not challenge the practice that state legislatures open public sessions with common prayers, led by a government appointed minister, first recited in the Congress in 1789.

73 Abbott (n 68) 68.

never challenged can become disturbing for the people of today.[74] It is argued by many, probably most vehemently by Justice Scalia, that the framers of the Constitution, the Founding Fathers of the United States, used different religious symbols and religion-based arguments many times in their speeches and during public events, and not even the early Congress refrained from these. As such, the text of the First Amendment could not aim to banish religious symbols from public life. However, according to Greenawalt, former historical practice and constitutionality as seen today may yield different results. In other words, modern practice may be different from that of the first Congress, since the notions and doctrines related to constitutionality have changed and developed in the meantime. Justices simply cannot focus strictly and narrowly on those practices which were acceptable at the time the constitutional guarantees were established.[75]

Almost all the opinions advocating the constitutionality of the symbols referred to the role religion has had in American history and society. Hence, these Justices not only concluded that the 'old' practice should be considered constitutional, but added that the role of the historic past must also be considered when assessing the cases. American history is rich not only in the instances of official use of Christian symbols but also in being open and tolerant towards religions in general. At the same time, the overall historical significance of the different Christian denominations in the United States is without doubt, and this ensures a certain extra protection to Christian symbols, even if this cannot be considered by the court as having any decisive importance.

The prohibition of governmental endorsement of religious views can hardly lead to the disregarding of cultural traditions, nor did the Supreme Court justices consider this to be desirable. Although no clear conclusion can be drawn based on the chain of decisions, certain individual decisions, nevertheless, explicitly emphasised the need for respect for religious tradition intertwined with social tradition (*Lynch*, *Van Orden*, *Buono*), and *Pleasant Grove City* explicitly took into account the traditions of the local community.

74 Greenawalt (n 69) 73.
75 *Ibid*, 76–77.

Based on all these cases, it can be concluded that the First Amendment is not violated if the symbols of certain religions enjoy a preferred position (with restricted scope and subject to special conditions) which is ensured by the government.

3.3.4. Cultural or Religious Symbols?

The huge distance between the present day and the time when the government started to use a certain symbol strengthens the argument that certain inherently religious symbols have become primarily secular with the passage of time; more precisely, the circumstances of usage of these symbols by the government puts the focus on the secular meaning evolved in the meantime. In other words, the official use of the Ten Commandments or the Christmas *crèche* primarily conveys not a religious message but the secular message of the government. In the case of the Ten Commandments, this secular message is respect for one of the fundamental bases of the US legal system, whereas in the case of the *crèche*, it was as a holiday able to be experienced by anyone; Christmas, the 'celebration of love', shorn of its religious content. When the court is about to judge the constitutionality of a once clearly religious practice, the court always searches for secular arguments whenever they argue for maintenance of the practice. A good example of this is the acknowledgement of Sunday as a mandatory non-working day.

Simultaneously with the secularisation of the arguments, the symbol itself also becomes secular. Apparently, this is the middle ground, since it helps to preserve the symbol, but at the same time, it does not allow a government message with religious content to penetrate the public sphere. However, in reality, it forces both opposing sides into serious compromises.[76] The *crèche*, the subject in *Lynch*, if viewed as a secular symbol, can become the symbol of a commercialised Christmas deprived of all its mysticism, or better, the memento of a historical event. However, this meaning desecrates the religion to those who believe the one lying in the

76 Seth Kurland, 'The Religion Clauses and the Burger Court', (1984) 34 *Catholic University Law Review* 1, 13–14.

crèche is the saviour of mankind. At the same time, by attaching a secular message to the symbol, the symbol itself is deprived of its religious nature, which communicates to the believers that their religion has no place in public life. On the other hand, all this does not completely placate those people who reject religions, since they may think that what they see is still primarily a religious symbol, and the secular message attached to it is only a disguise aimed at preserving the existence of the symbol in public life.

According to Stanley Fish, who always uses plain language, the Supreme Court is 'saving religion by emptying its content', and the symbols by 'leeching the life out of them'.[77] Fish argues that the principle of government neutrality is an anti-religious act. This anomalous interpretation totally misconstrues the meaning of these symbols, stating that the symbols can remain in their place if they become the antithesis of themselves and fit into the secular world view ('if you want to secure a role for religious symbols in the public sphere, you must de-religionise them').[78]

3.4. The Government Speech Doctrine

3.4.1. Government Neutrality

Fish is of the opinion that the approach of the Court in *Salazar v Buono* distorts the principle of 'plural neutrality' by forcing secular meanings onto religious symbols and thereby curtailing it of its real meaning or of any significance, which is detrimental not only for constitutional doctrine, but also for religion itself.[79] On the contrary, Justice Kennedy holds that the prohibition of governmental endorsement of religion, in the strict sense, is not neutral towards religions; what is more, it shows an unjustifiable hostility to them.[80] As such, secularity itself is an ideological rule as well, and while

77 Stanley Fish, 'When Is a Cross a Cross?', *NYTimes.com*, 3 May 2010, opinionator.blogs.nytimes.com/2010/05/03/when-is-a-cross-a-cross/?_r=0.

78 *Ibid.*

79 *Ibid.*

80 *County of Allegheny* (n 19), J Kennedy's concurring opinion.

it purports to be a principle that is a direct consequence of the necessary neutrality of the constitutional state, it is actually the very principle that violates the neutrality rule.

Joseph Weiler wrote of the self-evident neutrality of European societies and concluded that both religious practices and refraining from these are free choices based on the common European heritage. Religious diversity and the free choice of the individual are present in the United States as well, and have been ever since the foundation of the United States. To that end, Weiler's words that religious tolerance cannot include intolerance towards religions, national identities, community traditions or respect for the historic past can be interpreted in the American context as well.[81]

According to Garnett, the establishment prohibition included in the First Amendment does not mean that religious-based arguments as a whole can be excluded from public life or from discussions of public issues, or that the public policy decisions supported by such arguments should be annulled.[82] Michael McConnell emphasises that the government and the churches are necessarily linked to each other and cannot be separated completely. The real challenge is to define the ways in which they can interact with each other, and the ways in which they cannot. The purpose of forbidding religious-based arguments from public life is to prevent the success of divisive, absolutist and intolerant ambitions and the appearance of religious-based arguments in the debates of public affairs. However, according to McConnell, this is a position based on imprecise stereotypes and questionable epistemological premises which intends to deprive religious people of their full legal status within the community.[83]

Justice Kennedy believes in leaving room to accommodate divergent values within a constitutionally permissible framework.[84] Le-

81 JHH Weiler, 'State and Nation: Church, Mosque and Synagogue. The Trailer', (2010) 8(2) *International Journal of Constitutional Law* 162–3.

82 Garnett (n 70) 1718.

83 Michael McConnell, 'Five Reasons to Reject the Claim that Religious Arguments Should Be Excluded from Democratic Deliberation', (1999) *Utah Law Review* 639, 656–7.

84 *Salazar v Buono* (n 47), J Kennedy's concurring opinion.

slie Griffin also highlights that, within the meaning of 'constitutional tolerance', the symbols of other religions and philosophies could be displayed next to the Christian symbols during Christmas. This would result in less intolerant religions and more religious freedom.[85] However, in the American context, this approach cannot be applied in all cases, or sometimes only to some extent, since only a limited space is available for the government (on the wall of a public building, in a park or even at a Christmas Fair), not to mention that if it was made mandatory for the government to place any or all of these religious symbols in all these places, the government would be deprived of its right to communicate its messages at its own discretion to its citizens (which option must be ensured in line with *Pleasant Grove City*).

3.4.2. Government Speech in Religious Matters

Traditionally, the government is not viewed as the subject of freedom of speech, but as an entity responsible for respecting the freedom of speech granted to its citizens and for facilitating real possibilities in this field. However, the government inevitably conveys certain messages and opinions. The majority opinion expressed in connection with *Pleasant Grove City* demonstrated that these messages, too, are protected by the principle of freedom of speech, hence only the general rules of fundamental rights can be applied in terms of restriction of these messages. It should be noted that this interpretation of fundamental rights is distinct from European legal interpretation. According to the European approach to fundamental right, the rights of the citizens are ensured and protected by the state—protected, that is, primarily from itself. The expression of opinion by the state is thereby placed outside the system of fundamental rights and thus cannot be interpreted within that system.

According to Mary J Dolan, based on the 'government speech' doctrine created by the decision passed in *Pleasant Grove City*, the government is entitled to express its own viewpoint and reject

85 Leslie C Griffin, 'Fighting the New Wars of Religion: The Need for a Tolerant First Amendment', (2010) 62 *Maine Law Review* 23, 73–74.

alternative opinions in a way protected by the right to free speech.[86] This also involves the right of the government to convey messages about its identity, and not only written public policy views.[87]

Pleasant Grove City expressly ruled that if only a limited space is available for displaying symbols (and obviously, all public properties are of limited space), the government simply cannot avoid applying some sort of selection between the different ideologies and opinions. Hence, as far as permanent monuments are concerned, a public park is not a public forum where everyone should be allowed to express their opinion on equal terms but a place that's usage can be regulated by the government.

Some believe that the government can pass such decisions, thereby favouring some and disadvantaging others. Nevertheless, the Establishment Clause, specifies that the government is not allowed to convey and display messages or symbols with religious content. In other words, the government must reject, without further consideration, any requests filed for displaying religious symbols.[88] If the First Amendment prohibits the endorsement of religions, the government's right to free speech cannot include such messages either.[89] However, if, in the future, the court proceeds along the lines of its position expressed in *Pleasant Grove City*, citizens will be left without any constitutional protection against the establishment of churches.[90] According to Greenawalt, the government is doing the right thing when it teaches morality views or political theories as valid, but must not support the publication of statements quoting religious truths.[91]

86 Mary J Dolan, 'Government Identity Speech and Religion: Establishment Clause Limits After Summum', (2010) 19 *William & Mary Bill of Rights Law Journal* 1, 6.

87 *Ibid*, 35.

88 E Gregory Wallace, 'When Government Speaks Religiously', (2004) 21 *Florida State University Law Review* 1183, 1190–1.

89 Erwin Chemerinsky, 'A Dangerous Free Speech Ruling', (2009) 45 *Trial* 60.

90 Catherine MA McCauliff, 'Religion and the Secular State', (2010) 58 *American Journal of Comparative Law* 31, 48.

91 Greenawalt (n 69) 73.

According to Darnell Weeden, the equality principle resulting from the Establishment Clause does not ban the government from applying 'passive discrimination against religions', such as in the course of its decisions passed regarding the display of religious symbols, because the government has important values which are linked to the expression in public life of issues and affairs of historical significance or significance for the community.[92] Pleasant Grove City did not demonstrate hostile behaviour or religious intolerance *vis-à-vis* the Summum church when it rejected the request that the church filed for the erection of the monument. The City preserved the public park for recreational, historical, educational and aesthetic purposes. In the meantime, the City reserved its right to choose, at its discretion, from the monuments people wished to be erected. Moreover, if its decision really serves the above-mentioned purposes, it shall not violate the First Amendment, since the government is not allowed to promote or restrict any religions.[93] The total and absolute separation of State and religion is not possible.[94]

If we accept the government speech doctrine indicated in *Pleasant Grove City*, and in certain circumstances ensure a freedom of opinion to the government like that granted to its citizens, the question arises as to who should supervise the exercise of that right. According to Daniel W Park, supervision can only be achieved through a political process. In other words, it is at the time of democratic elections when the citizens can decide, among other things, about the correctness or errors of government speech. The government/state is accountable to its citizens.[95] This obviously passes the right to decide upon the appropriateness of government speech to the current majority, which in turn may result in an unfavourable situation for the religious minorities or the irreligious minority (if it is a minority at all).

92 L Darnell Weeden, 'A First Amendment Establishment Clause Analysis of Permanent Displays on Public Property as Government Speech', (2009–10) 35(2) *Thurgood Marshall Law Review* 217, 218.

93 *Ibid*, 232–3.

94 *Lemon v Kurtzman* (n 59), majority opinion.

95 Daniel W Park, 'Government Speech and the Public Forum: A Clash between Democratic and Egalitarian Values', (2009–10) 45 *Gonzaga Law Review* 113, 146–8.

3.5. Summary of the United States' Jurisprudence

Although the US cases are quite diverse, with strong and significantly divergent opinions on the part of the justices, having reviewed these decisions certain conclusions can be drawn. The common lesson of all these US judgments is that a secular purpose is always required whenever a religious symbol is used by the government. In other words, the symbol must also convey a secular meaning, and this meaning must be more important in the given context than the religious meaning of the given symbol. At the same time, the significance of the historic past and community traditions are also acknowledged by the court decisions. The latter means that long-used or existing symbols having a relevant secular purpose and meaning (Christmas, the memorial commemorating the soldiers who died in wars, recognition of local religious communities and traditions) are likely to meet the first criterion regarding the secular purpose. In this way, elapsed time does become a constitutionally significant factor for the purpose of judging the cases. Newer religious symbols that people wish to erect can be constitutional as well if a justifiable secular purpose is achieved through them. However, this 'pardon' comes at a price, since the religious message is dimmed. An interesting development of US judicial practice is the acknowledgement of the 'government speech doctrine', which also leads to a significant restriction, or rather restrictive interpretation of the government's (religious) neutrality.

The decisions reviewed and the principles and rules extracted from them may provide suitable grounds for newer debates; however, they are not sufficient to settle the most recent 'religious wars'. Hence, these decisions cannot be considered as the final word of the courts.

4. Europe and the Sign of the Crucifix

4.1. The *Lautsi* Decisions

4.1.1. The Facts of the Case

In the school year 2001–02, the two sons of the first applicant attended the state school in the Italian city of Abano Terme, where a crucifix was fixed to the wall in each of the classrooms. On 22 April 2002, during a meeting of the school's governors, the first applicant's husband raised concerns about the presence of religious symbols, particularly crucifixes, in the classrooms and requested their removal. On 27 May 2002, by a vote of ten to two with one abstention, the school's governors decided that the religious symbols may remain in the classrooms.

On 23 July 2002, the first applicant filed her claim with the Administrative Court of the Veneto Region. She designated as the reason for her complaint the infringement of the principle of secularism connecting it to the right to equality and freedom of religion under Articles 3 and 19 of the Italian Constitution, as well as the rule of impartiality of public administration authorities under Article 9 of European Convention on Human Rights (hereinafter: ECHR) and Article 97 of the Constitution.

On 3 October 2002, the Minister of Education, Universities and Research adopted Directive no 2666, instructing the competent services of his Ministry to take necessary measures to ensure that school governors guarantee the presence of crucifixes in the classrooms.

On 30 October 2003, the Minister joined the proceedings brought by the first applicant. He argued that the first applicant's claim was unfounded since the presence of crucifixes on the walls of state-run middle schools was based on Article 118 of Royal Decree no 965 of 1924 on internal regulations of middle schools and Article 119 of Royal Decree no 1297 of 1928 on the approval of the general regulations governing primary schools. Article 119 of the 1928 Decree required that a crucifix be displayed on the wall of each classroom. Article 118 of the 1924 Decree also required a crucifix, as well as a portrait of the king, be displayed on the wall of each classroom.

Many essays on the subject referred to these laws, arguing that they were from a 'fascist period', an argument which thereby weakened the Italian government's position. In fact, the roots of the regulation could be traced back to 1859. By its 14 January 2004 decision, the Administrative Court suspended the administrative proceedings and referred to the Constitutional Court the question of the constitutionality of the above-mentioned Decrees. By Decision no 389, dated 15 December 2004, the Constitutional Court declared the question inadmissible for technical reasons on the ground that the disputed provisions were not contained in statutes but rather in regulations that, under Italian law, could not be the subject of constitutional review.

Subsequently, on 17 March 2005, the Administrative Court dismissed the application. It emphasized that 'the principle of the secular nature of the state [was] now part of the legal heritage of Europe and the Western democracies'. However, it held that the presence of crucifixes in state school classrooms did not offend this principle. In the reasoning of the decision, the court explained that although the crucifix was undeniably a religious symbol, it was not solely a Catholic symbol but rather a symbol of Christianity in general. The court added that the crucifix was a historical and cultural symbol, possessing an 'identity-linked value' for the Italian people, and it represented the historical and cultural evolution that is a characteristic of Italy and Europe. The court further held that the crucifix should also be considered a symbol of a value system underpinning the Italian Constitution.

The first applicant appealed to the Supreme Administrative Court (Consiglio di Stato), which confirmed in its decision that the provisions at issue were compatible with the principles of secularism. The court found that Italian culture is characterised by the values of religious origin symbolised by the crucifix, such as tolerance, mutual respect, respect for individual values and the rights of others, consideration for one's freedom, the autonomy of one's moral conscience, human solidarity and the rejection of any form of discrimination. In that sense, when the crucifix is displayed on the walls of the classrooms, it fulfils a symbolic function, irrespective of the religious conviction of the pupils. On 13 April 2006, the Court dismissed the appeal. Subsequently, the complainant turned to the ECtHR claiming the infringement of both her and her children's right to freedom of religion (ECHR Article 9), as well as the right to education (ECHR Article 2 of Protocol no 1).

4.1.2. The First *Lautsi* Decision

In its opinion, the Second Section of the ECtHR concluded that the state's obligation to ensure freedom of religion prohibited it from trying, even indirectly, to influence its citizens as to which religion they should follow or to have them accept their teachings as true.[96] According to the ECtHR, among the many different meanings of the crucifix, its religious meaning was predominant (Paragraph 51). The sight of the crucifix may be emotionally disturbing to non-Christians or those who profess no religion (Paragraph 55). 'Negative freedom of religion' (the right to refrain from religions) is not restricted to the absence of religious services or religious education but also extends to freedom from symbols (Paragraph 55). The state has a duty to uphold religious neutrality in public education; the ECtHR could not see how the display of crucifixes could serve the maintenance of educational pluralism (Paragraph 57). The ECtHR further held that parents had the right to educate their children in conformity with their convictions, and children had the right to decide on what they believe. These rights were encroached upon by the requirement to display crucifixes (Paragraph 57). Consequently, the Italian state had infringed the applicant's right to the freedom of education and freedom of religion.

4.1.3. The Second *Lautsi* Decision

Upon the request of the Italian government, the case was referred to the Grand Chamber. The Grand Chamber reversed the first decision and dismissed the application.[97] In the reasoning of its

96 *Lautsi v Italy*, App no 30814/06, judgment of 3 November 2009.

97 *Lautsi and Others v Italy*, App no 30814/06, judgment of 18 March 2011 [GC].

decision, the ECtHR concluded that the freedom of religion (and, within that, the state's obligation to respect the religious and philosophical conviction of the parents) concerned not only the content of teaching and the way it was conducted but also all of the conditions that 'surrounded' public education and teaching, thus, even objects that can be found in the classroom (Paragraph 63). The Grand Chamber also found that the crucifix above all was a religious symbol. At the same time, it disagreed with the Second Section by finding that there was no evidence to support that the displaying of a religious symbol had an influence on pupils; the crucifix on the wall was a 'passive symbol' (Paragraphs 66 and 72). The applicant's subjective perception with respect to the occurrence of the injury was not in itself sufficient to establish such injury (Paragraph 66). Besides the fact that the crucifix is above all a religious symbol, it also contributes to Italian identity and is traditionally on the walls of schools. The decision whether or not to perpetuate this tradition falls within the margin of appreciation of the state. The doctrine of margin of appreciation of Contracting States is of fundamental importance in the jurisprudence of the ECtHR. According to its permanent practice, the ECtHR provides broader latitude to states in especially sensitive territories where there is no common European standard by deciding that it does not wish to fill in this gap and answer the arising questions in an activist manner.[98]

The ECtHR also took into account how diverse was the cultural and historical evolution of each European State (Paragraph 68). Thus, there is no uniform European standard as to whether or not religious symbols should have a place in public life and public education. Thus, it could not be established that the state infringed the ECHR.

98 The principle of discretion available to the Member States was first applied in connection with the derogation (Article 15) from the applicability of the Convention. See Oren Gross & Fionnuala Ni Aoláin, 'From Derogation to Scrutiny: Revisiting the Application of the Margin of Appreciation Doctrine in the Context of Article 15 of the European Convention of Human Rights', (2001) 23 *Human Rights Quarterly* 625.

4.1.4. Major Criticisms of the Decisions

According to the critics of the first judgment, the decision failed to take into account the pluralism of European states and societies, and wanted to set a 'One Size Fits All' European standard despite the fact that a number of different, and accepted, forms of the separation of church and state exist all across Europe.[99] According to Rob Lamb, the decision confirmed the secular principles of the ECHR over the moral principles of Christianity (upon which many European States were built).[100] In her concurring opinion to the second *Lautsi* decision, Judge Power, criticising the first decision, opines that the second decision only confirmed a body of settled jurisprudence with regard to the fact that mere 'offence' or 'feeling offended' by an undesired statement did not reach the level for which the ECtHR could provide protection for the offended individual.

According to the critics of the second judgment, the ECtHR's assumption regarding the passivity of the crucifix as a symbol was based on a misunderstanding. A symbol is necessarily passive in the sense that it is lifeless and incapable of action. However, the message is not passive and is sufficient to influence schoolchildren, which is impermissible.[101] There is no answer to the question as to why the crucifix can be considered more passive than the Muslim headscarf (with respect to which the ECtHR previously rendered several decisions).

Lorenzo Zucca also challenges the decision because it was based on the margin of appreciation principle. The ECtHR deferred to the decision-making competence of the states for the decision as to what manner they guarantee the right of parents to provide an education to their children in accordance with their convictions. According

99 JHH Weiler, 'Crucifix in the Classroom Redux', (2010) 21 *European Journal of International Law* 2–3.

100 Rob Lamb, 'When Human Rights Have Gone Too Far: Religious Tradition and Equality in *Lautsi v Italy*', (2011) 36 *North Carolina Journal of International Law and Commercial Regulation* 765.

101 Lorenzo Zucca, '*Lautsi*: A Commentary of the Grand Chamber Decision', *Social Science Research Network, working paper*, 14 April 2011, 2–4, papers.ssrn.com/sol3/papers.cfm?abstract_id=1809577.

to Zucca, the application of the margin of appreciation principle passes the decision to the majority in questions presented in the case or similar situations, and this encroaches upon the rights of the minority.[102]

In the concurring opinion of Judge Bonello, criticising Paragraph 63 of the reasoning of the Grand Chamber's decision, he raised the question as to whether the facts presented a human rights question; in other words, should not the ECtHR have declined to hear the case due to lack of jurisdiction?[103] Stijn Smet, similarly, has doubts as to whether displaying the crucifix should be considered such an education or teaching question that can be analysed from the ECHR's point of view.[104] And if there is no 'educational activity', the right to (neutral) education could not have been violated either.

4.2. Questions of the Relationship between State and Church

4.2.1. Interpretations of Secularism

The ideal of the secular public sphere is that crucifix and religious symbols in general have no place within the walls of state institutions. According to this view, social integration can only be achieved in a purely secular, non-religious environment. This rule, by analogy, also extends to state-run educational institutions. The fundamental right to freedom of religion also extends to freedom from religions and to the possibility, at least in the public sphere, that the person exercising this right be able to avoid an encounter with any religious concepts. Based on freedom of religion, everybody has the right to make an informed choice as to which religion they want to follow, which religion they want to reject, and whether they want to live without following any religion. With respect to this decision, the majority's will cannot influence or put any pressure on

102 *Ibid*, 10–12.

103 *Lautsi* (n 96), J Bonello's concurring opinion, para 3.2.

104 Stijn Smet, '*Lautsi v Italy*: The Argument from Neutrality', *Strasbourg Observers*, 22 March 2011.

them. According to the ideal of radical secularism, a non-religious, lay public sphere is the only solution to ensure equal treatment for the members of society and the peaceful coexistence of religious minority communities, agnostics and atheists.[105]

According to the critics of the Grand Chamber's decision in the *Lautsi* case, the ECtHR did not provide an adequate answer to the questions revolving around the interpretation of secularism, which necessarily arose in connection with the case. Namely, the decision considered secularism as an ideology or philosophical concept, one of many competing views. In contrast, the correct interpretation is that secularism is one of the principles that guarantees the functioning of the constitutional state. This view wishes to separate secularism from 'ideologies' presented in the form of religions, making it the guiding principle of the functioning of the state by basically placing it above them. According to Zucca, secularism is not the absence of something (in the present case, the absence of religious symbols in the public sphere) but rather it is a principle that makes liberty, equality and solidarity possible at a social level. The duty of the secular state is to protect the diverse society. Zucca acknowledges that secularism is not a 'neutral' choice, as no political view is, but he believes that this can provide the best default framework for the realisation of a diverse society.[106] Judge Malinverni's and Judge Kalaydjieva's dissenting opinion to the decision of the Grand Chamber was that the ideal of the secular state requires neutrality not only from the school curriculum but also from the whole educational system (actually, the majority opinion also agrees with this).[107]

In one of his former writings, Zucca drew attention to the dangers of secularism. In response to András Sajó's article,[108] he expressed that secularism could also serve to make dialogue impossible between different groups in society, and it could not

105 Gabriel Andreescu & Liviu Andreescu, 'The European Court of Human Rights' *Lautsi* Decision: Context, Contents, Consequences', (2010) 9(26) *Journal for the Study of Religions and Ideologies,* 47, 64–67.

106 Zucca (n 101) 5–8.

107 *Lautsi* (n 96), dissenting opinion, para 3.

108 Sajó (n 16).

deal with the characteristics of a pluralistic society. Instead of assisting in the resolution of existing problems, secularism sweeps them under the rug by banning religious issues from the public sphere. Zucca does not see how secularism could be able to serve simultaneously both the rights of freedom from religions as well as freedom of religion. Namely, banning religions from the public sphere inevitably conflicts with the right to practice one's religion. According to Zucca, the problem is not the existence of religions but the inability of States to manage the difficulties caused by the pluralistic society.[109]

The radical approach to secularism, in my opinion, is not appropriate for adequately managing the serious issues raised in today's Europe. According to Weiler, the tensions of present day Europe do not materialise primarily in the fight between religions; the division is much more extreme between religious and non-religious people. In this struggle, sending religion into exile from the public sphere cannot be considered a neutral response. Thus, removing the crucifix is not more neutral than leaving it untouched. According to Weiler, making the public sphere 'neutral' in this manner is an obstacle to peaceful coexistence and pluralistic society.[110] András Pályi quoted Tadeusz Gadacz, a Polish religious historian, according to whom:

> [today] two models compete: The post-Enlightenment French model and the model of Jagiellonian-Poland proclaiming religious tolerance in Europe for the first time ... today, the former seems to be prevailing. [Gadacz] describes the difference between the two the following way: 'In Jagiellonian times, there were Polish cities where next to the Catholic church and the Protestant chapel, a synagogue and mosque stood, and after the ceremony, the priests of each religion stepped out to the street in their own outfit, and lived their lives like that

109 Lorenzo Zucca, 'The Crisis of the Secular State: A Reply to Professor Sajó', (2009) 7 *International Journal of Constitutional Law* 509–14. See Sajó's response at András Sajó, 'The Crisis That Was Not There: Notes on a Reply', (2009) 7 *International Journal of Constitutional Law* 515–28.

110 Weiler (n 99) 3–5.

> in public. In contrast, the French model forces the priest to change into civilian clothes after the ceremony, and mingle in the crowd like that. Some call this tolerance. But it does not have much to do with tolerance. This is the new, secular ritual imposed upon everybody'.[111]

In connection with the *Lautsi* case, the debate surrounding the philosophical-ideological foundation of human rights becomes heated. While, according to some, the respect for human rights derives partially from the Judeo-Christian religious tradition, others consider human rights as an instrument against the social influence of religions. Despite the fact that the migration of religious and theological concepts into secular law can be clearly verified, and, therefore, the respect of human rights can only be separated from Christian traditions with great difficulty, followers of secularism are keen to use these rights in their arguments aimed at restricting the 'latitude' of religions. The crucifix-case provides an opportunity for a new clash between these conflicting views. Indeed, if human rights are closely linked with Christianity, it would be absurd to demand the removal of the crucifixes. However, if the respect for human rights is a 'secular religion', as Elie Wiesel claims, then their removal is clearly an obligation. At the same time, the possibility of the interpretation of secularism as a neutral 'rule of the game' is also becoming limited.[112]

In my view, adopting secularism has the direct consequence of religions and their practice are pushed into the private sphere. Obviously, it does not mean that, for example, the organisers of a religious procession would be denied permission to use the public areas, but religion would be exiled from the public sphere.

According to certain interpretations, freedom of conscience and freedom of religion are not considered 'communications rights', instead they belong primarily in the private sphere of the individual,

111 András Pályi, 'Kereszttel vagy kereszt nélkül?', *Élet és Irodalom*, 4 December 2009.

112 About this debate and Wiesel's comment, see Zachary R Calo, 'Pluralism, Secularism and the European Court of Human Rights', (2010–11) 26 *Journal of Law & Religion* 111–14.

and their public expression and practice is not necessary.[113] This is perhaps a less nuanced perception, as the public confession and outward expression of faith is, *by its nature*, an integral part of religions. Religion is not a private matter. Freedom of religion is an individual and collective right at the same time. If it did not also have a collective manifestation, then in the absence of institutionalised churches, its distinction from the other forms of free speech would be unwarranted (its external manifestation would be adequately protected by the right to freedom of speech, and its internal aspect by the protection of privacy).

According to Grégor Puppinck, if individuals are only entitled to freedom of religion with the restriction that they have to refrain from practising their religion publicly, this would only create the illusion of religious neutrality. Indeed, religions by nature are social phenomena; the denial of this or restriction of its consequences would ultimately undermine the right of the individual. According to this, the first *Lautsi* decision would have expected the Italian state to pretend that Italian society and culture was religion-free. By contrast, says Puppinck, the state and the people living there clearly have identities, which by extension have religious dimensions. Those who invoke the argument of liberty in *Lautsi* believe that with the right of freedom of religion, it follows that they are entitled to live in a public sphere free from religions.[114] In other words, they are really claiming that their freedom of religion is violated by others practising their right to freedom of religion.

My opinion is that if we restrict the freedom of communities in the name of protecting individuals' rights, this might undermine the rights of individuals belonging to the community. This is true for communities of any size, including families, schools and societies. However, Puppinck goes beyond this to raise the question of whether making individual autonomy absolute would lead to making the rights deriving from this absolute, and thus to the annihilation of

113 Gábor Halmai, *A véleményszabadság határai* (Atlantisz 1994) 112–15.

114 Grégor Puppinck, 'An Alliance Against Secularism', *L'Osservatore Romano*, 28 July 2010.

the state's interests.[115] According to Weiler, the balance must be found between the right to freedom from religion (negative freedom of religion) and the community identity of the nation as well as the interests of the state in its symbolic manifestation.[116] In contrast, according to Susanna Mancini, providing privileges to the religion of the majority or the culture connected thereto means discrimination against minorities. Accordingly, the first *Lautsi* decision was the appropriate move against the tyranny of the majority.[117]

In my opinion, the weak point in the views that are unable to accept the display of the crucifix is that they only consider worthy of protection individuals or entities living in a vacuum, outside the community or beyond this, as members of minority communities. Those individuals who are unfortunate enough to belong to a majority community would necessarily be restricted in their rights for the interest of protecting minorities and other individuals outside the community, do not receive the same, enhanced level of protection they would otherwise be entitled to because of the recognition of their human rights. This restriction contradicts the principles and objectives of equal human dignity. In other words, the right answer is not to totally offset the balance towards the direction of minorities and individuals but to find the appropriate balance between the interests of majority communities and others.

Thus, according to certain views, radical secularism is indispensably important for the functioning of the constitutional state. An alternative view is that it is nothing more than one of the competing ideologies, whose selection violates the ideological neutrality declared by the state. In the latter worldview, secularism is itself an ideology, and while it proclaims itself as the fundamental principle stemming from necessary neutrality and requiring predominance, it in fact violates neutrality. It does not require extraordinary courage to conclude that secularism does not have a uniform, generally accepted meaning in Europe. Accordingly,

115 *Ibid.*

116 Weiler (n 81) 161.

117 Susanna Mancini, 'The Crucifix Rage: Supranational Constitutionalism Bumps Against the Counter-Majoritarian Difficulty', (2010) 6 *European Constitutional Law Review* 16–17, 24.

with respect to the *Lautsi* case, I think that with the analysis of this principle (or ideology) alone, the question before the ECtHR cannot be answered.

4.2.2. Toward the Pluralistic Society

According to Zucca's commentaries to the second *Lautsi* decision, secularism (at least its interpretation that requires the non-religious public sphere) and social pluralism go hand in hand. A European society can only become pluralistic if the state 'frees itself from the grip of one religion'. As he writes, Italy had remained remarkably homogeneous (judging by the context, 'homogeneous' here is probably a negative value judgment), because the majority of the population are Catholic.[118]

In contrast, Weiler believes that European societies are naturally diverse. Due to the common European heritage, both freedom of and freedom from religion are protected. Europe accepts and respects the French (based on the principle of *laïcité*) and English (built on the Anglican Church of England) models for the realisation of freedom of religion, as it also accepts the Swedish, Danish, Greek and Italian approaches. A given state (through its elected representatives) can decide that from now on they follow the French model, but the ECtHR cannot make this mandatory for any state. Moreover, religious tolerance cannot include intolerance against religions or national identity. According to Weiler, the first *Lautsi* decision did not manifest the pluralism and diversity of the ECHR but the values of *laïcité*.[119]

At the same time, Zucca in another study drew attention to the fact that while the model of the French *laïcité* cannot be considered the general practice of secular states (its rigor is not typical elsewhere), the English and Italian approaches referred to by Weiler are secular with respect to the division of state and church (we cannot say that in these societies the church would have an excessive influence on

118 Zucca (n 101) 9.
119 Weiler (n 81) 162–3.

the public sphere).[120] Thus, secularism is present everywhere in Europe to a greater or lesser extent. Zucca accepts that the state has the right to decide which manner and form of secularism it chooses. Thus, *laïcité* cannot be forced onto any of them.

The differences between Zucca's and Weiler's views can be basically traced back to the debate surrounding the definition of secularism. If we believe in radical secularism, then it seems natural that one of the building blocks of a diverse society capable of peaceful coexistence and cooperation must be a religion-free public sphere. If, however, we understand a diverse Europe as a basic attribute (and in my opinion, we cannot justifiably do anything else), then just to the contrary, we can perceive this strict secularisation as a factor inevitably undermining this diversity.

Exposure to religious views may increase tolerance toward them and the potential to understand and accept them. This could be especially important during the encounters between Islam and Europe. If the public sphere is stripped of religions, this could suggest to religious people (the pupil participating in public education) that the public sphere 'does not welcome' but only tolerates religions or banishes them into the private sphere. Weiler says that freedom from religion cannot be an absolute right, because by making it absolute, we would encroach upon others' right to practice their religion.[121]

Pasquale Annicchino notes that the bare wall stripped of the crucifix is also harmful because it prevents children attending school from being exposed to religious symbols (perhaps even to more than one at the same time) and beginning to familiarise themselves with different religions and, therefore, with serious issues and problems facing society. The description of the bare wall as neutral sweeps these under the rug. Democracy is not an empty space but a ground where respect for, and acceptance of, differences must be achieved. According to Annicchino, the removal of the cross facilitates the termination of the discourse and cannot serve the principle of

120 Lorenzo Zucca, 'Crucifix in the Classroom: The Best Solution to the *Lautsi* Case', working paper (Social Science Research Network August 2010), papers.ssrn.com/sol3/papers.cfm?abstract_id=1667496.

121 Weiler (n 81) 160.

pluralism.[122] According to the Coalition of Professors intervening before the ECtHR in the *Lautsi* case, the displaying of the crucifix on the wall of the school means not the end of an argument but an invitation for dialogue.[123]

According to Weiler, pluralism would be facilitated if everybody could display their own religious (or other ideological) symbols in the classroom. The school cannot prohibit this without infringing the principle of pluralism. Modern European societies must show respect toward the different religions and worldviews, and children must be raised accordingly. Respect is not achieved by making all these symbols disappear. If the educational program attaches importance to the representation and presentation of the values of tolerance and mutual respect, then religious symbols may have a place on classroom walls.[124]

Smet, in his paper commenting on the decision of the Grand Chamber, also took a stand for open neutrality. Open neutrality would not ban the use of religious symbols from the public sphere (like its opposite, closed neutrality), but, to the contrary, it would allow all symbols into the public sphere.[125]

Benedek Varsányi raises the question as to whether a solution allowing the display of all religious symbols (say, per the request of children going to the given class or their parents) would be in line with the first *Lautsi* decision. He takes it from the ECtHR's reasoning that under the interpretation of the first decision, the obligation of religious neutrality would prohibit this, too. As he writes, 'this direction of reasoning shows the tendency that the pluralism argument is separated from its original consideration (the respect for the parents' religious and ideological convictions), as well as from the objective institution-protection approach connected to

122 Pasquale Annicchino, 'Is the glass half empty or half full? *Lautsi v Italy* the European Court of Human Rights', *Stato, Chiese e pluralismo confessionale,* May 2010, 18.

123 Comments of Third-party Intervenor Coalition of Professors of Law, 2010, para 6, strasbourgconsortium.org/document.php?DocumentID=4944.

124 Weiler (n 99) 5.

125 Smet (n 104) 10.

freedom of conscience and religion, and it becomes a separate, "laicity" type, imperative neutrality principle'.[126]

According to Zachary Calo, we will be able to close the debate on the appropriate interpretation of secularism and pluralism satisfactorily when we rise above the scope of earlier interpretations, and the age of 'post-secularism' arrives. This is because it would not be impossible to reconcile respect for religious tradition and human rights, even if, besides the numerous commonalities, there is a lot of tension hidden in their relationship. If we look at religious tradition as a system of norms, which is different from the system based on the respect for human rights, but is capable of enriching the discourse about the nature of human rights and the moral foundations of the modern world, then we can leave undecided the debate where the main question is whether secularism itself is an ideology or indeed a neutral 'organising principle'.[127]

Thus, we can choose the best solution for maintaining the pluralistic state depending on which interpretation of secularism we believe in and on whether we can rise above the 'traditional' narratives of secularism (see Calo). If, however, we accept Weiler's and Smet's arguments regarding the walls open for symbols, we have to answer one additional question: How can we fit in, can we fit in at all, the principle of 'open neutrality' that although the display of all religious symbols is permitted, there is one among these, whose display is mandated by the state. Another question is whether the display by the state of non-religious (cultural) symbols is permissible? In other words, can religious and 'purely' cultural symbols be treated differently in this respect?

4.2.3. The Meaning of State Neutrality

What does the principle of state neutrality mean with respect to the representation of religions in the public sphere? As we have seen, from radical secularism it would follow that religions cannot

126 Benedek Varsányi, 'Az erősebb "nem" jogán? Az állam semlegessége, lelkiismereti és vallásszabadság a Lautsi-ügy tükrében', (2010) 14(4) *Fundamentum* 93.

127 Calo (n 112) 18, 114–17.

be present in any manner in the public sphere. Thus, it does not only mean that the state cannot prefer one religion to the detriment of the others or against the others, but that it cannot allow the representatives, symbols, rituals and other acts within the, broadly interpreted, territory of the state. The 'softer' interpretation of secularism would not ban religions from the public sphere, but it would not allow the state to treat any of them differently from the others. In other words, the rules of equal treatment would have to prevail in this respect, too. It follows from both views that the crucifixes could not stay on the classroom walls of state schools.

However, there is another interpretation of state neutrality. Pursuant to the constitutional law principle of neutrality, the state is not allowed to select from among the available ideologies and value judgments. It must treat them equally.[128] Thus, it cannot give one a more favourable position, in any form, than the other. The principle of neutrality, however, can only be maintained as long as it guarantees that everybody can freely choose from among the available ideas. In other words, the state cannot force anybody when making this decision. The state, however, cannot be completely independent, and this principle does not expect indifference from it. It does not follow from the principle of pluralism that the state cannot designate priorities based on value judgments at all. However, it does follow that it cannot demand exclusivity and cannot say that only the ideology it prefers is correct.

Individuals are not born into a vacuum. The surrounding cultural environment provides individuals with the possibility of value selection, and the state has an important role to ensure that the choice of the different alternatives are available, with an emphasis on those that feature the values most characteristic of their own citizens, and compared with other options, to support them with more emphasis. The man of modern times condemns the destruction of the several thousand years old Buddha statutes in Afghanistan by the Taliban, irrespective of whether or not he is a Buddhist. Another example is the condemnation of the destruction of the

128 Jeroen Temperman, 'The Neutral State: Optional or Necessary? A Triangular Analysis of State-Religion Relationships, Democratisation, and Human Rights Compliance', (2006) 1(3) *Religion & Human Rights* 269.

statues of Notre-Dame during the French revolution, and believing in renovating the cathedral via public funds irrespective of being a member of the Catholic church or accepting Christianity.

Deciding on what days the state should designate as public holidays, what they teach in schools, whether they should maintain a ministry of culture, all require choices of value judgments, which are absolutely necessary and desirable.[129] The task should be carried out even if at a given moment only a smaller proportion of the community deems it necessary or important. —Its value does not depend on how many recognise it, after all we also cling to democracy, although we probably will never reach the point when joint decisions will really be made by the majority and based really on careful consideration, after a debate of rational and carefully considered arguments. It would be worthwhile to maintain libraries and galleries even if only a few would be interested in them, simply because the protection of values that must be preserved based on a certain consensus made in the past, even if that consensus is no longer clearly apparent or widely debated. Of course, it cannot mean the formal reduction of the state's latitude to, for example, determine cultural public policy by referring to some sort of a timeless cultural tradition. However, the state (the government) must necessarily consider even as a matter of its own interest these traditions.

The state and the actual government cannot distance themselves from the history and traditions of the given country or nation. However, obviously, a state decision that would call for the removal of crucifixes in the private sphere based on changed social circumstances is not inherently prohibited. At the same time, it is a question whether an international court has such degree of authorisation to influence state policies. Respect for the principle of state neutrality thus cannot mean an exit from the cultural traditions and their forced removal from the territory of the state. Religious tradition is inseparably intertwined with cultural traditions, and this

129 Sanford Levinson, 'The Tutelary State: "Censorship", "Silencing", and the "Practices of Cultural Regulation"' in Robert Post (ed), *Censorship and Silencing: The Practices of Cultural Regulation* (Getty Research Institute 1998) 195–220.

is a given fact in every Western state.[130] Consequently, the principle of state neutrality is not violated *per se* if representatives of certain religions and certain churches in some contexts enjoy (to a limited extent) a preferred status, which they gain from the state.

Meanwhile, the state preserves its neutrality by refraining from 'conversion'. In other words, it does not influence the thinking of its citizens and does not expect them to identify with the churches that are placed into more favourable positions. Of course, 'placing into a more favourable position' itself may have a direct influence. In other words, with respect to certain religions, the state takes a position, and by supporting it, makes it clear that it values the activities of the religion or its representative church.[131] This, at the same time, does not mean that the state is applying pressure toward its citizens, but stems from the recognition of the cultural tradition as described above. The representative of Buddhist teachings is treated the same way as Christians. The Catholic Archbishop and the guru have equal rights; only the organisations they represent have different social importance and cultural relevance. Exactly for this reason, based on objective considerations, the state may rationally differentiate between government funding for Buddhist or Catholic schools. In contrast, the state cannot discriminate against the non-beneficiary Churches and religions. For example, the Buddhists may receive government funding for maintaining educational or social institutions, and the pupils may also study about Buddha, and so forth.

Under this interpretation, state neutrality is compatible with the compulsory display of crucifixes in state schools. As Weiler writes,

130 See, in the context of human rights and democracy: Larry Siedentop, *Inventing the Individual: The Origins of Western Liberalism* (Allen Lane 2014); Michael J Perry, *Toward a Theory of Human Rights: Religion, Law, Courts* (Cambridge University Press 2006), and George Weigel, *The Cube and the Cathedral: Europe, America, and Politics Without God* (Basic Books 2006).

131 Leni Franken, *Liberal Neutrality and State Support for Religion* (Springer International 2016), and András Sajó, 'Constitutionalism and Secularism: The Need for Public Reason', (2009) 30 *Cardozo Law Review* 2401, 2407.

displaying portraits of 'heroes' of the secular state in the classroom (in other words, 'purely' cultural symbols') also does not comply with the broad interpretation of state neutrality (according to which this space must be free from religious symbols). Why is it more neutral to hang Voltaire's portrait on the wall promoting the ideals of 'Liberty, Equality and Fraternity' than to display the crucifix? Why does it not violate the principle of neutrality if other ideological symbols (such as the universally used peace sign) are displayed instead of religious ones?[132] However, there is one dividing line. Namely, that the national-historical tradition does not have a transcendent aspect, while the religious does. Therefore, the latter points from the 'historical-cultural' reality toward a higher sphere. At the same time, the formation and evolution of the European States were inextricably intertwined for centuries with religions and churches, and only as the result of a fairly new historical development have churches been somewhat excluded from the public sphere. Thus, the religious and cultural meanings of certain symbols used in certain context inseparably intertwine. According to Paolo Carozza, cultural tradition exists whether we want it or not, and we cannot erase or rewrite it entirely, only perhaps revise the current one[133] (but, obviously, not by a simple, central decision and from one day to the next).

Judge Bonello writes in his concurring opinion to the decision of the Grand Chamber that '[a] court of human rights cannot allow itself to suffer from historical Alzheimer's'.[134] Judge Bonello refers to the ECtHR's decision in the *Akdaş v Turkey*, according to which the decision banning the distribution of one of Guillaume Apollinaire's rather pornographic novels violated the right to freedom of speech enshrined in Article 10 of the ECHR.[135] The ECtHR (the same Second Section that rendered the first *Lautsi* decision) found that the novel is part of the European literary heritage.[136] If this is so (and in my opinion this is indeed the case), then the question is why Christian

132 Weiler (n 81) 159.

133 Carozza's opinion is quoted by Eric Rassbach, 'The Persistence of Memory', *The Becket Fund*, 25 March 2011 (no longer available online).

134 *Lautsi* (n 96), J Bonello's concurring opinion, para 1.1.

135 *Akdaş v Turkey*, App no 41056/04, judgment of 16 February 2010.

136 *Lautsi* (n 96), J Bonello's concurring opinion, paras 4.1–4.2.

tradition was not worthy of a few thoughts in the reasoning of the first *Lautsi* decision.

According to Sajó, the interpretation of state neutrality according to which certain religions and churches receive government funding and favoured status because of tradition, 'in reality, is only a bias in favour of the preservation of the *status quo*'.[137] In this view, religious neutrality can only aim at full equality, and neither 'size' nor 'historical-national merits' are permissible considerations in determining the manner and extent of government funding. I argue in this chapter as well as in Chapter 2 that this view leaves me with a sense of void, considering that we cannot deprive the state and society of their religious and cultural traditions with simple, administrative decisions; the interruption of the transfer of religious traditions in this manner would be the denial of the historical past, which would result in the lack of understanding the processes of the present.[138]

According to Puppinck, it follows from the spirit of the first *Lautsi* decision that the ECtHR should not close at Christmas and Easter, and should adopt a new calendar that avoids any references to Jesus Christ (as was done by the French revolutionaries some two hundred years ago; and as a matter of fact, Judge Bonello addresses a similar question to the applicant). Puppinck states that the religious identity of a society cannot be 'neutralized'. It can be denied, fought against and replaced, but it cannot be neutralized. In light of this, it is questionable whether a supranational body can make an attempt to modify the religious identity of a country.[139]

In my opinion, it is very difficult to make a consistent and principled distinction between religious and cultural symbols and in the question regarding the permission to display. This is because, on one hand, religious symbols are also at the same time cultural symbols. For example, if we display in a classroom a

137 András Sajó, 'Concepts of Neutrality and the State' in Ronald Dworkin et al (eds), *From Liberal Values to Democratic Transition: Essays in Honour of János Kis* (CEU 2004) 107–45.

138 See also Calo (n 112) 109.

139 Puppinck (n 114) 21.

picture of the statue of the founder of the Hungarian state, King Saint Stephen, in which he is holding in his hands the apostolic double cross, then do we have to consider it as a religious or cultural symbol? On the other hand, cultural symbols also represent clear positions in a debate about values similarly to religious symbols, and, thus, if displaying the latter violates the neutrality of the state, then it would be difficult to defend the former, too. Displaying the state coat of arms on the walls of public institutions already represents a position (yet, it has not occurred that it would be impermissible).

Weiler notes that the Italian state's argument in *Lautsi* (according to which the crucifix is primarily a cultural symbol) undermines its significance; as a result, the state indirectly admits that religious symbols have no place in the public sphere.[140] However, in one of his other papers, Weiler acknowledges that the crucifix is not solely a religious symbol.[141] I agree with the notion that if we strip the crucifix of its religious meaning, we offend those believing in it. However, I think that religious symbols cannot necessarily be completely separated from cultural symbols, because religions have been shaping and are still shaping culture. Hence, it is not necessary to choose between one or the other meaning of the crucifix; both can be accepted simultaneously (or acknowledged by those who reject the religious meaning).

In summary, one of the possible interpretations of state neutrality continues down the path of the interpretation called radical secularism and would banish all religious symbols from the public sphere. The other view is more permissive than this, and says that based on historical-cultural traditions, the state can treat certain religions as more important than others, if it does so with appropriate caution and by avoiding discrimination against other religions. However, it does not necessarily follow from the latter view that the state would have the right to require the display of crucifixes on the walls of state institutions. Those who acknowledge this right have to also look for additional arguments.

140 Weiler (n 99) 3.
141 Weiler (n 81) 162.

4.2.4. 'Freedom of Speech' of the State

The analyses in the previous parts of this chapter built upon each other and led together to the issue of the state/government's 'freedom of speech'. In my opinion, there is no such uniform definition of secularism generally accepted in Europe that could serve as a basis for the decision of an international court in a case similar to the *Lautsi* case. The argument continues that a pluralistic and diverse Europe distinguishes between and permits many forms of state attitudes towards religion. Religious practice cannot purely be a 'private matter', because it necessarily has community and, what is more, social manifestations. State neutrality does not mean indifference toward religions, and the state's conduct arising from the obligation of neutrality may reflect the cultural traditions of the given state. The next step, which will round off the argument, is the recognition of the state's 'freedom of speech' in issues concerning the cultural (and religious) traditions of its citizens. The state obviously cannot be the subject of fundamental rights, including freedom of speech, but it can have objectives and interests that require public communications on its part. If we consider the state (or more precisely its different representatives, together forming a rather diverse group, the Parliament, the government, the education policy, the cultural policy, etc.) as the representative of society 'who' acts in the name of society, then it can assume a role in the communication and expression of the opinion of its citizens. Judge Rozakis, in his concurring opinion (joined by Judge Vajić), referred to the right of the social majority, based on which it can express its religious conviction. According to the Judge, the state's decision regarding the display of crucifixes aims at the expression of the opinion of the majority community.[142]

We cannot think of the state as the subject of freedom of speech but rather as an entity that is capable of restricting freedom. *Lautsi* also focused on the state restricting freedom of religion and education. The state (primarily, the Parliament and organs executing certain public policies) has the right (and in a number of cases even the obligation) to take a stand in disputed (even in 'life or death')

142 *Lautsi* (n 96), concurring opinion of J Rozakis, s (iii).

issues. We have already mentioned these obligations of the state in the course of our analysis of the content of state neutrality. The state institutions make the decision, for example, as to how much money is spent in support of culture, and in what proportion it is distributed among theatres, museums and film production companies; they decide what should constitute the curriculum of public education; they decide on how much money they give to institutes of higher education and what courses the money should be spent on, etc.

Nobody disputes the fact that a society (or a nation, people, or community) has the right to maintain its self-identity and preserve its cultural tradition, and in doing so, it may receive assistance from the state. It is also hardly disputable that the majority communities in society may receive a larger proportion from this assistance than other communities. We also have to accept that 'the state', in the context of the crucifix-case, based on democratic authorisation, includes the various public bodies and persons (e.g., Parliament, the government, and the institution executing education policy) charged with representative rights and making decisions in the name of the majority. It follows from all this that when the state decides to make it compulsory to display the crucifixes on classroom walls of state schools, it conveys the opinion of its citizens. It recognises a religious tradition, deems it worthy of support, and expresses the importance thereof. Further, it does this without forcing anybody to accept it. For me the question is not whether this purpose of the state is legitimate (as we have seen, the state in many contexts and subjects cannot even avoid to openly take a position), but whether it oversteps the scope of the permissible exercise of rights by making the display of the crucifix compulsory.

Regarding the latter issue, I believe that if the state does not try to force anyone to accept the views it thinks to be sensible or cultural traditions it thinks to be worthy of its protection, and it only offers these as options for its citizens, then the state does not overstep the boundaries of its permissible latitudes. In the judgment of the crucifix-case, the 'reasonable observer' category of the US jurisprudence might provide some assistance. The 'reasonable observer' is greatly similar to the 'reasonable reader' of British defamation lawsuits. The courts describe this 'reasonable reader' as someone who 'does not live in an ivory tower', can read between the lines, and can interpret the entire text with its connections and in context.[143] The hypothetical standard of the average person, the average reader, 'the man on the Clapham omnibus', or the 'reasonable reader' is relevant for the determination of the injury. Accordingly, the 'reasonable observer' is a person who, when he encounters a cross at a public place, can properly judge what the symbol means as well as why and in what circumstances it was erected.

In *Salazar v Buono*, the different courts involved argued about what the 'reasonable observer' would think about the cross at issue in the case. I think that the hypothetical average European person knows exactly that with crosses standing in public places the state does not want to convert him. The majority of crucifixes have been in place for long decades and centuries, and in most cases, the religious meaning of the crosses indeed fades and becomes secondary to the cultural meaning. If a hypothetical average European sees a church with scaffolds, he does not think about how much money the state might pull out from the taxpayers' pockets with the renovation, but that based on what he observes, the state properly undertakes its conservation obligations. In other words, pursuant to my conclusion, if the exercise of the state's 'freedom of speech' does not exceed an acceptable limit and does not put pressure on its citizens with respect to choose between the various views, the expression of cultural traditions and presence in the public sphere can be acceptable.

5. Conclusions

Presumably, Weiler, who supports the display of various different symbols upon request, is not really satisfied with the consequences of the Bavarian crucifix decision. The new rule orders the crucifix to be removed if a complaint is submitted and not to display other symbols equally according to needs and on request; in this way (though crucifixes typically may stay where they are), the state

143 *McQuire v Western Morning News* [1903] 2 KB 100 (CA); *Hall v Brooklands Auto-Racing Club* (1933) 1 KB 205; *Lewis v Daily Telegraph* [1964] AC 234, HL.

responds to complaints with empty walls, thus it immediately closes rather than starts the discussion. As opposed to this, Zucca finds that the best solution to the Italian crucifix case would be that while the display of the symbol would remain mandatory, parents would be entitled to protest it. In addition, the question of whether the crucifix can remain, the wall should be empty or other symbols should also be added alongside the crucifix would be decided at a forum of debate after a well-established reasoning and common reflection; this is a mixture of the Bavarian solution and the ideas of Weiler.[144]

The facts of the Bavarian case and *Lautsi* essentially differ from the majority of US cases on one issue. In the two European decisions, the debate was not about the installation of one single symbol but the display of the same symbol in all classrooms. In this sense, the Bavarian and the Italian state 'interfered' with the lives of students more powerfully than a city or a government that erects one single religious symbol in one place. However, the European cases are largely similar to *Stone v Graham*. Based on the latter, we might come to the following conclusion: Presumably both the Bavarian and the Italian regulations would have failed the test before the court in the United States. However, beyond that, a comparison of the argumentations, the justification or reasoning given by the court in the European cases and the analogies of US cases other than *Stone* would also teach us some lessons.

The justification given by the Second Section (first *Lautsi* judgment) overlaps the justification of Judges Brennan, Stevens, Ginsburg and others regarding the characteristics of the secular state. According to these judges, religious symbols should not be present in public life and it is not permissible for the state to use them. At the same time, the Grand Chamber (second *Lautsi* judgment) emphasised the passive character of the symbol, that is, the fact that there was no state force to use it. The 'passive nature' of symbols and therefore their freedom from expressing the opinion of the state or the lack of pressure being exerted by the state were also arguments raised in the US cases. The Italian state referred to the cultural and historical significance of the crucifix, in the same

144 Zucca (n 120).

way as the US judges agreeing upon the constitutionality of the erection of symbols raised the secular 'message' of the state, devoid of its religious content. This exposed the Italian state to criticism, according to which depriving the crucifix of its religious content is too high a price for its preservation; secularising religious symbols can only lead to the dissatisfaction of both the opposing parties.[145] According to Marie E Roper, emphasising the secular content of symbols violates the rule of religious neutrality from the perspective of religions. For her, it also seems absurd if the court allows the use of religious symbols in public life only if the symbol also has a secular meaning.[146] As opposed to this, the German Constitutional Court deemed the Bavarian regulation as unconstitutional due to the 'inviting' character of the crucifix and showing the religious content symbolised by the crucifix as an example worth following, which makes the two decisions different from one essential aspect.[147]

At the same time, the Grand Chamber, in the statement of reasons for its decision, mentioned Italian traditions as well, thereby providing an opportunity for drawing parallels between its judgment and the US decisions respecting historical traditions. Of course, respect for historical traditions as the decisive argument also projects the view that while churches might preserve or protect their remaining bastions surviving from the past (symbols in public places), they have no chance of erecting new ones.

Zucca challenged the second *Lautsi* judgment because he disapproves of the fact that it was based on the principle of the margin of appreciation. He thinks that applying the margin of appreciation principle leaves the question to be decided by society's majority in the given question or in similar questions,

145 Weiler (n 99) 3.

146 Marie Elizabeth Roper, 'Secular Crosses and the Neutrality of Secularism: Reflections on the Demands of Neutrality and its Consequences for Religious Symbols: The European Court of Human Rights in *Lautsi* and the US Supreme Court in *Salazar*', (2012) *Vanderbilt Journal of Transnational Law* 841, 874–6.

147 Tobias Lock, 'Of Crucifixes and Headscarves: Religious Symbols in German Schools' in Myriam Hunter-Henin (ed), *Law, Religious Freedoms and Education in Europe* (Ashgate 2011) 354.

which curtails the right of the minority.[148] This problem was also raised concerning the analysis of consequences of the government speech doctrine outlined in the majority reasoning of *Pleasant Grove City*.

Although the US cases are rather diverse with markedly and significantly differing opinions put forward by judges (moreover, the two *Lautsi* judgments also contradict one another), certain conclusions might be drawn after making an overview of them. The common lesson of all these US judgments is that a secular purpose is always required whenever a religious symbol is used by the government. In other words, the symbol must also convey a secular meaning and that meaning must be more important in the given context than the religious meaning of the given symbol. At the same time, the significance of the historic past and social and community traditions are also acknowledged by the court decisions. The latter means that the symbols that have been used or have existed for a long time and have a relevant secular purpose and meaning (Christmas, the memorial commemorating soldiers killed in wars, recognition of local religious communities and traditions) are likely to meet the first criterion regarding the secular purpose. As such, elapsed time becomes a constitutionally significant factor in the process of judging the cases. Newer religious symbols that people wish to erect can also be constitutional if a justifiable secular purpose is achieved through them. However, this 'escape' takes its toll, since the religious message is obscured. Secularising originally religious symbols in order to save them will essentially contribute to secularisation gaining ground, at the expense of religions, and we cannot rule out the possibility that, in the long run, it will prove to be too high a price for churches.[149] At the same time, transforming religious symbols into cultural symbols is not a generally accepted position. Rejecting the 'profanation' of the Cross was part of the reasoning of the German Constitutional Court, it is true that this led to declaring the regulation prescribing the mandatory placement of crucifixes in classrooms as unconstitutional.

148 Zucca (n 101) 10–12.

149 Steven D Smith, 'Religious Symbols and Secular Government', (2013) 46(2) *Israel Law Review* 193, 205.

A very interesting development of US judicial practice is the recognition of the 'government speech' doctrine, which under certain circumstances authorises the state to convey messages with religious content. However, this right is not unlimited. Its exercise is limited by traditions and the will of the majority of society and its abuse might be punished in the course of the political process, that is, at national and local elections. The recognition of the freedom of government speech essentially leads to a significant restriction of the rule of the religious neutrality of the state, or rather it leads to a restricted interpretation of it. The *Lautsi* case, so far the only decision by the ECtHR similar to the US cases, basically caused similar arguments to appear and finally, within certain limits, accepted the freedom of the state to decide on questions regarding the use of symbols. These decisions, and the principles and rules that can be derived from them, provide suitable orientation in new debates; however, they are not sufficient (neither in Europe, nor in the United States) to help these modern 'wars of religion' come to an end; these decisions therefore cannot be taken as the courts' last words.

In the *Lautsi* case, only a sufficiently measured judgment was appropriate and therefore the first judgment left a lot to be desired in the eyes of those reading it. The second judgment avoided taking positions on the really essential questions, in a way which is not unacceptable, taking the jurisprudence of the court and the interpretation it has of its own role into account. However, we may draw some conclusions.

The first is that secularism has no generally accepted European definition which could serve as the basis for a supranational court's decision-making process; hence, it is not at all clear which interpretation brings us closer to the appropriate functioning of a multifaceted and diverse state. From this it also follows that we cannot claim with full certainty that freedom of religion (and freedom of education) can only be achieved through radical secularisation (e.g. 'bare walls').

The second is that the neutrality of the state cannot be a synonym for indifference and the state might take a stand in debates over values, but it cannot force anybody to take any decision in this area. In the process of the state prioritising values, which is necessary, the demand of the minority cannot be synonymous with an automatic 'veto' of the will of the majority (expressed indirectly). Minority rights do not include the ability to block any majority will unconditionally.

The third conclusion is that tradition and history do count; religion is part of our traditions which must be considered. We cannot pretend that traditions do not exist. Traditions change from country to country, which again makes the task of international courts more burdensome.[150]

If there is no uniform concept of secularism, generally accepted in Europe; if pluralistic and diverse Europe also differentiates between and allows for the various kinds of attitudes the state shows toward religions, and if exercising one's religion unconditionally cannot be a purely private matter, because it necessarily has community as well as societal manifestations, and the neutrality of the state does not mean indifference to religions, the conclusion is that the conduct of the state, determined by the obligation to remain neutral, might reflect the cultural traditions of the given society. The next step is the recognition of the 'freedom of government speech' in questions which deal with the cultural and religious traditions of its citizens. Naturally, the state cannot be the subject of fundamental rights, and so it does not have the right to freedom of speech in the traditional sense of the concept, but it might have objectives and interests which require public communication on the parts of the state. If we consider the state (more precisely its individual representatives, who otherwise are rather diverse, such as the national assembly, the government, education policy, cultural policy, etc.) as the representative of society, on whose behalf it acts, then it might participate in conveying and expressing the opinions of its citizens.

In his concurring opinion, Judge Rozakis (joined by Judge Vajić) refers to the right of the majority of society, on the basis of which they can express their religious convictions. According to

150 As regards similar conclusions, see, e.g., John Witte, 'Lift High the Cross? An American Perspective on *Lautsi v Italy*', (2011) 13(3) *Ecclesiastical Law Journal* 341–3.

the judge, the decision of the state on displaying crucifixes aims to express the opinion of the majority community.[151]

But, again, we cannot think of the state as the subject of freedom of speech, it is rather an entity having the ability to limit freedom. In *Lautsi*, too, the state limiting freedom of religion and education was the focus of analyses. Nevertheless, the state has the right, and in several cases the obligation to take a stand in disputed questions.

151 *Lautsi* (n 96), J Rozakis's concurring opinion, s (iii).

Chapter 2

The Freedom of the State in Integrating Religious Studies in Public Education

1. Introduction

The decisions of the state adopted during organising public education are usually not considered to be manifestations of the freedom of expression. When fulfilling this obligation, the state carries out an indispensable task, and cannot avoid the expression of values when determining who is entitled to teach, in which institutions and which disciplines, with which content and in what type of system. Although the leeway for deciding these questions is quite extensive, it is not unlimited as the freedom of education and the fundamental rights of the persons receiving the education must be ensured and are binding on the state in this context like any other. Appropriately integrating religions in the education system entails a certain choice of values on the part of the state. There is no dispute in the Western world that religious studies are an important element of public education. Moreover, there seems to be a European consensus on certain aspects of religious education in schools, as summarised in the Toledo Directives compiled at the request of the Organisation for Security and Cooperation in Europe.[1] There is no such agreement, however, on whether mandatory attendance of religious education lessons can be required, and if so, under what conditions. When a state decides to prescribe such an obligation, it simultaneously adopts an unequivocal stance on the role of religion in public life. Although such a stance cannot be viewed as exercising the freedom of expression, it still qualifies as an 'opinion' in the

1 ODIHR Advisory Council of Experts on Freedom of Religion or Belief, Toledo Guiding Principles on Teaching About Religions and Beliefs in Public Schools. OSCE/ODIHR, 2007.

public eye. It is for this reason that this chapter has a place in a book discussing the relationship between the freedom of expression and religious beliefs.

2. Teaching Religion

2.1. The Different State Regulations

In a monograph by Norman Doe, European states are grouped according to their treatment of religious education in state schools. As expected, the results are extremely variegated. Doe's categories are as follows:

(i) Mandatory Christianity studies: The curriculum envisages classes in religious studies based on Christian fundaments, but there is no distinction between the various Christian denominations. The Danish and British education systems follow this.[2]

(ii) Mandatory Christianity studies of a single denomination: The content of the classes is determined by the dominant Christian denomination in that state. In Malta, this is the Catholic Church, while in Greece and Cyprus, it is generally the Orthodox Church, in respect of state schools in the entire country. Compulsory religious education in Austria, Germany and Belgium is not limited to a single denomination, and if there are a sufficient number of students belonging to the same denomination in a school, religious classes must be provided for each of these groups separately, in accordance with their denomination.[3]

(iii) Optional religion lessons based on the teachings of one of the Christian denominations: In this case, the state's obligation is to organise education, but the key point is its non-compulsory nature, so student attendance is discretional. This is the case in Italy, Spain, Portugal and many of Central Eastern European countries.[4]

2 Norman Doe, *Law and Religion in Europe. A Comparative Introduction* (Oxford University Press 2011) 191–2.

3 *Ibid*, 192–4.

4 *Ibid*, 194–6.

(iv) Denomination-neutral teaching of religion: The classes discuss religions in general, and therefore lack an explicit Christian focus in their content. Attendance in these classes is mandatory in Sweden, whereas in Bulgaria, the school is under an obligation to provide such classes at the request of the students.[5]

(v) Prohibition of religious teaching: It is prohibited to conduct any kind of religious studies on school premises, but students who wish to participate in such classes may do so outside of school. The French educational system allows students to leave school premises during school time on weekdays for the purpose of attending religious classes. In Slovenia, it is permitted to organise religious education on school premises if it is separated from public educational activities.[6]

Where the state does not prohibit religious education, it also undertakes to assume the expenses of providing it. However, the 'mandatory' nature thereof does not mean that exemption on request is not possible in any of these countries. The most important argument for the constitutionality of 'mandatory' religious education and its non-discriminatory nature is that nobody may be forced to participate in any kind of education against their will. In some cases, general ethics classes are provided as an alternative; in other cases, the student is simply exempted from attending school while religious education classes are being held. Exemption may be requested by the parents, or even by the student after reaching a certain age limit. The recognition of faith schools, however, is an altogether separate question from the matter of religious education in state schools. The state supports institutions operated by churches by, on the one hand, acknowledging the education conducted by them as equal to the state system and, on the other hand, by financial subventions. Naturally, faith schools do not have to be neutral when it comes to religious values if respect for the rules of non-discrimination is otherwise observed.[7]

5 *Ibid*, 196.

6 *Ibid*, 197.

7 *Ibid*, 199–203.

In Germany, each province may freely decide on the nature of its school system within the boundaries set by the *Grundgesetz*. The state is neutral from a religious point of view, but state schools may be either denomination-neutral or denomination-affiliated. With the exception of the former, religious studies are mandatory in all state schools.[8] According to the resolution of the Constitutional Court of Germany, which was adopted in 1975, the existence of state schools with Christian values is not against the constitution, even if parents have no alternative schools available to send their children to.[9] In this specific case, the aggrieved parent complained that the child was obliged to attend a denomination-affiliated school, where education is based on Christian values, as the constitution of Baden-Württemberg sets out that this is the only type of school that the province operates.

According to the Federal Constitutional Court, the federal constitution does not prescribe to the provinces the types of schools they must maintain. It is permitted for the province legislature to operate only schools with Christian values. However, 'coercive measures' must be minimised in such institutions; in other words, pressure cannot be put on students to accept and follow a certain religion. The schools must be open to other ideologies, religious convictions and values and the province cannot limit its education-related goals to serving only those who are affiliated with one of the Christian denominations. The Christian character of a school primarily means the acknowledgment of the historic and social importance of Christianity in shaping Western civilization, and its purpose is to demonstrate this role in education. This is not to be considered as discriminatory against those who are members of a minority because they are not followers of any Christian denomination, as long as the education serves the purpose of fulfilling individual autonomy while acknowledging religious freedom. The operation of schools which provide for an objective discourse of all philosophical and religious views, even if such schools have a distinct ideological orientation, does not lead to unreasonable conflict with the freedom of religion and conscience of the non-Christian students and their parents (section C I.3 of the resolution).

8 Grundgesetz, Art 7(3).

9 41 BVerfGE 29 (1975).

The different states of the US may only operate religiously neutral schools. However, there were several examples in the past where some states intended to prescribe that schools must respect certain aspects of a religion in the context of their curriculum. In the first half of the twentieth century, several states punished teaching the Darwinian theory of evolution with criminal sanctions. A teacher was convicted in Tennessee for denying the veracity of the Biblical creation. The restriction was upheld by the Federal Supreme Court.[10] In 1968, the Federal Supreme Court declared similar legislation in Arkansas to be unconstitutional. The majority of the judges were of the opinion that the First Amendment does not allow the states to organise their education system around the tenets of any religious group or dogma.

The movements preaching the theory of creationism, which is rejected by many influential churches, have succeeded in obtaining great influence in many US states.[11] For example, in Louisiana the state legislation prescribed that if the schools set out to teach the theory of evolution, they must also mention the 'science of creationism'. The Supreme Court invalidated this statute, too, in *Edwards v Aguillard*.[12] The state pleaded for the freedom of education by saying that the intent behind the rule was to ensure that those teachers who believe the theory of creationism will not be put into an unfavourable position when

10 *Scopes v State* 393 US 97 (1927)—it must be noted, however, that the Supreme Court did not review the constitutionality of the rule for procedural reasons, thus failing to resolve the most important question of all.

11 Creationism is the generic term for all views, according to which not only was the world and life created by a wilful power (this being the common denominator of all major religions), but that such different geneses should be interpreted literally. Creationism's followers mainly belong to various fundamentalist religious movements, who deny the modern scientific findings on the creation of life. One of these movements is Christian or Biblical creationism, which is extremely popular in the United States. The Catholic Church also finds that the Biblical genesis story is compatible with the achievements of modern day science.

12 *Edwards v Aguillard* 482 US 578 (1987).

having to teach the theory of evolution. However, those teachers were, in any case, entitled to this freedom of education without the need for such a regulation as they were free to introduce other views when teaching the Darwinian theory of evolution. The aim of the legislation was clearly to favour the creationism theory, in other words, the secular goal required by the *Lemon* test was absent.[13] For example, it was prescribed that certain educational materials are to be prepared and that a research service be provided for teachers in relation to creationism, while such aid was not provided in relation to the teaching of the theory of evolution; moreover, the opinions expressed during the discussions preceding the passage of the law and the background materials both reflected such a bias.

A similar endeavour followed this with the attempted introduction of the Intelligent Design (ID) theory into the education system.[14] According to the district court, the compulsory demonstration of ID in education qualifies as the 'support of religion', just like creationism, and is therefore unconstitutional.[15] In summary, one is free to talk about religion in the schools of the United States and to teach the viewpoints of religious communities, but the state may not prescribe that any of these viewpoints be taught in a compulsory fashion, including religious studies which are denomination-neutral.[16]

13 In *Lemon v Kurtzman* 403 US 602 (1971), the state's activity (1) must serve a secular purpose; (2) may not have as a primary effect the advancement or disadvantaging of any of the churches, and (3) shall not connect in an excessive manner the operation of state and church. The state must obey all these elements in order for its conduct not to qualify as a breach of the Establishment Clause of the First Amendment.

14 According to the ID theory, Darwinism does not explain the creation of the world, as that requires an 'intelligent designer'. This theory is basically the same as creationism, but dressed in a scientific mask.

15 *Kitzmiller v Dover Area School District* 400 F Supp 2d 707 (MD Pa 2005).

16 For more on practice in the USA, see Eric Barendt, 'Teaching Evolution, Creationism, and Intelligent Design in US Schools (With Some European Comparisons)' in Myriam Hunter-Henin (ed), *Law, Religious Freedoms and Education in Europe* (Ashgate 2011) 267–81.

2.2. The Jurisprudence of the European Court of Human Rights

The European Court of Human Rights (hereinafter: ECtHR) adopted three important decisions regarding the clash of religious education in public schools and the freedom of religious beliefs. In *Folgerø and Others v Norway*[17] a request was filed by parents and children belonging to the Norwegian Humanist Society because the children were not allowed full exemption from attending religious education classes, and because the conditions of partial exemption were quite limited. As of autumn 1997, religious education was gradually introduced to the primary education curriculum in Norway, replacing a class called 'Christianity and Life Philosophy'. In March 1998, the Norwegian Humanist Society, together with eight sets of parents, lodged a procedure before the Oslo City Court at the request of the parents, because their children's exemption from attending religious education classes had been rejected by way of an administrative process. In their opinion, the process violated the freedom of religious beliefs as well as the right to education (Article 2 of Protocol no 1 to the European Convention on Human Rights (hereinafter: ECHR)). The latter states: 'No person shall be denied the right to education. In the exercise of any functions which it assumes in relation to education and to teaching, the state shall respect the right of parents to ensure such education and teaching is in conformity with their own religious and philosophical convictions'. The Grand Chamber of the ECtHR resolved, by nine votes for and eight against, that the right to education had been violated by the Norwegian authorities by rejecting the parents' request to have their children exempted fully from attending religious lessons.

The need to respect parents' religious and educational convictions can be derived from the fundamental right pertaining to schooling, and no distinction can be made in this respect between state and private schools. In the exercise of any functions, the state must respect the right of parents to freedom of conscience. 'Respect' in this sense is more than just 'acknowledgement' or 'take into

17 *Folgerø and Others v Norway*, App no 15472/02, judgment of 29 June 2007.

account', as this is a positive obligation prescribed on the part of the state. In addition, the term 'conviction' holds more weight than an opinion or an idea, and it denotes views that attain a certain level of cogency, seriousness, cohesion and importance. It is in the discharge of a natural duty towards their children—parents being primarily responsible for the education and teaching of their children—that parents may require that the state respect their religious and philosophical convictions. Although setting and planning the curriculum falls, in principle, within the competence of the Contracting State, it must nonetheless ensure that the information or knowledge included in the curriculum is conveyed in an objective, critical and pluralistic manner (Paragraph 84).

In this connection, the ECtHR noted that the operation of the partial exemption arrangement presupposes that the parents concerned are sufficiently informed of the details of the lesson plans to be able to identify, and notify the school in advance, of those parts of the teaching that would be incompatible with their own convictions and beliefs. This could be a challenging task, not only for parents but also for teachers. To do so must have been even more difficult where it was the general Christian leaning of religious education lessons that posed a problem (Paragraph 97).

In order to obtain an exemption, parents had to give reasonable grounds for their request. According to the ECtHR, information on personal religious and philosophical convictions concerns some of the most intimate aspects of private life, and imposing an obligation on parents to disclose detailed information to the school authorities about their religions and philosophical convictions may constitute a violation of the ECHR. Despite the fact that, in the present case, there was no such obligation, the ECtHR found, nonetheless, that inherent in the requirement to give reasonable grounds was a risk that the parents might feel compelled to disclose their own religious and philosophical convictions. In addition, the question as to whether a request for exemption was reasonable was apparently a potential breeding ground for conflict, a situation that parents might prefer simply to avoid by not expressing a wish for exemption (Paragraph 98).

The ECtHR noted that, even if a parental request were deemed reasonable, this did not necessarily mean that the student concerned would be exempted from the part of the curriculum in question. Based on the national legislation, the teacher was expected to apply a flexible approach. For a number of activities, it was proposed that observation by attendance could suitably replace involvement through participation. In the ECtHR's view, this must not only have been complicated to operate in practice but would also diminish the effectiveness of the right to a partial exemption as such (Paragraph 99).

In light of the above, the ECtHR found that the system of partial exemption was capable of subjecting the parents concerned to a heavy burden, with a risk of undue exposure of their private life, and that the potential for conflict was likely to deter them from making such requests (Paragraph 100). By this, the right to education set out in the ECHR had been violated.

In the joint dissenting opinion of eight judges, there was no violation of Article 2 of Protocol no 1. In the opinion of the dissenting judges, a review of the case requires that two factors be taken into consideration, on the one hand, the increasing number of Norwegian citizens with different ethnicities and religious beliefs, and on the other, that when devising the curriculum, one cannot overlook the many centuries of Norwegian history. Christianity has a very long tradition in Norway, both as a religion and a school subject. The Norwegian Constitution guarantees freedom of religion, but also states that the Evangelical Lutheran Church, of which 86 per cent of the population are members, is the official religion of the state. The Constitution confers on the adherents of the Church an obligation to educate their children likewise.

Acknowledgements of religious pluralism should not prevent a democratically elected political majority from giving official recognition to a particular religious denomination and providing it with to public funding, while subjecting it to regulation and control. This does not in itself mean that the state does not respect parents' religious and philosophical convictions in the education of their children, nor does it affect their exercise of freedom of thought, conscience and religion. The authors of the dissenting opinion were not convinced of the strong Christian leaning of the religious education classes, and, according to them, it was also not unreasonable to expect those parents who intended to receive exemption for their children to obtain information about the content of the lessons. Considering the above, the dissenting judges did not share the view that the conditions for partial exemption place an excessive and undue burden on the parents who wish to request such exemption.

In *Hasan and Eylem Zengin v Turkey*, Hasan Zengin filed a request in his own name and on his daughter's behalf.[18] He presented that he and his family are adherents of Alevism, which has deep roots in Turkey, and is one of the branches of Islam representing the second most widespread faith after the Hanafite (Sunni) branch. He submitted a request to the Provincial Directorate of National Education, seeking to have his daughter exempted from 'religious culture and ethics classes'. The state authority rejected his request. The ECtHR unanimously established that Turkey had breached the right to education.

Pursuant to the decision of the Turkish Ministry of Education, the syllabus for teaching in primary schools and the first cycle of secondary school, as well as all of the textbooks, give greater priority to knowledge of Islam than they do to knowledge of other religions and philosophies. In the ECtHR's view, this in itself cannot be viewed as a departure from the principles of pluralism and objectivity, considering the fact that Islam is the majority religion practiced in Turkey (Paragraph 63).

The ECtHR—in agreement with the applicants—considers that, in the absence of instruction in the basic elements of Alevism in primary and secondary school, the fact that the life and philosophy of two individuals who had a major impact on its emergence are taught in the ninth grade is insufficient to compensate for the shortcomings in this teaching (Paragraph 67).

Where the Contracting States include the study of religion in the subjects on their school curricula then, irrespective of the arrangements for exemption, students' parents may legitimately expect that the subject will be taught in such a way as to meet the criteria of objectivity and pluralism, and with respect for their religious or philosophical convictions (Paragraph 68). The school

18 *Hasan and Eylem Zengin v Turkey*, App no 1448/04, judgment of 9 January 2008.

subject 'religious culture and ethics' cannot be considered, in general, to meet the criteria of objectivity and pluralism and, more particularly, in the applicants' specific case (Paragraph 70). The ECtHR notes that, under Article 24 of the Turkish Constitution, 'religious culture and ethics' is one of the compulsory subjects and only children 'of Turkish nationality who belong to the Christian or Jewish faiths' have the option of exemption, 'provided they affirm their adherence to those religions' (Paragraph 72). This in itself may raise concerns with respect to Article 9 of the ECHR (Paragraph 73).

The ECtHR considers that the exemption procedure is not an appropriate method and does not provide sufficient protection to those parents who could legitimately consider that the subject taught and their own values are likely to give rise in their children to a conflict. This is especially so where no possibility for an appropriate choice has been envisaged for the children of parents who have a religious or philosophical conviction other than that of Sunni Islam, where the procedure for exemption is likely to subject the parents to a heavy burden and to the necessity of disclosing their religious or philosophical convictions in order to have their children exempted from the lessons in religion (Paragraph 76).

In *Grzelak v Poland*,[19] the applicants were the parents and their child who—in conformity with the wishes of his parents—did not attend classes of religious instruction at a state school. The school did not offer an alternative class in ethics, as such a need had not arisen from other students, and therefore such a course could not be started. During the period of religious instruction, the child was left without any supervision in the corridor or the school library or in the school club. The student was subjected to discrimination and physical and psychological harassment because he did not follow religious instruction and subsequently changed schools. The next institution signalled to the parents that the student frequently mocked religious symbols and the children who attended religious instruction. The parents requested again that a course in ethics be arranged, but, owing to the lack of sufficient numbers of interested

19 *Grzelak v Poland*, App no 7710/02, judgment of 22 November 2010.

students, it was not possible. With respect to the above, in the place reserved for a mark for 'religion / ethics', on the school report there was a straight line (due to the lack of any results). The applicants claimed that, as there were no marks in the school reports of the student in the place reserved for 'religion/ethics', it became apparent that he did not attend religious instruction, which violates his freedom of religious beliefs. He objected to being deprived of his freedom of thought, conscience and religious beliefs, which he substantiated by the overall impact of the following circumstances—the obligation to submit a declaration stating that he would not follow religious instruction; the impossibility of his following a class in ethics owing to organisational difficulties; the presence of a straight line instead of a mark on his school reports; the fact that teachers tolerated his humiliation and the failure of the state authorities to react to these problems.

According to the ECtHR, the state violated the third applicant's (the student's) right to non-discrimination in relation to his freedom of religious beliefs. The ECtHR did not find the parents' (the two first applicants') request admissible, as the violation of rights only affected their child. The ECtHR emphasised that the manifestation of religious convictions entails a negative characteristic as well, namely that the subject of that right is entitled to refrain from manifesting their conviction entirely. Article 9 ensures non-believers have certain rights if there is an interference with the negative aspect of this provision, when the state brings about a situation in which individuals are obliged, directly or indirectly, to reveal that they are non-believers (Paragraph 87).

The ECtHR's stance was that the absence of a mark for 'religion/ethics' on the school reports falls within the ambit of the negative aspect of freedom of thought, conscience and religion, and should be considered as a disclosure of his lack of religious affiliation (Paragraph 88). It follows that Article 14 on the prohibition of discrimination taken in conjunction with Article 9 is applicable in this case. The ECtHR observed that, in the present case, the parents of the third applicant systematically requested that the school authorities organise a class in ethics for him, as provided for in the Ordinance. However, no such class was organised for the third applicant throughout his entire schooling at primary and secondary level. The reason was the lack of sufficient numbers of students interested in following such a class, in accordance with the requirements set out in the Ordinance (Paragraph 91).

The ECtHR takes the view that the requirement, according to which a mark must be given for 'religion/ethics' courses, cannot as such be considered to infringe Article 14 taken in conjunction with Article 9, as long as the mark constitutes neutral information on the fact that a student followed the courses offered at a school (Paragraph 92). The absence of a mark for 'religion/ethics' would be understood by any reasonable person as an indication that the third applicant did not follow religious education classes and that he was thus likely to be regarded as a person without religious beliefs. This finding takes on particular significance in respect of a country like Poland, where the great majority of the population owe allegiance to one particular religion (Paragraph 95).

From 1 September 2007 onwards, the situation of students like the third applicant became even more problematic due to the entry into force of a provision according to which the marks obtained for 'religion/ethics' would be included in the calculation of the average mark in a given year. This rule may have a truly adverse impact on the situation of students like the applicant who could not, despite their wishes, follow a course in ethics. Such students would either find it more difficult to increase their average mark, as they could not follow the desired optional subject, or might feel pressurised—against their conscience—to attend a religion class in order to improve their average (Paragraph 96).

With respect to the above, the ECtHR found that the absence of a mark for 'religion/ethics' on the third applicant's school certificates throughout the entire period of his schooling amounted to an unwarranted stigmatisation of the applicant (Paragraph 99). It is important to note the element of the majority decision according to which it remains within the national margin of appreciation left to the states to decide what particular system of instruction should be adopted, provided that the freedom of religion and conscience is respected. Consequently, the failure to provide ethics classes as an alternative to religious instruction to the applicant does not in itself constitute an infringement of Article 9 (Paragraph 104).

Judge Björgvinsson attached the only dissenting opinion to the judgment. In this opinion, the judge argued that, since the failure to ensure an ethics class does not infringe the freedom of religion and the right to non-discrimination, the only circumstance which may give rise to concerns of discrimination is the absence of a mark. However, the absence of a mark merely indicates that the person did not attend the religious instruction. Those who receive a mark actually attend the classes, so the discrimination does not happen in relation to the treatment of people in relevantly similar or analogous situations, which would substantiate the infringement of Article 14 (dissenting opinion, Paragraph 7).

Summarising the jurisprudence of the ECtHR, religious education (teaching *about* religions) plays an important role in public education. The compulsory nature of religious education *per se* is not contrary to the freedom of religion and the right to education, provided that it does not aim to indoctrinate, in other words, it does not pressure the students to accept and identify with the teachings of a particular religion. The possibility to be absent from compulsory religious education must be real and easy to achieve. At the same time, the state cannot be obliged to provide schooling to all, according to their individual personal religious and philosophical views; moreover, it shall not be put under the obligation to provide an alternative class to religious education (if denying such an alternative class is justly founded, as it was in the *Grzelak* case due to the lack of interested students).

The anti-discrimination argument raised in *Grzelak* is cause for some concern, however, if we accept that the exemption from attending religious instruction resulting in the absence of a mark qualifies as negative discrimination, as the person affected is bound to disclose their lack of religious affiliation against their will, the question arises as to why other practices leading to a similar disclosure do not qualify as discriminatory. For instance, if an individual indicates that they do not want to attend religious instructions and will be absent from the classes, they automatically unveil their lack of religious affiliation and vice versa. It is safe to assume that a person is religious if they do not exercise their right to absent themselves (although there could be other reasons for attending religious instruction). The difference between the Polish case and the above example lies first and foremost in the proportionality aspect: The school reports may be disclosed to other third parties during the course of the affected person's life, other than school staff, and may even influence that individual's future career (especially in a country where the majority is religious, as the ECtHR also highlighted). However, if the ECtHR considered that the prevention of discrimination lies in the impediment of 'disclosure', then religious education as such would be made impossible. It should be noted that nine years before the *Grzelak* case, in another Polish case, the ECtHR did not establish the infringement of the ECHR in relation to similar provisions in a similar situation.[20] According to Peter Cumper, the ruling in the latter case were not very successful in establishing the distinction between the two cases, the difference was simply that the applicant of the case in 2001 protested against only one school report whereas in the *Grzelak* case, several reports issued by several different schools were objected to.[21]

3. Public Communal Prayers

3.1. The Different State Regulations

As a general rule, communal prayers in the United Kingdom are compulsory in state schools.[22] In addition to this, it is the obligation of the schools to advance the spiritual, moral and educational development of the pupils.[23] In other words, the British schooling system does not entrust the parents and families entirely with the religious education of pupils. The regulation is 'entirely or primarily' of a Christian character, prescribing a daily prayer which does not, however, distinguish between denominations. In other words, it is denomination-neutral.[24] The daily communal prayer does not necessarily have to be recited in the morning, and does not require the participation of the entire school community to perform it

20 *Saniewski v Poland*, App no 40319/98, judgment of 26 June 2001.

21 Peter Cumper, 'Religious Education in Europe in the Twenty-First Century' in Hunter-Henin (n 16) 213–14.

22 'Collective Act of Worship'—School Standards and Framework Act 1998, s 70.

23 Education Reform Act 1988, s 1(2).

24 Schools Standards and Framework Act 1998, Sch 20(3).

jointly; praying may be done in classrooms and in smaller groups. It is not an obligation for the prayer to be of a Christian character, the notion of 'primarily' may be interpreted by the schools with substantial flexibility.[25] It is the right of parents to withdraw their children from the act of worship, and also to take their children, if they wish, to another location for prayer if that is not possible on school premises.[26] Similarly, the teachers or even the entire institution may choose to opt out from this obligation.[27]

In Germany, there is no similar obligation in place; the federal states and the schools are free to decide on whether to prescribe such prayer. The Federal Constitutional Court adopted a resolution in 1979 according to which the obligation of communal prayer is not against the constitution.[28] This Resolution by the Constitutional Court decided on two cases at once. In the first case, a parent complained that the prohibition by the authorities of school prayers infringed on the child's freedom of religion but, on the decision of the Constitutional Court of the State of Hessen, school prayers may not be allowed if a student or a parent protests them. In the second case, the subject of the complaint was the exact opposite, namely that compulsory school prayers violate fundamental rights. The Constitutional Court of North Rhine-Westphalia decided that 'negative freedom of religion' may not be given priority over 'positive freedom of religion', meaning that the right to opt out of communal prayers may not restrict others from expressing their faith within the school community.

These two matters were brought before the Federal Constitutional Court for a final decision. The first senate was of the view that mandatory school prayers were not in violation of the constitution. According to the *Grundgesetz*, the planning of the schooling system falls under the competence of the states, and they are allowed to establish state schools with a 'religious affiliation'. Schools, and

25 Rex Ahdar & Ian Leigh, *Religious Freedom in the Liberal State* (Oxford University Press 2nd edn 2013) 257.

26 Schools Standards and Framework Act 1998, ss 71(1), (3), and (4).

27 *Ibid*, s 59, Sch 20(4).

28 52 BVerfGE 223 (1979).

indeed the entire national education system, must be neutral when it comes to religious beliefs but this does not mean that religions must be expelled from the school grounds (section C I.1 of the resolution). It is clear that prescribing a Christian prayer in schools 'encourages' the acceptance of Christianity and therefore becomes a component of education which passes beyond the mere demonstration of the cultural and educational significance of Christianity. However, as long as participation in the act of prayer is voluntary, so that the pupil may opt out, the general prescription on this does not infringe the right of the states to plan their schooling systems freely, as set out in Article 7(1) of the Constitution (C I.2c). At the same time, however, the states are not obliged to provide the option of school prayers; parents may not demand its provision, just as they cannot request that the state establishes a school with a specific religious or philosophical affiliation (C I.4).

The pupil or their parents may only protest against school prayers successfully if the school does not ensure pupils' right to decide freely on attendance for those who do not wish to participate in the act of prayer (C I.3). There are various ways for pupils to withdraw from the act of prayer. The pupil may either choose not to be present in the classroom during the course of the prayer or may enter the classrooms, but remain silent. Without a doubt, standing out like this (especially if the student is the only one) sets that pupil apart from the majority, and risks them being considered by the others as an outsider and potentially being subjected to detrimental consequences (C I.3a–b). Even so, it cannot be said that such withdrawal from worship generally and frequently puts these pupils in the untenable position of an outsider. The school circumstances in which this act of prayer takes place—as part of a large group of pupils in classrooms, which decreases the risk of segregation and the role of teachers in such situations—are such that the board concluded that it should not be feared that those pupils who wish to opt out from prayers will be discriminated against (C. I.4).[29]

29 Inke Muehlhoff, 'Freedom of Religion in Public Schools in Germany and in the United States', (2000) 28 *Georgia Journal of International & Comparative Law* 405, 469–71.

There are several Supreme Court decisions in connection with the matter of school prayers in the United States. *Engel v Vitale* in 1962 laid down the basic constitutional guidelines on the subject matter.[30] The procedure was launched by the parents of certain pupils attending public schools in New Hyde Park, as they claimed that the obligatory joint recitation of the prayer beginning 'God Almighty' at the start of school days is unconstitutional. The wording of the prayer was determined by the State of New York. The district and the circuit appellate courts rejected the pleading, but the Washington Supreme Court reversed the decisions of the lower courts by a six to one vote and declared the morning prayer to be in violation of the Establishment Clause. According to the Court, prayer is by nature a religious act and prescribing it infringes upon the provisions of the First Amendment, which sets forth the religious neutrality of the state. The panel rejected the school's argument, which had been accepted by the lower courts, according to which worship is voluntary and participation is not compulsory, and it also found it irrelevant that the text of the prayer is denomination-neutral.

According to the Court, endorsement of religious beliefs in general is sufficient to state unconstitutionality, regardless of the fact that the state's support is not aimed at one specific religion or denomination. On behalf of the majority, Justice Black wrote that 'The First Amendment ... tried to put an end to government control of religion and prayer'.[31] The framers of the Constitution wished to build a wall of separation between the church and the state, and therefore denomination-neutrality and the voluntary nature of participation is not sufficient to ensure compliance with the Constitution. Justice Black also rejected the notion that forbidding school prayers would create an impermissible hostility towards religion. According to the Court, forbidding the state to write a prayer and to organise communal prayer cannot be considered hostile.

Justice Stewart, the only justice with a dissenting opinion, brought up the many religious references made by the state, such as the Declaration of Independence, the inauguration speeches of almost

30 *Engel v Vitale* 370 US 421 (1962).

31 *Ibid*, 425.

all presidents and the slogan 'In God We Trust' found on American coins since 1865. Stewart argues that these manifestations cannot be viewed as 'establishing a religion' in the constitutional sense, just as prayers, in the case at hand, cannot be either. The state does not endorse religion in an intolerable manner when allowing someone to say a prayer if they want to.[32] To deny students of the joint recitation of a prayer is to deny them the opportunity of sharing in the spiritual heritage of the American Nation.[33]

A year later, in *Abington School District v Schempp*,[34] the Court corroborated its stance. Edward Schempp turned to the District Court for the Eastern District of Pennsylvania claiming that the state legislation which stipulates that ten verses of the Bible must be read at the opening of each school day in every public school is unconstitutional. The district court declared the statute as unconstitutional, which was then appealed by the school. In the meantime, the State of Pennsylvania amended the legislation with a supplement, under which pupils can be excused from Bible reading upon the written request of their parents. Due to the change in legislation, the appellate court referred the case back to the court of first instance, where it once again rejected the applicant Schempp's claim. The case was finally decided by the federal Supreme Court, which held the statute unconstitutional. The Court also decided in this ruling on the constitutionality of a statute in the state of Maryland which, although it did not prescribe compulsory Bible reading, made it possible for the local boards of education to decide on religious activities at the start of school days in public schools. The plaintiff, Mrs Murray, objected to regulations passed on the basis of the authorisation mentioned above, according to which all schooldays in Baltimore start with Bible readings. This regulation was also found unconstitutional by the Supreme Court.

According to the Court, it is the state's constitutional obligation to stay neutral when it comes to religious affairs, protecting all but not endorsing any of them. The state may not prescribe any rules which would coerce any person to manifest their religion, faith or the lack

32 *Ibid*, 445.

33 *Ibid*.

34 *Abington School District v Schempp* 374 US 203 (1963).

thereof. The state cannot support a religion against the faithless, and cannot in any sense discriminate among the religions. Justice Clark, who authored the majority opinion, established a two-step test. In order for a piece of legislation to be in compliance with the First Amendment, 'there must be a secular legislative purpose and a primary effect that neither advances nor inhibits religion'.[35] Justice Stewart was once again the only one with a dissenting opinion, rejecting the assumption that school boards lack the qualities of inventiveness and good will so much as to render it impossible for them to devise a practice compliant with the Constitution.[36]

Several decades passed by until the next similar case followed. Notwithstanding, the decision in *Wallace v Jaffree* did not deviate from the previous approach.[37] Legislation in Alabama authorised teachers to spend one minute at the beginning of each school day with 'meditation or voluntary prayer' in the classroom. Three children of an Alabama resident attended public schools in Mobile County. The youngest of the three children was regularly bullied for not attending morning prayers and so the parent turned to the Southern Alabama District Court requesting the repeal of the statute endorsing religious practices, as it violates the First Amendment. The district court rejected the claim, but the appellate court amended this decision, and declared the statute in question unconstitutional. Following this, the Federal Supreme Court declared by a six to three majority that the statute was indeed violating the First Amendment.

According to the Court, the purpose of the statute was to endorse religion, and it restricted individuals from manifesting or veiling their religious convictions or the lack thereof at their own discretion, without being subjected to any pressure. In the Court's view, in order for legislation regulating religious affairs to be compliant with constitutional requirements, it must have a secular purpose. As based on the First Amendment, regulations which have as a primary aim the endorsement of a religion are considered

35 *Ibid*, 222.

36 *Ibid*, 230.

37 *Wallace v Jaffree* 472 US 38 (1985).

unconstitutional.[38] The aim of this statute is, in practice, to bring back the custom of voluntary prayer to schools. In other words, the religious purpose is unambiguous.[39] The goal of the statute subject to the review was to endorse a religion and, when adopting that legislation, the legislator was not driven by any secular purpose. The statute violated the rule of the neutrality of the government in religious matters and was therefore unconstitutional. As stated by Justices O'Connor and Powell, it is evidently not forbidden to allow students to pray during the school day silently, as the one-minute period of common silence would also not be unconstitutional if it was aimed at contemplation and meditation without any further religious purpose.[40]

All of the previous cases examined the constitutionality of everyday school practices, and regarded the provisions endorsing religion as unconstitutional. However, it remained a question as to whether in individual cases, on special occasions such as school events, a communal prayer may be recited in a way that complies with the First Amendment. The answer came with the decision adopted in *Lee v Weisman*[41] where the preliminary facts were that the principal of the Nathan Bishop Middle School in Providence invited a Jewish rabbi to recite a prayer at the graduation ceremony. The parents of one of the students requested a temporary restraining order from the Rhode Island District Court to prohibit the rabbi's speech from taking place, but the Court denied the request. The ceremony was held, but the case continued. The appellate court sustained the Weismans' request. The school then turned to the Supreme Court, arguing that participation in the prayers was voluntary and was denomination-neutral; the students were not coerced to stand up during the recitation of the prayer; moreover, attendance at the ceremony was not obligatory either. However, the Court ruled five to four that the Weisman claim was well founded and the school practice was unconstitutional.

38 *Ibid*, 56. This requirement which was already established in *Schempp* (n 34) was corroborated in the meanwhile by the *Lemon* test. See *Lemon* (n 13).

39 *Ibid*, 56.

40 *Ibid*, 62, 73–4.

41 *Lee v Weisman* 505 US 577 (1992).

In the Court's opinion, government involvement in the recitation of the prayer was so pervasive that it created 'a state-sponsored and state directed religious exercise in a public school'.[42] There is no real choice when the pupil may either elect to stay absent from their own graduation ceremony for not wanting to participate in its religious aspects or, by going, being made to feel that they had to participate in such religious practices by listening to the prayer silently and thereby expressing agreement.[43] The government may not coerce students into a choice where they either elect to agree with the prayer or protest against it in a manner that represents an undue burden for them. According to the Court, the government may not force anybody to endorse any religion or religious activity, or to participate in it or to have to act in any other way so as to acknowledge that religion.

The dissenting opinion of Justice Scalia, similar to Justice Stewart's previous opinions, emphasised historic traditions when arguing for the constitutionality of this type of school prayer. Based on the fact that the framers of the Constitution did not object to prayers being recited at solemn occasions held by all three branches of power, it may be concluded that they would not have had any objections against similar practices at school festivities.[44]

A similar judgment was delivered in a similar subsequent case. *Santa Fe Independent School District v Doe*[45] was initiated after the School District Board of Santa Fe adopted a policy which authorised the students to recite a prayer before each home varsity football game. After two former students and their parents filed a complaint against that practice before the District Court, the school changed its approach and introduced a two-round voting system. Subsequently, they held a vote on delivering a joint invocation before each game. In the event that the majority decided to deliver an invocation, there was another vote on who would deliver the prayer. The Court accepted this practice, provided that the prayer was denomination-neutral and of a non-proselytising nature. Both parties appealed

42 *Ibid*, 587.

43 *Ibid*, 595.

44 *Ibid*, 633–5.

45 *Santa Fe Independent School District v Doe* 530 US 290 (2000).

against the decision; the parents requested the complete abolition of the rule, and the school requested that the limiting conditions be reversed. The appellate court was of the view that the conditions were indispensable, and decided that a prayer may only be recited at school festivities and sport events. The case was finally brought before the Supreme Court, who declared the prayers held before the sport games to be unconstitutional.

The Court stated that the prayer was recited on school grounds at events sponsored by the school and were disseminated through school loudspeakers, based on a policy which expressly supported the recitation of public and communal prayer. The Court did not accept the argument that the prayer qualifies as private speech. The average outside observer identifies the prayer with the school, regardless of whether the audience agrees with or objects to it.[46] The rule is not rendered constitutional by the fact that the students held a vote in relation to it. As Justice Stevens argued, the regulations do nothing to protect the minority; that minority is subjugated to the majority. However, 'fundamental rights may not be submitted to vote'.[47] The practice clearly endorses a religious message. In the Court's view, imposition of coercion was also realised, despite the fact that the Board of Education claimed that attending varsity football games was voluntary to begin with. Attendance for many of the participants, such as the athletes and cheerleaders, is obligatory, and for many other students, there may be social pressure to be present. As such, to claim that there is no considerable pressure or strong personal motivation to attend is formalistic in the extreme.[48]

The subsequent and the last to date of the cases brought before the federal Supreme Court also originated in a school environment, but the subject thereof was not the act of prayer but the recitation of the Pledge of Allegiance recited communally in the mornings (the oath pledges to the state, and is recited by US citizens at solemn occasions or by students at the beginning of the school day). The

46 *Ibid*, 308.

47 *Ibid*, 304–5, referenced by *West Virginia State Board of Education v Barnette* 319 US 624, 638 (1943).

48 *Ibid*, 311.

Pledge of Allegiance was written in the nineteenth century and, pursuant to a decision of Congress, it has been the official 'oath of loyalty' since 1942. In 1954, the Cold War motivated the modification of the text so that it was supplemented with the phrase 'under God' in order to distinguish American citizens from atheist communists, and since then the text has read: 'I pledge allegiance to the Flag of the United States of America, and to the Republic for which it stands, one Nation under God, indivisible, with liberty and justice for all'.

The above text was challenged by an atheist parent in *Elk Grove Unified School District v Newdow*.[49] Newdow claimed that the public institution attended by his daughter violated the Establishment Clause because it made it mandatory for its students to recite the Pledge of Allegiance together each morning. The Supreme Court did not consider the case of merit but ceased the procedure as a matter of procedural law (Newdow was not a custodial parent of the minor as he was not married to the mother of the child and therefore did not have standing in the case).

However, several justices expressed their concurring opinion in relation to the decision, and proceeded to examine the substance of the case. Justice O'Connor argued that the Court should have examined the case, and also added that the phrase referring to God in the text of the oath of allegiance is an expression of ceremonial deism compatible with the Constitution; more specifically, the manifestation of faith traditionally expressed at solemn occasions which—with the lapse of time—became a formality and represents the respect of traditions and the acknowledgement of the historic role of Christianity, thereby losing its religious content. Ceremonial deism cannot be viewed as an impermissible endorsement of religion by the government. For instance, see the motto on the dollar bill or the joint prayer by the legislative bodies at their opening sessions.

In Justice O'Connor's opinion, in order to establish whether any manifestation qualifies as the endorsement of religion by the government four questions must be evaluated: (1) historic and ubiquitous character; it is an argument pro permissibility if a text has been recited for a historic period of time, while more recent

49 *Elk Grove Unified School District v Newdow* 542 US 1 (2004).

texts with religious references are less likely to pass the test; (2) whether the recitation of the text qualifies as worship or prayer; (3) whether the text refers to a specific religion; (4) what portion of the text carries religious content.[50]

The Pledge has been recited since long ago and cannot be considered as a prayer; it does not refer to any particular religion and only a small portion of it (two words) carries religious sentiment. Based on this, Justice O'Connor would have declared the disputed regulation as constitutional. Although O'Connor's opinion is not binding due to the majority decision of the Court, the test drawn by her is of importance and has become a point of reference.

However, Douglas Laycock disputes the O'Connor test. He writes that when students are coerced into reciting the Pledge of Allegiance, they are forced to express their faith in God (the government is prohibited from doing so) or if they are not believers, they 'take the Lord's name in vain' which is impermissible from a religious point of view.[51] He also disagrees with O'Connor's conclusion: Although the Pledge only contains two words relating to religion ('under God') these words represent a personal creed which is recited by students in schools everyday under orders.[52]

It is noteworthy that two Supreme Court decisions already existed regarding the mandatory recital of the Pledge. While in 1940, the justices were of the view that the mandatory morning recital of the Pledge may be allowed in schools,[53] in 1943 they decided that the compulsory salutation before the flag placed in the classrooms and recital of the Pledge of Allegiance is unconstitutional.[54] The case was important is laying down the foundations for the 'right to reticence'. The facts of the case, however, differ considerably from those in *Elk Grove*: There was no real possibility in 1943 to obtain an exemption from reciting the Pledge of Allegiance, whereas nowadays a student

50 *Ibid*, 37–44.

51 Douglas Laycock, 'Theology Scholarships, the Pledge of Allegiance, and Religious Liberty: Avoiding the Extremes but Missing the Liberty', (2004) 118 *Harvard Law Review* 155, 225.

52 *Ibid*, 227.

53 *Minersville School District v Gobitis* 310 US 586 (1940).

54 *West Virginia State Board of Education* (n 47).

or parent who wishes to be exempted is entitled to request it. Furthermore, the religious content was not part of the text in 1943.

Justice Scalia made a reference in *Lee* to the act of prayer before the sessions of the various bodies pertaining to the different branches of power as an argument for the constitutionality of the prescription of similar prayers in schools. However, the context of the sessions of the legislative body and of schools are fundamentally different. Nevertheless, it is without doubt that the Supreme Court was more lenient when judging the mandatory act of prayer of the legislative bodies. In the first of these cases, the *Marsh v Chambers* case, Nebraska State Senator Ernie Marsh lodged the suit because he found that the practice of the government, according to which a chaplain paid by the government (employed by the state) recites a prayer before sessions, is unconstitutional.[55] The District Court held that the prayer did not violate the Constitution, but that state support for the chaplain did. The circuit court of appeals found that both practices were unconstitutional. In a six to three decision, the Supreme Court resolved that the state position of chaplain has traditionally been closely tied to the work of state legislature and, with respect to the acknowledgement of this historic circumstance, the prayer recited by the chaplain and the state support thereof cannot be considered unconstitutional. The Court noted that even the framers of the First Amendment started their sessions with a prayer and did not find the practice unconstitutional. Hence, the fact that this has been the practice in the legislature for more than two hundred years substantiates its constitutionality sufficiently.[56]

Justices Brennan and Marshall disapproved in their joint dissenting opinion of the fact that the Court failed to employ any of its previously established tests. They were of the opinion that it is unconstitutional that the non-believer congressman/woman either stays in the congressional hall despite their lack of religious faith or, if they decide to leave, their absence will likely be subject of public discussions. They criticised the reference made to the sessions of the framers two hundred years earlier when noting that legislators, influenced by the passions and exigencies of the moment and the

55 *Marsh v Chambers* 463 US 783 (1983).

56 *Ibid*, 786–92.

pressure of constituents and colleagues, do not always pass sober constitutional judgment on every piece of legislation they enact.[57]

More than thirty years later, in its most recent decision the *Town of Greece v Galloway* case, the Court held a similar position, although in a much closer, five to four vote.[58] The decision did not establish the unconstitutionality of the prayer recited at the opening of sessions of the Greece city legislature. The Court reiterated its previous arguments, according to which this practice has a long historic past which is followed by Congress and other state legislatures. According to the Court, the prayer does not serve the purpose of proselytising or to persuade the acceptance of a certain religion. It has no coercive effect on those who do not wish to listen to similar prayers; it has no discriminative nature and also does not degrade non-believers or religious minorities. The Court stated that to hold that invocations must be non-sectarian would force the legislatures sponsoring prayers and the courts deciding these cases to act as supervisors and censors of religious speech.[59]

Justice Kagan, with whom Justices Ginsburg and Sotomayor joined, highlighted three main deviations from the *Marsh* decision in her dissenting opinion, while not debating the sustainability of its content: (1) the Greece city town hall is not only a legislative congress but also a place for ordinary citizens to engage with their government, in other words, others can attend the meeting and not only the members of the board; (2) consequently, the prayers were not addressed to the legislator congressmen only but to all persons present who were there to take care of their own matters with the board; (3) the prayers were tied to a single religion, that is, Christianity. For this reason, the four justices in the minority did not find the city's practices constitutional. They were of the view that the problem could have been easily solved if the prayer had been denomination-neutral or if the representative of more than one religion had been invited to say a prayer, thereby ensuring openness towards as many citizens as possible.[60]

57 *Ibid*, 814.
58 *Town of Greece v Galloway* 572 US _ (2014).
59 *Ibid.*
60 *Ibid.*

4. Conclusion

Religious instruction cannot be absent from public education because religions have fundamentally shaped history, literature and arts alike. However, outright religious education, the teaching of a specific religion as a separate class, is an old tradition which raises certain human rights issues. These concerns are confronted by each state in consideration of their own cultural and educational heritage, although there are some common approaches which can be perceived in the underlying legal regulations and jurisprudences.[61] In order to protect the negative aspect of the freedom of religion, mandatory prescription of religious education is characterised by the requirement to allow non-attendance by those who are believers of another religion or are non-believers. This possibility must be real, easily obtained and free from discrimination. Furthermore, religious education must be objective, critical and neutral in the sense that it does not put the students under pressure to accept or follow a religion.

Any given state is free to give prominence to a single religion over all the rest because of its own traditions; it is the Catholic Church or other Christian denominations that may receive such preferential status in some European countries. This *per se* does not infringe the freedom of religion, at least according to the German Constitutional Court, and the ECtHR also did not hold a contradictory stance on this. This is the case even if the compulsory religious education is organised around content that reflects the philosophy of that specific church. The historically and socially influential role of Christian denominations will not be eliminated quickly with ease by human rights doctrines which only started gaining shape a few decades ago. However, even if a religion or a church receives such preferential status, students' freedom of choice, the pluralism of education and openness are still to be observed.

Similar principles apply to mandatory school prayer. This type of tradition still exists in some states or certain parts of a country. It

61 Carolyn Evans, 'Religious Education in Public Schools: An International Human Rights Perspective', (2008) 8(3) *Human Rights Law Review* 449, 462–70.

must be noted, however, that regardless of the most recent developments in the protection of human rights, it is common for manifestations previously considered to be of a religious nature (school prayers, singing of songs with religious content at official events, certain religious holidays becoming public holidays, etc.) to now be formalities, emptied of their sacramental character. These are the customs which the American terminology calls Ceremonial Deism, which are regarded as constitutional practices precisely because they have lost their religious character. If the fading of their religious character is the price to be paid for allowing religious practices to remain in public life, it is safe to assume that this will not be accepted by the churches or their followers, because it is the very essence of these acts, actions and customs which is curtailed by such a requirement. However, if we were to emphasise their religious character, the requirement to protect the negative freedom of religion would be brought to the surface. There is no way to handle this matter that will please everyone, and therefore it is the government that must take a stance on which of the opposing values it chooses to endorse and how it intends to balance them out.

Chapter 3

Limitations on Wearing Religious Clothing and Symbols: Headscarves and Crosses

1. Introduction

It is indisputable that in certain situations freedom of religion can be restricted and individuals might be obliged to refrain from wearing the clothing prescribed by their religions. Such situations include taking photographs for identity cards, which has appeared in the jurisprudence of the European Court of Human Rights (hereinafter: ECtHR),[1] and in connection with traffic rules[2] or security controls[3] (e.g., at airports). In these cases, taking a photograph enabling the person concerned to be identified, or carrying out a security check are not possible without taking off any piece of clothing covering the face, and obliging the person concerned to obey these rules, i.e., limiting their fundamental rights for the shortest time necessary, is justified for reasons of public order and public safety.

1 *Karaduman v Turkey*, App no 16278/90, admissibility decision of 3 May 1993; *Mann Singh v France*, App no 24479/07, admissibility decision of 13 November 2008.

2 *X v the United Kingdom*, App no 7992/77, admissibility decision, 12 July 1978. In this case, a man of the Sikh faith, was fined because, due to his turban, he did not wear a crash helmet while riding his motorbike. Since then, British regulations were amended (Road Traffic Act of 1988, s 16(2)) and today it is allowed for Sikhs to wear turbans—and, as such, to disregard road traffic rules—in such cases as well.

3 *Suku Phull v France*, App no 35753/03, admissibility decision, 11 January 2005; *El Morsli v France*, App no 15585/06, admissibility decision of 4 March 2008.

It is less clear, however, whether bans with a more general scope can be established which ensure the right balance between freedom of religion and the recognition of needs justifying the restriction of this right. In the recent past, the debate on Muslim headscarves (veils) concealing the face has flared up in several European states. At first, the agenda was the restrictions of rights allowed in the school environment, which was followed in more recent years by the introductions in some countries of total prohibitions on wearing headscarves. There is a growing fear in some quarters of the rise of Islam in Europe, and Muslim women walking in the streets wearing *burqas* or *niqabs* are considered by some as symbols of this growing influence.[4] Accordingly, debates have focused primarily on the freedom of religion of members of the Muslim community, but recently questions pertaining to the restriction of Christian symbols from being worn in public have also surfaced. This chapter will provide an overview of the issues surrounding this topic.

2. Wearing Religious Clothing at School

2.1. Regulations in Individual European States

The French National Assembly adopted the Act on Wearing Religious Symbols on 10 February 2004 and it was ratified by the Senate on 3 March 2004.[5] Pursuant to the provisions of the law, symbols emphatically expressing the religious conviction and identification of students with a religious community or religious dogma cannot be worn in state-run institutions of public education. Clearly, this is not a general ban on wearing religious symbols. The provisions of the ministerial circular contains an explanatory memorandum and interpretation which refers to the Muslim headscarf, the *kippah* and large crosses. Traditionally worn religious symbols with a discreet

4 *Submission*, a dystopic novel by Michel Houllebecq, the renowned French author, on the Muslim takeover in France came out on 7 January 2015, the very day of the attack against the *Charlie Hebdo* editorial offices.

5 Loi no 2004-228 du 15 mars 2004. This legislation, of course, had a significant history.

appearance (e.g., smaller jewellery) are not banned, nor is wearing the kind of clothing and accessories worn by students irrespective of their religious affiliation. The scope of the Act covers all primary and secondary public education institutions (but not tertiary), and all extramural activities organised by the institution (such as school trips). Private schools do not fall under the scope of the Act.

In France, secularism is one the major foundations of the state; the emphasis on secularity at the level of the state is an inherent feature of the French public sphere, and so restrictions on wearing religious symbols or clothing in the public sphere are a necessary feature of the legal system. What is perhaps surprising about the stringent legislation on religious clothing is that it was passed to solve a problem that affected only a tiny proportion of Muslim women living in France. According to estimates, one per cent of Muslim school children (1,256 girls) had earlier worn headscarves covering the whole face, but the overwhelming majority were not 'problematic' in this regard.[6]

In Germany, the judgment of the Federal Constitutional Court delivered on 24 September 2003 in the *Ludin* case was the first to respond to the question of whether it is possible to ban teachers working at state schools from wearing headscarves.[7] In this case a constitutional complaint was upheld, which had been submitted by a teacher of Afghan origin, a German citizen who was not admitted to public service for a probationary period, due to her wearing a headscarf. As the restriction had no legal basis, this measure violated her right to freedom of religion. If a teacher is prohibited from expressing their religious affiliation by wearing certain items of clothing and thus their right to freedom of religion enshrined in Article 4 of the Basic Law, the person concerned will face a serious dilemma: They have to either disobey the rules of their religion, or stop working as a public employee. If they cannot find a job in a

6 Susana Mancini & Michel Rosenfeld, 'Unveiling the Limits of Tolerance: Comparing the Treatment of Majority and Minority Religious Symbols in the Public Sphere' in Lorenzo Zucca & Camil Ungureanu (eds), *Law, State and Religion in the New Europe. Debates and Dilemmas* (Cambridge University Press 2012) 175.

7 2 BvR 1436/02.

private institution they will have to leave their profession entirely. A restriction of this kind can only be prescribed by a law of the appropriate level.

The decision of the court avoided taking a substantive stance, and concluded that a compromise had to be established by legislators in states, either by banning headscarves from being worn, with reference to the principle of neutrality, or by allowing the wearing of headscarves at schools, on the grounds of upholding teachers' freedom of religion. That is, the unconstitutional nature of the decision appealed against was derived only from the absence of the proper legal basis, which could be remedied by adopting (potentially restrictive) provisions at the level of states. The tasks of the state legislator is to strike the right balance between the freedom of religion of teachers and the rights and interests of students, by determining the degree of adjustment expected from the former. Accordingly, in individual German states, various pieces of legislation have been adopted and various practices have emerged.

Bans on wearing religious symbols were introduced in eight *Länder*.[8] Pursuant to legislation in Baden-Württemberg, for example, teachers are obliged to refrain from expressing political, religious, or ideological views which would disturb peace at school and in education and compromise the neutrality of school *vis-à-vis* students and their parents, especially if those views or manifestations can be interpreted as a demonstration against human dignity and anti-discrimination. At the same time, regulations and related practices allow Christian and Jewish symbols to be worn, because

8 A ban on wearing headscarves was introduced in the following states (with the date of the introduction of the ban in brackets): Baden-Württemberg (1 April 2004), Lower Saxony (29 April 2004), Saarland (23 June 2004), Hessen (18 October 2004), Bavaria (23 November 2004), Berlin (27 January 2005), Bremen (28 June 2005), and North Rhine-Westphalia (13 June 2006). Brandenburg, Rhineland-Palatinate and Schleswig-Holstein were also contemplating the introduction of the ban on headscarves, whereas Hamburg, Mecklenburg-Western Pomerania, Saxony, Saxony-Anhalt, and Thuringia opted for freedom of religion to be granted to teachers, see www.uni-trier.de/index.php?id=24373.

the religious views embodied in these symbols, according to public opinion, are compatible with the values cherished by the state.[9]

The decision of 27 January 2015 of the first Senate of the Federal Constitutional Court triggered essential changes in the legal settlement of this issue.[10] The Constitutional Court decided in the cases of two teachers from North Rhine-Westphalia. The Constitutional Court ruled that the general and complete ban on female teachers working in public education wearing the headscarf as an expression of their respect for the rules of the Muslim religion is in contravention of the German Basic Law. The complainant concerned in case 1 BvR 471/10 had worked at a state school as a specialist youth worker since 1997. After the prohibition of wearing headscarves took effect in North Rhine-Westphalia, the management of the school called upon her not to wear a headscarf in the course of her work. The complainant complied with this warning by replacing her headscarf with a pink beret and covering her neck with a high-neck pullover. For this she received a disciplinary sanction from the management of the school which she responded to by launching labour law proceedings, but these were unsuccessful. The complainant concerned in case no 1 BvR 1181/10 had been teaching concurrently at various state schools in North Rhine-Westphalia, in Turkish, from 2001. At first, only disciplinary sanctions were imposed upon her for wearing a headscarf in class, but later she was dismissed. She also lost the labour law proceedings.

The School Act of North Rhine-Westphalia (SchulG NW), Article 57(4) stipulates that male as well as female teachers are obliged to refrain from expressing political, religious, ideological or similar views which would disturb the ideological neutrality of the state and would jeopardise or disturb the peace at school. Especially inadmissible is to have an appearance which might create the impression in students or parents that the teacher is opposed to human dignity and equality as enshrined in Article 3 of the Basic Law, on the fundamental liberties, or as embodied in the free and democratic political regime. This provision is the legal basis for the ban on wearing headscarves adopted in German states. The right to

9 Mancini & Rosenfeld (n 6) 175.

10 1 BvR 471/10 and 1 BvR 1181/10.

freedom of religion stipulated in Article 4 of the Basic Law grants, for teachers working at state schools open to religious convictions, the freedom to comply with the strictures of their religions related to clothing.

State institutions may examine cases and decide whether the conduct or behaviour in question really falls under the scope of exercising one's right to freedom of religion as enshrined in Article 4 of the Basic Law. The courts in these cases were also obliged to examine this. The complainants argued that for them, this is a religious obligation affecting their personal identity and, pursuant to Article 2(1) of the Basic Law, every person shall have the right to free development of their personality insofar as they do not violate the rights of others or offend the constitutional order or the moral law. Since from the ban it follows that all other Muslim women in a similar situation will be prevented from working at schools which they would otherwise be qualified to do, the ban also violates the provisions on gender equality in Article 3(2) of the Basic Law.

The Constitutional Court stated in its decision that the purpose of the legislator in North Rhine-Westphalia was legitimate when it adopted the challenged provision, the purpose of which was to ensure the peaceful and smooth running of schools, and safeguard the ideological neutrality of the state. For teachers, to wear religious clothing *per se* is not capable of restricting the negative freedom of religion of students granted in Articles 4(1)–(2) of the Basic Law (the opportunity to refrain from religions). As long as the teacher does not explicitly profess their religious conviction and does not attempt to influence the students in this respect, the wearing of religious clothing shall remain the manifestation of the positive exercise of the teacher's freedom of religion. The activity and presence of teachers following other religions and having different ideological creeds will make the school environment balanced. It does not follow from the provisions of the Basic Law (Article 6(2)) on the parents' rights with regard to the care and upbringing of their children that parents have the legitimate interest of keeping their school-aged children away from teachers who follow religion-based rules on clothing.

Pursuant to Article 7(1) of the Basic Law, the entire school system shall be under the supervision of the state, which shall also include the obligation to preserve the ideological neutrality of the state. The exercise of the positive religious freedom of teachers by wearing headscarves does not in general violate the above provision. The state can legitimately prohibit a form of conduct derived from a religious rule and manifested in an appearance only if it endangers the peace at school, the smooth running of the institution, and the ideological neutrality of the state. In the concrete cases, wearing items of clothing *per se* did not constitute such a danger. Certain teachers wearing headscarves does not mean that the state identifies with the given religion. The obligation of the state to remain ideologically neutral is not identical to the strict separation of the state and the church, but should be manifested in open, comprehensive and supportive behaviour ensuring the same degree of freedom for each religion. This also applies to the role played by the state in the education system.

The Constitutional Court stated that, in the concrete cases, it was not realistic to assume that the smooth running of the school and the ideological neutrality of the state were at risk; at the same time, the fundamental right of the complainants to freedom of religion had been breached. The task of the legislator is to draw up suitably differentiated legislation in this regard. The Constitutional Court declared the third sentence of Article 57(4) of the School Act null and void on the grounds that it provided a more favourable treatment for Christian-Western values and tradition by exempting its symbols from the ban. From the ruling of the Constitutional Court, it directly follows that there is an obligation to re-legislate the issue in all the German states concerned.

In December 2016, the Constitutional Court ruled that conservative Muslim girls must take part in mixed swimming classes at school, finding against an 11-year-old pupil who had argued that even wearing a *burqini*, or full-body swimsuit, breached Islamic dress codes.[11]

Turkey, based on its Constitution, is a secular state, which is neutral in questions relating to religion. Due to this fact, for constitutional reasons, any form of wearing headscarves was banned for a long time for girls and women studying or working at schools. The Republic of

11 BvR 3237/13.

Turkey first banned the wearing of the *fez*, the Turkish headdress, in 1925 in a law,[12] then in an act adopted in 1934, it banned all religious clothing in order to facilitate the westernisation of the country.[13] At the beginning of the 1990s, several bills made attempts to lift this ban, but the Constitutional Court systematically blocked them.[14] In 2000, a Turkish student appeared at a college exam wearing a headscarf, for which she was sentenced to six months' imprisonment, as she disturbed the prevailing order of education.[15]

In February 2008, the Turkish Parliament adopted a law which sought to amend two constitutional provisions in order to allow headscarves to be worn in institutions of tertiary education, as this ban prevents a large number of women from receiving proper education. Act no 5735 would have amended Article 10 of the Turkish Constitution on equality before the law, with the addition that the state and administrative authorities should proceed to ensure equal treatment in proceedings and the use of public services alike. In addition, it would have amended Article 42 of the Constitution on the right to study, stipulating that no student can be denied access to education, except if this is explicitly provided for by law. The amendment of the Constitution ignited strong protests from supporters of secularism who turned to the Constitutional Court with the request to annul the adopted legislation. The Constitutional Court, with reference to the neutrality of the state, declared the law unconstitutional, adding that permitting headscarves to be worn would lead to tension between the communities of Islamic and non-Islamic believers, and it would put emphasis on a symbol of the oppression of women, which would go against human rights.[16]

Despite all this, the Turkish Council of Higher Education (Yükseköğretim Kurulu Başkanlığı) announced in 2010 that they

12 Şapka İktisası Hakkında Kanun 28/11/1925 – 230.

13 Bazı Kisvelerin Giyilemiyeceğine Dair Kanun 13/12/1934 – 2879.

14 Theresa Perkins, 'Unveiling Muslim Women: The Constitutionality of Hijab Restrictions in Turkey, Tunisia and Kosovo', (2012) 30 *Boston University International Law Journal* 551.

15 *Ibid*.

16 Judgment of June 5 2008, E: 2008/16, K: 2008/116, Anayasa Mahkemesi (Constitutional Court).

would ensure that nobody should be discriminated against and banned from higher education for wearing a headscarf. Students were asked to report any discriminative treatment they suffered because of wearing headscarves immediately to the Council; at the same time, they announced that they would launch proceedings against the leaders of institutions who dismissed students for wearing headscarves.[17] As a result, the institutions withdrew their prohibitive rules on wearing headscarves, and in 2013, the Turkish government made it possible to wear headscarves in state institutions. The Act adopted on 8 October 2013 amends the Regulations on the Dress Code of Staff Working at Public Institutions.[18] Members of the police, the judiciary, the prosecution authority and the military continue to be governed by special rules banning the wearing of headscarves.

In the United Kingdom, there is no legislation which restricts the wearing of religious clothing or symbols in public, since this type of prohibition would be alien to the British legal culture. State schools have individual dress codes in place with respect to the clothing worn by students and teachers, and in any case, in the British education system, students traditionally wear uniforms. The first relevant notable British case was that of Shabina Begum,[19] a student at Denbigh High School in Luton. The overwhelming majority of students were Muslim, and therefore the school offered three types of uniforms for the students to choose from. The governors of the school, after consultations with the parents and the local imam, offered a garment known as the *shalwar kameez,* which complies with the requirements prescribed by Islam.

Shabina Begum, however, complained about the uniform, saying that she had a strong preference for *jilbab,* which covers more of

17 'YÖK head gives guarantee to all Turkish students on headscarves', *Hürriyet Daily News,* 13 October 2010, www.hurriyetdailynews.com/default.aspx?pageid=438&n=yok-head-gives-personal-guarantee-to-all-students-2010-10-13.

18 Regulation on the Dress Code of Staff Working at Public Institutions (No 8/5105) 1982-10-25.

19 *R (Begum) v Headteacher and Governors of Denbigh High School* [2006] UKHL 15.

the body and which she claimed is more in line with the strict rules of her religion. The governors of the school, however, rejected her complaint, then she applied for a judicial review on the grounds that her right to freedom of religion had been violated. She lost the case in the court of first instance, and then the Court of Appeal decided in favour of Begum; the question was ultimately decided by the House of Lords which, in their judgment, stated that the institution had the right to set rules pertaining to clothing, which the school did with due care, accommodating criteria defined by various religious and other customs and traditions. The Law Lords rejected Begum's application on various grounds.

The majority shared the opinion according to which the school environment is a 'specific situation', which justifies the more stringent restriction of freedom of religion. At the same time, they did not elaborate why they think this is so, what makes this environment 'specific'.[20] The Law Lords approvingly referred to the jurisprudence of the ECtHR (see Section 2.2 below), but did not point out that whereas university students (the applicants in the cases before the ECtHR) attended the education institutions of their own choice, for Begum, it was mandatory to participate in public education.[21] Three Law Lords were of the opinion that, as Begum could choose the school in the full knowledge of its dress code (she had the opportunity to learn about it), and in theory, she had the opportunity to attend another school that respected her religious clothing (which in the end she did, though that school was further away from her place of residence), the decision of the school did not interfere with her freedom of religion.[22] According to the statement of reasons, the Law Lords also examined whether the clash between Begum's right to freedom of religion and the school's decision and the resulting restriction can be justified or not, if we assume that

20 Mark Hill, 'Bracelets, Rings and Veils: The Accommodation of Religious Symbols in the Uniform Policies of English Schools' in Myriam Hunter-Henin (ed), *Law, Religious Freedoms and Education in Europe* (Ashgate 2011) 318–19.

21 *Ibid*, 318.

22 Erica Howard, *Law and the Wearing of Religious Symbols* (Routledge 2012) 67.

such a clash exists. The Law Lords claimed that the school had made serious efforts to review the dress code in order to bring it in line with various religious convictions; the school board even requested expert opinions from two mosques, according to which the dress code was compatible with mainstream Muslim thought.[23] The Law Lords noted that there were three schools in the neighbourhood which would have accepted Begum, even with her specific clothing. The Law Lords were not convinced that Begum had been wearing the dress out of her free will and not under the pressure of her male family members.

In *R (on the application of X) v Y School*[24] the applicant was a 12-year-old girl, who wanted to wear the veil called *niqab* at school in the presence of a male teacher or other men. This case did not get as far as the House of Lords; the ruling was delivered by the High Court (Queen's Bench). The Court again ruled that the prohibition by the school of wearing a headscarf is not in breach of the freedom of religion and, even if it was, the restriction could be justified. This decision was also based on the fact that the school environment is a special one, and therefore specific rules are applicable to it. The Judge of the High Court claimed that freedom of religion had not been disrespected, because the complainant had other opportunities to exercise it, which would not have brought about unjustified or unreasonable difficulties or inconvenience (she could also have chosen another educational institution to attend without having to change her clothing habits), and the complainant accepted the dress code of the school based on free will.

The complainant of *R (on the application of Playfoot (a Child)) v Millais School Governing Body* wanted to wear a so-called 'chastity-ring', indicating that she had taken a vow of chastity until her wedding.[25] According to the court, although the conviction of the complainant can be considered to be of a religious nature, the wearing of the ring was not closely related thereto (i.e., her conviction did not oblige her to wear the ring), and the prohibition from wearing it cannot be considered as a limitation on her freedom

23 *Ibid*, 68.
24 *R v Y School* [2006] EWHC (Admin) 298.
25 *R v Millais School Governing Body* [2007] EWHC (Admin) 1698.

of religion.

The case of Aishah Azmi, a primary school teacher, raised a storm.[26] Azmi worked as a classroom assistant at an institution run by the Church of England. During her job interview and induction training, she wore a *burqa* which did not conceal her face. However, later she asked for permission to wear a *niqab,* which covers the whole face except the eyes, in the presence of her male colleagues. Although initially the school permitted Azmi to wear a headscarf covering her face in the presence of a male person, later, due to complaints, permission was withdrawn on grounds that the facial expressions of teachers are of outstanding importance in the teaching process, and consequently, Azmi was dismissed. Azmi turned to the labour court to appeal against this decision on the grounds of discrimination, but her appeal was rejected, because the discrimination was of an indirect nature and was justified by a legitimate interest, that of maintaining the order of education and the interests of students.

2.2. The Jurisprudence of the European Court of Human Rights

In the jurisprudence of the ECtHR, there have been several important decisions delivered with respect to restrictions on clothing worn at school and related to one's religion. According to the position of the Court, reflected in the decisions, states are free to introduce limitations and bans in this context and such limitations are not considered to be in breach of the freedom of religion.

The applicant in *Dahlab v Switzerland*[27] was a primary school teacher working in the canton of Geneva, who converted from the Catholic religion to Islam in March 1991, then married and started to wear a Muslim headscarf according to the rules of the Quran. Some years later, at the school where she worked, she was requested to stop wearing a headscarf while carrying out her professional

26 *Azmi v Kirklees Metropolitan Borough Council* [2007] IRLR 434 (EAT).

27 *Dahlab v Switzerland,* App no 42393/98, admissibility decision of 15 February 2001.

duties. The request was based on the grounds that such a practice contravened the Public Education Act and constituted 'an obvious means of identification imposed by a teacher on her pupils, especially in a public, secular education system'. The applicant was not willing to comply with this request and she argued that she had worn a headscarf earlier, and nobody had complained about it. After exhausting national fora for legal remedy, the Second Section of the ECtHR declared the application to be inadmissible and so the Court did not deliver a substantive decision.

The Court accepted that wearing the headscarf was an act derived from exercising one's religion, i.e., its restriction curtails the right to freedom of religion; accordingly, it examined whether the degree of limitation was necessary in a democratic society. It concluded that the federal court substantiated the restriction by referring to the potential violation of the religious conviction of the students studying at the school and that of their parents. The decision of the federal court did not include any objection to the religious conviction of the applicant; it only focused on the circumstances of her employment when assessing the legitimacy of the restriction. Taking into account the right of the teacher to manifest her religious conviction freely and the right of students to maintain religious harmony, the measure taken by the state was not ill-founded. Teachers at a state school represent the state, and therefore it is of extreme importance for them to carry out their duties in such a way that the state maintains its religious neutrality. The main objective of the restriction was to preserve the religious neutrality of the state, and the decision took into account the fact that the pupils taught by the applicant were easy to influence due to their age, and as such, wearing the headscarf might have a proselytising effect. The ECtHR found this important, even if on the other hand concluded that the actual impact had not been possible to assess. The Court also mentioned that the fundamental principles of the equality of sexes, tolerance, equality and the prohibition of discrimination are difficult to reconcile with the teachings of the Quran, and a teacher in a democratic state has to represent these values to their pupils. Hence, according to the body, the requirement which obliges a teacher to take off her headscarf while carrying out her professional duties is 'necessary in a democratic society'. Peter Cumper and

Tom Lewis critically remark that the ECtHR made this conclusion without proving any intention of the applicant to proselytise, either politically or in a religious context.[28] The applicant did not make any attempt in any way to convert her pupils; she did not require them to participate in any religious activities (e.g., praying). As Carolyn Evans puts it, it is difficult to discern how the teacher could have put any improper pressure on her pupils.[29]

In another case, also affecting a Muslim university professor (*Kurtulmus v Turkey*), the applicant taught at the University of Istanbul, and wore an Islamic headscarf while exercising her profession.[30] In 1998, disciplinary proceedings were launched against her in order to make her respect the regulations on the dress code of civil servants. As she was not willing to observe the rules, she was first barred from promotion, then, as she continued to wear her headscarf while performing her professional functions, she was deemed to have resigned. National courts dismissed her claim, and the ECtHR declared it inadmissible. According to the position of the Court, the measure had indeed restricted her freedom of religion, but it served a legitimate aim. In line with this, in a democratic society, the state has the right to restrict the wearing of the headscarf with the purpose of safeguarding the rights and freedoms of others. The Court also stated that the applicant had chosen to become a civil servant; the 'tolerance' shown by the authorities, upon which the applicant relied, did not make the rule at issue any less legally binding. The dress code in question, which applied without distinction to all members of the civil service, was aimed at upholding the principles of secularism and neutrality in state education. In conclusion, the ECtHR in the two cases affecting teachers considered the restrictions on wearing religious clothing to be legitimate, in order to protect the neutrality of the state and protect pupils and students from

28 Tom Lewis & Peter Cumper, 'Taking Religion Seriously? Human Rights and Hijab in Europe: Some Problems of Adjudication', (2009) 24 *Journal of Law and Religion* 599, 609.

29 Carolyn Evans, 'The "Islamic Scarf" in the European Court of Human Rights', (2006) 7 *Melbourne Journal of International Law* 3, 10.

30 *Kurtulmus v Turkey*, App no 65500/01, judgment of 1 January 2006.

proselytising. Although these arguments are less applicable to pupils in the education system, similar conclusions were drawn in the cases affecting them.

The applicant of *Şahin v Turkey* studied at the University of Istanbul as a practising Muslim; she considered wearing a headscarf covering her face her religious duty.[31] A circular issued at the university prohibited wearing similar headscarves during lectures and examinations. The applicant failed to comply with the rules contained in the circular and so she was denied participation in exams on several occasions. After this, she moved to Vienna. According to the Grand Chamber of the ECtHR, the right of Leyla Şahin to freedom of religion was affected by the restriction, but that was neither unacceptable nor unnecessary. According to the Court, it would have been clear to the applicant, from the moment she entered the University of Istanbul, that there were restrictions on wearing the Islamic headscarf on university premises and, from the date of issuing the circular letter, that she was liable to be refused access to lectures and examinations if she continued to do so. The right to manifest religious convictions freely cannot lead to the legal protection of all acts influenced by this conviction. This especially applies to manifestations which go against secularism which is protected by the Constitution, which is consistent with the values underpinning the ECHR (Paragraph 114).

According to the Court, when examining the question of the Islamic headscarf in the Turkish context, it is important to bear in mind the impact which wearing such a symbol, which is presented or perceived as a compulsory religious duty, may have on those who choose not to wear it (Paragraph 115). The Court, in mentioning this, referred to certain 'extremist political movements' which seek to impose their own religious symbols on society, or those Muslim women concerned, who might be unfavourably affected by wearing a headscarf as a symbol of oppression, even if they see others do it. Measures taken by relevant state authorities against these and the upholding of the pluralistic and secular nature of an education institution might be interests which justify the restriction on exercis-

31 *Şahin v Turkey*, App no 44774/98, judgment of 10 November 2005.

ing the right to freedom of religion (Paragraphs 115–16). Therefore, according to the Court, the restriction can be considered necessary in a democratic society.

Judge Tulkens was the sole member of the Court to attach a dissenting opinion to the judgment. He was of the opinion that the majority of judges erred by accepting the argumentation of the Turkish state, according to which the measure against the applicant was necessary in order to protect secularism and equality between the sexes. As opposed to this, there was no sign indicating that Şahin had worn the headscarf to exert pressure, provoke, proselytise or spread religious propaganda, nor was there any indication that wearing the headscarf would have disrupted teaching at the university. As regards the argument put forward by the majority with regard to the disturbing effect of wearing the headscarf on those who chose not to wear it, Judge Tulkens concluded that it is a fundamental principle, with respect to the freedom of expression, that the disturbing effect *per se* does not constitute sufficient grounds for restricting the freedom of expression, that is, the majority deemed freedom of religion as inferior to the freedom of expression. While the majority opinion creates the impression of wishing to protect the applicant from the obligation to wear a headscarf, there was no evidence to indicate that the applicant was hiding the truth and was wearing the headscarf against her free will, for reasons other than the intention to fulfil her religious duties.

The applicants in *Köse and 93 Others v Turkey* were pupils at a religious school founded by the state who wore Islamic headscarves at school as an expression of their own and their parents' religious convictions.[32] On 12 February 2002, the Istanbul Governor's Office issued a directive which banned the wearing of headscarves at school and prescribed uniforms to be worn, in order to ensure the neutrality of the state. These rules were also adopted by the institution attended by the applicants who contested them. After domestic legal proceedings, the applicants turned to the ECtHR, but the Second Section also declared this application to be inadmissible. The decision made reference to the case of Leyla Şahin, according to which

32 *Köse and 93 Others v Turkey*, App no 26625/02, judgment of 24 January 2006.

the right to manifest a religious conviction does not automatically bring about the legal protection of any act motivated by this religious conviction. The Court stated that the primary objective of the rule on school uniforms is to ensure pluralistic education, which is of fundamental importance from the perspective of safeguarding a democratic society. The school concerned is a state school, the primary objective of which is to train future religious functionaries. However, parents enrolling their children at such schools are not necessarily motivated by the wish to see their children become religious functionaries but to make sure that their children are provided with religious-oriented education. Since these schools are not denominational but state schools, they are not exempt from the principles of secularism and religious neutrality. The competent authorities, in order to protect the 'rights of others' and respect pluralism, must take great care to ensure that the manifestation of pupils' religious beliefs within schools, if it is permitted, does not take on the nature of an ostentatious act which may constitute a source of pressure and exclusion. The Court believed that the rule in which pupils are not permitted to wear headscarves on the school premises (except during Quran classes) did not deprive parents of the ability 'to guide their children in a direction which accorded with their own religious or philosophical beliefs'.

In two cases adjudicated on the same day, *Dogru v France*[33] and *Kervanci v France*,[34] the applicants were Muslim French citizens who were expelled from school for refusing to take off their headscarves in physical education and sports classes. According to the justification given by the school, wearing headscarves was incompatible with physical education classes. The pupils were able to continue their studies by correspondence courses only. The Fifth Section of the ECtHR admitted the application, but in the substantive decision, it concluded that the right to freedom of religion had not been breached. The Court made reference to its previous decisions, and again stressed that the state had to observe the fundamental principles of pluralism and the freedom of others. In this case, the

33 *Dogru v France*, App no 27058/05, judgment of 4 December 2008.

34 *Kervanci v France*, App no 31645/04, judgment of 4 December 2008.

conclusion of domestic authorities that the Islamic headscarf is incompatible with sports classes for reasons of health and safety is not unreasonable. Regulations on wearing religious symbols and clothing at school tend to vary between European states. The state can restrict the manifestation of religion if practicing that religion conflicts with the objective of protecting the rights and freedoms of others, or with ensuring public order or public safety. According to the Court, respecting the fundamental values of secularism, neutrality and pluralism served as a clear and legitimate reason for not admitting pupils wearing headscarves to classes, after they had refused to remove these garments, despite the relevant internal rules of the school. The Court is of the opinion that the sanction imposed upon them was not motivated by their religion but by their reluctance to obey the internal rules of the school. The ban related only to physical education, and so it cannot be considered to have been extremely stringent and it was proportionate to the aim pursued.

The facts of the six cases adjudicated in 2009 in Strasbourg were identical (*Aktas v France*,[35] *Bayrak v France*,[36] *Gamaleddyn v France*,[37] *Ghazal v France*,[38] *Jasvir Singh v France*[39] and *Ranjit Singh v France*[40]). At the beginning of the 2004–05 academic year, some Muslim girls went to school wearing headscarves covering their hair, and some young Sikh boys wore Sikh *keski*, that is, first turban. Since they refused to take off the unlawful items of clothing, pursuant to the French law restricting the wearing of religious symbols, they were not admitted to the classroom and were subsequently expelled from school, compelled to continue their studies only via correspondence courses. The ECtHR did not admit these applications, because the restriction of the pupils' right to manifest their religious affiliation

35 *Aktas v France*, App no 43563/08, judgment of 30 June 2009.

36 *Bayrak v France*, App no 14308/08, judgment of 30 June 2009.

37 *Gamaleddyn v France*, App no 18527/08, judgment of 30 June 2009.

38 *Ghazal v France*, App no 29134/08, judgment of 30 June 2009.

39 *Jasvir Singh v France*, App no 25463/08, judgment of 30 June 2009.

40 *Ranjit Singh v France*, App no 27561/08, judgment of 30 June 2009.

was in compliance with legislation which had the legitimate aim of protecting the rights and freedoms of others and public safety. The Court again reiterated the neutral role of the state as an organiser with respect to exercising various religions, beliefs and faiths. Unlike in the cases affecting teachers, in these cases the Court found that the major reasons for the restrictions were the protection of public order, the interests of education and the peace and security of the other pupils.

In *Osmanoğlu and Kocabaş v Switzerland*, the Court reinforced its previous case law, and decided that by refusing to exempt two Muslim pupils from compulsory (and mixed) swimming lessons, the competent Swiss authorities had not infringed the applicants' right to freedom of religion.[41] The authorities would even have allowed for the pupils to wear a *burqini*, but the parents had refused to accept this offer. The Swiss authorities were allowed to give precedence to the children's obligation to follow the school curriculum.

Although it is homogeneous, the ECtHR jurisprudence raises several serious questions that have been left unanswered by the decisions. No response has been provided to the question of why freedom of religion can be subjected to restrictions of a much broader scale than freedom of expression. In other words, why is it sufficient to have the rather abstract, distant notions of threat and the violation of public order, which do not even emerge in the concrete, specific cases, to restrict the latter fundamental right? Neither are the questions answered of whether it is appropriate to display such a paternalistic attitude to applicants or not, and whether the right point of departure would be the assumption that the right to freedom of religion also includes the right to wear clothing in accordance with one's religious conviction, which the state can prohibit only for compelling reasons? A further question is whether it is possible, in a school environment, to establish that a pupil or teacher wearing such clothing does indeed harm or pose a threat to others, even if the person wearing such clothing does not wish to exert any influence in matters of religion. The different treatment of pupils and teachers in this respect and the degree

41 *Osmanoğlu and Kocabaş v Switzerland*, App no 29086/12, judgment of 10 January 2017.

and consequences of differentiation are not well-established in the Court's jurisprudence either. Is it not plausible that encountering various convictions might have a positive influence on pupils' acceptance of religious equality and cultural diversity, and serve to increase their tolerance, experience and knowledge of other religions.[42]

3. Wearing Religious Symbols at Work

Specific questions, similar to those relating to the wearing of symbols by teachers, surround the issue of wearing symbols at work (other than at schools). Generally speaking, the possibility of indoctrination is not a realistic threat in the workplace since, in relationships between adults, the vulnerability of one of the parties is not obvious and can only be realistically argued in a limited number of cases (e.g., in the relationship between hospital staff and seriously ill patients). Another characteristic feature of this problem area is that, as opposed to the context of primary schools, there is a stronger chance of the regulation of wearing symbols covering the relationship between private parties. Whereas the overwhelming majority of schools are state-run institutions, and denominational or ecclesiastical schools can, by their nature, adopt rules on wearing religious symbols at school, private undertakings in theory can adopt codes of conduct for their employees, but these, in a secular environment, might clash with the right to exercise one's religion. One example of this is the *Eweida and Others v the United Kingdom* case, one of the main issues of which was the horizontal scope of fundamental rights (freedom of religion).[43]

The *Eweida* case is in fact made up of four individual cases raising similar problems of fundamental rights, of which two (the applications of Nadia Eweida and Ms Chaplin) are related to the wearing of religious symbols in public, whereas the other two (Ms Ladele and Mr McFarlane) are related to refusing work for reasons of religious conviction. Lilian Ladele, a marriage registrar, refused to

42 Lewis & Cumper (n 28) 609.

43 *Eweida and Others v the United Kingdom*, App nos 48420/10, 59842/10, 51671/10 and 36516/10, judgment of 15 January 2013.

participate in acts establishing the civil partnership (an act similar to marriage proceedings) of same-sex couples. Gary McFarlane similarly refused to provide sexual counselling for same-sex couples. While these cases touch upon important issues of freedom of religion, they are not directly related to exercising the freedom of expression.

Eweida, a practising Christian, had been a member of the check-in staff of British Airways since 1999. As a requirement of the job, she was obliged to wear a uniform, which, initially was a high-neck top, later followed by a V-necked top. In addition, a detailed dress code on the uniform stipulated that all jewellery and accessories in the shape of religious symbols had to be concealed. Eweida wore a small cross openly as a pendant on 20 May 2006, as a symbol of her religion, and refused to cover it up. Consequently, in September 2006 she was sent home from work, and was not paid for the time lost. In October 2006 she was offered an administrative job, not involving personal contact with customers, where she would not have been covered by the dress code, but she rejected the offer. As of 1 February 2007 a new dress code was enacted, which allows crosses to be worn, but the company did not offer to compensate Eweida for the loss of income over the preceding period of time. After exhausting, unsuccessfully, the domestic fora for redress, Eweida turned to the ECtHR to address the violation of her freedom of religion and discrimination she felt she had suffered. Section IV of the Court, by five votes to two, concluded that the right enshrined in Article 9 (freedom of religion) of the ECHR had been breached, and imposed a fine of 2,000 euro on the state to be paid in moral damages; furthermore 30,000 euro was to be paid in compensation for legal expenses.

The ECtHR again stated, as a universally applicable rule, that not all acts motivated or inspired by the manifestation of beliefs can be considered as the exercise of freedom of religion, that is, an act protected legally under Article 9(1).[44] In order to count as a

44 *Skugar and Others v Russia*, App no 40010/04, admissibility decision of 3 December 2009; *Arrowsmith v the United Kingdom*, App no 7050/75, admissibility decision of 12 October 1978; *Zaoui v Switzerland*, App no 41615/98, admissibility decision of 18 January 2001.

'manifestation' within the meaning of Article 9, the act in question must be intimately linked to the religion or belief. An example would be an act of worship or devotion which forms part of the practice of a religion or belief in a generally recognised form. However, the manifestation of religion or belief is not limited to such acts; the existence of a sufficiently close and direct nexus between the act and the underlying belief must be determined on the facts of each case and acts that are only distantly related to the teachings of a religion shall not fall under the protection of Article 9(82). This approach is of primary importance and differs significantly from the previous Strasbourg jurisprudence mentioned above, according to which the protection of the manifestation of religious belief provided for a more limited scope of acts, as necessary for practicing that religion or mandated by it.[45]

Although, in theory, the applicant had been afforded the opportunity to change jobs, the Court considered that instead of this response to the interference in her religious practices, a better approach would be to weigh that possibility in the overall balance when considering whether or not the restriction was proportionate, and thus the possibility of changing jobs in itself is not of decisive importance (Paragraph 83). On the other hand, it is important that the act in dispute was carried out by a private company and was not therefore directly attributable to the respondent state; the Court must consider the issues in terms of the positive obligation on the state authorities to ensure the rights under Article 9 to those within their jurisdiction (Paragraph 84). The Court considered that Eweida's behaviour (wearing a cross visibly) was a manifestation of her religious belief, and as such, attracted the protection of Article 9(89). The Court considered that the refusal by British Airways between September 2006 and February 2007 to allow the applicant to remain in her post while visibly wearing a cross amounted to an interference with her right to manifest her religion. Since the interference was not directly attributable to the state, the Court must examine whether in all the circumstances the state authorities complied with their positive obligation under Article 9. In other words, the Court had to determine whether Eweida's right to freely

45 Daniel J Hill & Daniel Whistler, *The Right to Wear Religious Symbols* (Palgrave MacMillan 2013) 107–16.

manifest her religion was sufficiently secured within the domestic legal order and whether a fair balance was struck between her rights and those of others (Paragraph 91).

In common with a large number of European States, the United Kingdom does not have legal provisions specifically regulating clothing and the wearing of religious symbols in the workplace. The Court does not consider that the lack of specific protection under domestic law in itself meant that the applicant's right to manifest her religion by wearing a religious symbol at work was insufficiently protected (Paragraph 92). The Court concluded that in weighing the proportionality of the measures taken by a private company in respect of its employee, the national authorities, specifically the courts, operate within a margin of appreciation. Nonetheless, the Court has reached the conclusion in the present case that a fair balance was not struck. On one side of the scales was Eweida's desire to manifest her religious belief, a fundamental right. A healthy democratic society needs to tolerate and sustain pluralism and diversity. On the other side of the scales was the employer's wish to project a certain corporate image. The Court considers that, while this aim was undoubtedly legitimate, the domestic courts accorded it too much weight. Eweida's cross was discreet and cannot have detracted from her professional appearance. There was no evidence that the wearing of other, previously authorised, items of religious clothing, such as turbans and *hijabs*, by other employees, had any negative impact on British Airways' brand or image. Moreover, the fact that the company was able to amend the uniform code to allow for the visible wearing of religious symbolic jewellery demonstrates that the earlier prohibition was not of crucial importance (Paragraph 94). The Court therefore concluded that the domestic authorities had failed to protect sufficiently the applicant's right to manifest her religion.

Judges Bratza and Björgvinsson (the former is the member of the body delegated by the UK), in their joint partly dissenting opinion, concluded that the rights of Eweida had not been violated. They based their opinion on the following reasoning: The company's dress code had for two years caused no known problems to any employee including the applicant herself; when she changed her mind and wished to wear the cross, she was not willing to wait for the results of a formal grievance complaint which she had lodged with the company. Furthermore, the issue was conscientiously addressed by British Airways, which offered the applicant a temporary administrative position within the company, the dress code was reviewed, in consequence, the applicant was reinstated in her original post.

The second applicant, Shirley Chaplin is also a practising Christian who has worn a cross on a chain around her neck since her confirmation in 1971, and has worked as a nurse at a hospital since 1981. The hospital had a uniform policy based on guidance from the Department of Health. That policy provided that 'no necklaces will be worn to reduce the risk of injury when handling patients'. In 2007, a V-neck uniform was introduced, after which the applicant was asked to remove the necklace. After lengthy disputes, she was moved to another position, for a set period of time, then after the expiry of this period, her employment relationship was terminated. The applicant exhausted the domestic fora for legal remedy, then turned to the Strasbourg Court. The ECtHR concluded in the case of Chaplin that there was no interference with her right to freedom of religion.

The Court considered also in this case that the second applicant's determination to wear the cross and chain at work was a manifestation of her religious belief and that the refusal by the health authority to allow her to remain in the nursing post while wearing the cross was an interference with her freedom to manifest her religion (Paragraph 97). A major difference between the cases of Eweida and Chaplin is that in the latter one, the employer was a public authority, and the wearing of jewellery was restricted in order to protect the health and safety of nurses and patients (Paragraph 98). The Court considers that this reason is of a much greater magnitude than what Eweida's employer was able to demonstrate in order to substantiate the interference. The area in question (the public health care system) is a field where the domestic authorities must be allowed a wide margin of appreciation. The hospital managers were better placed to make decisions on clinical safety than a court, particularly an international court (Paragraph 99). It follows that the Court was unable to conclude that the measures of which Chaplin complains were disproportionate. It also follows that the interference with her freedom to manifest her religion was necessary in a democratic society, and that there was no violation of Article 9 in respect of Chaplin (Paragraph 100).

In the case of Eweida, the ECtHR considered that in the case of a conflict between the interest of a private company to maintain its 'corporate image' and the right to freedom of religion, with respect to the facts of the case, the latter should be attributed greater importance. Wearing a small cross visibly does not undermine the image of the company, which is also confirmed by the fact that the company subsequently amended its own dress code. However, in the case of Chaplin, the argument against the right to exercise one's freedom of religion freely, being the protection of the health and safety of others, was attributed greater importance by the Court. The Court accepted the reasoning of national authorities who claimed that patients can easily and accidentally tear off the pendant hanging from a necklace, that it might cause injuries and could come into contact with an open wound causing a risk of infection. However, there is a risk that the protection of 'health and safety' will become a *carte blanche* for interfering with the right to freedom of religion.[46]

A major step forward in the jurisprudence of the ECtHR is that it accepted in both cases without disputing that wearing the cross shall qualify as the exercise of one's freedom of religion. According to previous practices,[47] the protection within the meaning of Article 9 had not covered every act motivated or influenced by religion, and it was the applicant who had to prove that their conduct was necessary or mandatory with respect to practising their religion.[48] According to the *Eweida* decision, the existence of a sufficiently close and direct nexus between the act and the underlying belief might be sufficient to invoke Article 9 (Paragraph 82). As is also pointed out by Jeroen Temperman, in the case of Eweida, an

46 Ian Leigh & Andrew Hambler, 'Religious Symbols, Conscience, and the Rights of Others', (2014) 3 *Oxford Journal of Law and Religion* 2, 4.

47 See *Arrowsmith v the United Kingdom* (n 44).

48 See also *Valsamis v Greece*, App no 21787/93, judgment of 16 December 1996.

extremely important circumstance is the fact that—given that the restriction on wearing the symbol was prescribed by a private company—the state did not directly interfere with the right of the applicant to freedom of religion; the classic concept of human rights, namely that the state must refrain from curtailing the rights of its citizens, is not affected in this case. At the same time, the state has positive, active obligations (i.e., not only prescribing refraining from something), on the basis of which the state can impose obligations on private parties in order to ensure that they respect the fundamental rights of others.[49] In this case, we encounter the problem of the horizontal scope of fundamental rights, that is, those which are also applicable to private parties. In reaction to the joint partly dissenting opinion of Judges Bratza and Björgvinsson, a dress code that can easily be amended overnight can hardly be considered a necessary restriction.[50]

As regards the case of Chaplin, since the protection of 'public health' as possible grounds for limitations is explicitly included in Article 9(2) of the ECHR, we might also suppose that assessing the application could not have posed serious difficulties. If it can reasonably be assumed that there is a connection between the restriction and the protection of public health, the restriction is permitted. However, being aware of the specific facts of the case, we have every reason to worry. The endeavour of a hospital or health authority to protect the health of patients and health workers is a legitimate and self-evident aim. At the same time, the threat referred to in this case is rather distant and abstract. Is it a real threat that a patient will unintentionally seize and pull the necklace of the nurse, and this poses a health risk for both? This is contradicted by the fact that Chaplin offered to wear a necklace and cross attached to each other with a magnet, so that in the event of any unwanted interference the two immediately come apart, thereby preventing injury, but the hospital rejected this idea as well. It also came to light that workers had been wearing identity badges, and strangely

49 '[T]he state does not face human rights obligations here. Indeed, positive obligations in this area entail a duty to protect the right to manifest a religion *vis-à-vis* non-state actors'. Jeroen Temperman, 'Of Crosses and Homophobia', (2013) 2 *Arbeidsrechtelijke Annotaties* 87, 96.

50 *Ibid*, 97.

enough, no similar safety concerns were raised with respect to those. All in all, the ECtHR accepted the reference to the rationale of health protection without any criticism or evidence being presented. This is rather alarming if interference with fundamental human rights needs to be substantiated, and raises the issue of whether the protection of public health in the future can easily be used as grounds for any restriction of fundamental rights protected by Article 9.[51]

In the context of the *Eweida* case, it is important to emphasise that it brought the problem of wearing Christian symbols in public to the attention of the ECtHR. While the questions of the Islamic headscarves of Muslim women caught the attention of the European public, legislators and those applying the law more intensively, this must not overshadow the fact that the appearance of Christianity in the public sphere also raises fundamental and moot questions. This is also reflected in the Resolution of the Parliamentary Assembly of the Council of Europe (2015), which called upon European states to combat intolerance and discrimination against Christians, asking them to facilitate reasonable accommodation to the exercise of religion.[52]

In the recent *Ebrahimian v France* case, the applicant, a social worker in a public hospital, was informed that her contract would not be renewed, a decision based on her refusal to remove her veil and complaints made by a number of patients.[53] The authorities had identified problems created by her attitude within the department in question, and had attempted to persuade her to refrain from displaying her religious convictions. According to the ECtHR, that did not lead to the breach of her Article 9 rights, as state regulations gave precedence to the rights of others, the equality of treatment of patients and the functioning of the service over manifestations of religious beliefs.

51 *Ibid*, 99; Andrew Hambler, *Religious Expression in the Workplace and the Contested Role of Law* (Routledge 2015) 87.

52 Tackling intolerance and discrimination in Europe with a special focus on Christians. Resolution 2036 (2015) of the Parliamentary Assembly.

53 App no 64846/11, judgment of 26 November 2015.

The European Court of Justice (ECJ) will decide in two cases in the near future, where the facts are very similar to the abovementioned ECtHR cases, but the two Advocate Generals' preliminary opinions completely differ. Both cases involve dress codes at the working place, which ban the full-face veil. In one of the cases, Advocate General Sharpston argues that 'an entirely neutral dress code policy may also constitute indirect discrimination which will be justified only if it is proportionate to the pursuance of a legitimate aim, including the interests of an employer's business'.[54] According to him, there is nothing to suggest that the applicant was unable to perform her duties as a design engineer because she wore an Islamic headscarf, so her dismissal constituted direct discrimination, to which none of the derogations provided for by the relevant EU directive apply.[55] In the other case, according to Advocate General Kokott, 'if the ban is based on a general company rule which prohibits political, philosophical and religious symbols from being worn visibly in the workplace, such a ban may be justified if it enables the employer to pursue the legitimate policy of ensuring religious and ideological neutrality'.[56] In any case, the ECJ will soon decide which path to choose.

4. General Bans on Wearing Religious Clothing in Public

4.1. Regulations in Individual States

In addition to restricting religious clothing at school, in several European states, after debates on such bans, a complete and general ban was introduced on wearing clothing covering the face in public, legislation which effectively meant that the *burqa*, *niqab* and other similar pieces of clothing cannot be worn in the street. In Belgium,

54 Advocate General's Opinion in Case C-188/15 *Bougnaoui and ADDH v Micropole SA*.

55 Council Directive 2000/78/EC of 27 November 2000 establishing a general framework for equal treatment in employment and occupation.

56 Advocate General's Opinion in Case C-157/15 *Samira Achbita and Centrum voor gelijkheid van kansen en voor racismebestrijding v G4S Secure Solutions NV*.

a law prohibiting headscarves covering the whole face was adopted in June 2011.[57] According to the regulation amending the Penal Code, it is prohibited to wear attire in the street which makes it impossible to recognise one's face. In December 2012, the Belgian Constitutional Court dismissed the complaints lodged against the law.[58] The Constitutional Court, with respect to the interference with freedom of religion and expression, explained that the adoption of the law was necessary to maintain public safety, facilitate social cohabitation and ensure equality between men and women. The decision considered gender equality and individualisation to be enabled by leaving the face uncovered and recognisable as a fundamental value of a democratic society.[59]

In France, Act no 1192 on the complete ban of *burqas* was adopted in 2010. According to the text of the law, nobody can wear clothing covering the face in public places, because this practice contradicts the values constituting the basis of cohabitation, and endangers the dignity of the individual wearing such clothing. The law defines public places thus: 'public places comprise the public highway and any places open to the public or assigned to a public service'. The fine imposed for the violation of this rule cannot exceed 150 euro. The law also criminalises the act of forcing someone to cover up their face. Pursuant to the new provision inserted concurrently into the Penal Code, the act of forcing someone to cover up her face due to her gender shall be punishable with imprisonment not longer than 1 year and a fine of 30,000 euro. If the victim is a minor, the punishment will be twice as severe.

After a huge national scandal and heated debates, the French Conseil d'État overturned the *burqini* (a swimsuit for women, which

57 1er juin 2011, loi visant à interdire le port de tout vêtement cachant totalement ou de manière principale le visage.

58 Decision of the Constitutional Court of Belgium, Arrêt 145/2012 du 6 décembre 2012, http://strasbourgobservers.com/2012/12/14/belgian-constitutional-court-ban-on-face-coverings-does-not-violate-human-rights/#_ftn1.

59 For the English extract of the Belgian Constitutional Court decision, see the reasoning of the *SAS v France* case, App no 43855/11, judgment of 26 June 2014, para 42.

covers the whole body except the face, the hands and the feet to make it suitable for conservative Muslim women) ban in a coastal town of France.[60] The bans affected many French towns and cities besides the one, Villeneuve-Loubet, which the court explicitly addressed, as many had adopted ordinances to prohibit Muslim women from wearing these bathing suits. The French court concluded that the idea of a *burqini* ban insulted 'fundamental freedoms' such as the 'freedom to come and go, the freedom of conscience and personal liberty'.[61]

There are states where the idea of introducing a similar ban has also been raised, but so far the courts with jurisdiction have prevented its implementation. In Spain, in the city of Lérida in the province of Catalonia, a measure of this kind was adopted, then the Spanish Supreme Court, overruling provincial courts, declared it null and void for formal reasons in 2013, but in addition, they declared that neither the protection of public safety or public order, nor that of the rights of others or even gender equality are appropriate grounds for a complete ban on headscarves.[62] The supreme judicial forum was of the opinion that there is no evidence to prove that wearing this type of clothing violates public interests, whereas the restriction does actually and specifically violate freedom of religion. In addition, the ban contributes to the isolation of and discrimination against the women concerned.[63]

After facing a serious migration crisis in 2015–16, the German government is now expected to pass a motion proposing a ban on the full-face veil in many areas of public life such as courts, schools and universities, as well as in road traffic and during police checks.[64] Still, a general, French-type ban on the veil in Germany is

60 Nos 402742, 402777, order of 26 August 2016.

61 James McAuley, 'France's Top Administrative Court Overturns Burkini Ban', *Washington Post*, 26 August 2016.

62 *Ahmet Arslan and Others v Turkey*, App no 693/2013, judgment of 6 February 2013.

63 For the English extract of the Spanish Supreme Court decision, see the reasoning of *SAS v France* (n 59), paras 43–47.

64 Philip Oltermann, 'Angela Merkel Endorses Party's Call for Partial Ban on Burqa and Niqab', *The Guardian*, 6 December 2016.

unlikely to be introduced, as the human rights standards set by the Constitutional Court would prevent this.

4.2. The Jurisprudence of the European Court of Human Rights

As of today, there are two ECtHR decisions related to wearing headscarves in public spaces and their outcomes differ. The 127 applicants in *Ahmet Arslan and Others v Turkey* were members of a religious group named *Aczimendi tarikatÿ*, who attended a religious ritual event in Ankara in October 1996.[65] They toured the streets of the city while wearing the distinctive dress of their group, which comprises a turban, '*salvar*' (baggy '*harem*' pants), a tunic and a stick. Following various incidents on the same day, they were arrested and placed in police custody. They were later sentenced for breach of anti-terrorist legislation for wearing clothing items covering their heads and, in general, for wearing religious clothes outside their religious rituals. The ECtHR stated that Article 9 of the Convention had been breached, as it found that it was not proven that the applicants jeopardised public order or that they had pursued any missionary activity, putting passers-by under duress. According to the judgment, the wearing of certain clothing items in 'public places' and in 'public establishments' differs. Whereas in schools and other state establishments the ban on such clothing serves a legitimate state aim, such an aim cannot be established in a public place, with respect to the peaceful members of a religious community. An important condition was that the applicants were private persons, and not civil servants, whose conduct did not violate the principle of state neutrality. As such, interference with the right to freedom of religion was not necessary in a democratic society.

From this judgment, the conclusion could be drawn that the French regulations on the general ban on wearing headscarves in

65 *Ahmet Arslan and Others v Turkey*, App no 41135/98, judgment of 23 February 2010.

public places would not stand the test of the ECtHR.[66] However, contrary to this, the Court ruled against the applicant in *SAS v France*.[67] The applicant in this case was a practising Muslim and a French citizen, who objected to not being allowed to wear a veil covering the entire face as a result of the legislation banning the covering up of the entire face in public places. The applicant emphasised that the religious clothing is worn of her own free will without pressure from anyone. It was also underlined that she has worn the veil in the past, even if not all the time, and wishes to wear it freely in the future as well, at any time she pleases. Finally, she pointed out that her intent was not to disturb anyone but to 'find her inner peace' (Paragraph 12).

The ECtHR stated that the present case differs significantly from *Ahmet Arslan and Others* in the fact that the full-face Islamic veil has the particularity of entirely concealing the face, with the possible exception of the eyes, whereas this does not apply to the members of the Turkish religious group (Paragraph 136). For reasons of security, any state may prohibit wearing clothes which restrict identification of a person but a blanket ban to that effect is acceptable only if the risk to public order can generally be identified (Paragraph 139). The French government could not demonstrate such a risk. Another possible rationale for limitation is the 'protection of the rights and freedoms of others'. In this respect, the French government pointed out that concealing one's face makes living together impossible for the affected members of society and is 'against the minimum norms of civility which are necessary for social interaction' (Paragraphs 25 and 141). The ECtHR accepted the above as legitimate arguments, asserting at the same time that 'allowing full-face veils in public places is a choice to be made by society' (Paragraph 153).[68] The question raised by this point was the proportionality of the restriction. With respect to the broad discretionary right of the state, as well as the

66 L Ragep Powell, 'The Constitutionality of France's Ban on the Burqa in Light of the European Convention's *Arslan v Turkey* Decision on Religious Freedom', (2013) 31 *Wisconsin International Law Journal* 118.

67 *SAS v France* (n 59).

68 'It can thus be said that the question whether or not it should be permitted to wear the full-face veil in public places constitutes a choice of society'.

absence of a European consensus on the subject matter and the low value of the penalty applicable in the event of a breach, the Court deemed that the French restriction is neither disproportionate nor unnecessary.

Judges Nussberger and Jäderblom attached a dissenting opinion to the decision (which was passed by 15 to 2), in which they explain that, contrary to the majority opinion, they believe that the applicant's freedom of religion and right to privacy had been violated. According to the dissenting opinion, the majority forced its opinion on the minority through the disputed legislation in the name of abstract values ('living together', 'civility'), which are insufficient grounds to justify the restriction of fundamental rights. These abstract values cannot be considered as 'the rights of others', which are acknowledged grounds for the limitation of rights under the ECHR. Wearing a full-face veil does not limit living together; everyone has the right to be an 'outsider' (dissenting opinion, Paragraph 8). Seeing the face of another is important in human communication but its absence does not make it impossible to communicate (dissenting opinion, Paragraph 9).

Thus, the two cases testing the compatibility of the general ban with the jurisprudence of the ECtHR had different outcomes. It is surprising that the majority accepted the limitation of freedom of religion in *SAS* based on such weak reasoning. This reserve is probably attributable to the sensitive nature of the matter at hand, to which Europe has yet not given unequivocal responses, and to which the Strasbourg Court was not willing to provide answers either. John Adenitire believes that the decision has resulted in the exact opposite consequences to those it intends to achieve: Enhancing the restriction actually hinders social interaction.[69] Nevertheless, it is questionable (in particular in the light of *Ahmet Arslan*) whether freedom of religion can be restricted outright based on the customs practised by the majority without proving actual endangerment. This approach is in opposition with the dogmatic order of fundamental rights; these rights are to be exercised by the individual against the state, that is, for example, the government

69 John Adenitire, '*SAS v France*: Fidelity to Law and Conscience', (2015) 22 *European Human Rights Law Review* 78.

authorised by the majority. In this case, the perceived will of the majority—embodied by the legislator—overruled the rights of the individual without proving the existence of a compelling interest.

5. An Overview of Arguments Relating to Restrictions

5.1. Protection of Safety, Public Order and Peaceful Cohabitation

One of the possible reasons behind the restrictions on dress codes may be the fight against terrorism and the intent to avoid a terrorist attack. Some believe that a Muslim woman concealing her face represents a threat to Western societies, as they associate such attire with terrorism. For Europeans, wearing a *burqa* or a *niqab* may lead to an association with radical Islam and with religious fundamentalism.

Evidently, there may be circumstances where the identification of the individual is necessary to maintain a secure environment. These may be, for example, security checks at airports or when taking photographs for identification documents. Moreover, there are situations in a school or university environment where wearing a headscarf that conceals the face may render educational activities impossible. A practical point of consideration may be if the headscarf makes communication with the teacher difficult or if attendance at class or exams cannot be verified otherwise.[70] It is yet another question whether these points of consideration merit a full restriction or if there may be other ways of tackling these problems where lesser limitations on freedom of religion are available. One thing is certain: Acknowledgement of special situations like these ones cannot justify a general restriction, applicable without exception, on dress codes, as is currently effective in Belgium and France. For one, banning clothes that conceal the face does not particularly make it more difficult to execute terrorist attacks, and it is also a cause for concern that such a general restriction identifies

70 Erica Howard, *Law and the Wearing of Religious Symbols* (Routledge 2012) 34.

any and all Muslim schoolgirls as terrorists. Experience shows that the majority of girls and women wearing such attire do not support terrorism or suicide attacks and do not consider themselves to be Islamic fundamentalists.[71]

However, Europe and/or the 'Western world' are undoubtedly afraid of or at least worried about Islam. This fear is not necessarily identical to concerns about suicide attackers, but to doubts about the growing presence of the Islamic culture, legal system and civilisation in Europe. Accordingly, the headscarf concealing the face might symbolise the fact that certain varieties of Islam are not compatible with the western legal and institutional system, and endanger the liberal social order.[72] The headscarf is not itself dangerous and does not become an important issue as such, but it is the symbol of a cultural clash, of a conflict between various social and political concepts. The stance of Europe and the United States is also different in this matter, as the fear of Islamic culture is less dominant in North America. The United States was founded as a melting pot of different cultures, and therefore builds its identity on this characteristic; fear of the impact of diverse mentalities is therefore not typical, either in society or at the legislative level: terrorism is the primary fear.[73] By contrast, the European approach is worried about the identity of the secular state and principally fears extremist political movements,[74] and secondly all cultures that are far from European culture if they jeopardise the generally accepted form and rules of 'living together'.[75] According to this, the restriction of freedom of religion is justified by the protection of general European freedom.

71 Dominic McGoldrick, *Human Rights and Religion: The Islamic Headscarf Debate in Europe* (Hart 2006) 21.

72 Peter G Danchin, 'Suspect Symbols: Value Pluralism as a Theory of Religious Freedom in International Law', (2008) 33 *The Yale Journal of International Law* 1, 6.

73 Robert A Kahn, 'The Headscarf as Threat: A Comparison of German and US Legal Discourses', (2007) 40 *Vanderbilt Journal of Transnational Law* 417.

74 *Şahin v Turkey* (n 31), paras 129–30.

75 *SAS v France* (n 59), paras 141–2, 153.

At this point, it is important to note the attitude of the state to Christianity; European states wish to keep Islam away from the public sphere in the same way that they managed to 'expel' Christianity from the most important areas of public life and public sphere, in the process of establishing the secular, religion-neutral state.[76] This is why in *Dahlab*, a point of consideration was that—and according to the ECtHR it substantiated the restriction—the potential proselytising effect of teachers wearing headscarves would be in breach of the principle of the neutrality of the state (the Court accepted this in spite of the absence of any evidence showing proselytising intent or activity). At the same time, it also holds true that rules limiting the wearing of certain attire can obviously be considered as a response to certain varieties of Islam, though in the normative texts of these regulations any specific reference to the Islamic religion is avoided (when talking about the general ban of concealing one's face). Problems that have arisen so far in relation to Christian symbols and customs of dress are much more limited in scope, but they do exist and therefore the issue was not triggered exclusively by the appearance of Islam in Europe.

Nevertheless, the neutrality of the state does not entail depriving the citizens of that state of the opportunity to exercise and represent their religion, either in public life or in public places. It is the state and not its citizens that should be neutral with regard to religions. This also belongs to the fundamental characteristics of liberal, western societies which respect freedoms and liberties. It means that by decreasing the level of freedom granted to others without a genuine need and a compelling reason, we undermine our own habitual universe and hard-fought freedom. It is fundamentally incompatible with the ideal of human rights to put at a disadvantage, by decreasing their level of legal protection, a vulnerable minority, small in number (Muslim women wishing to wear the banned items of clothing) without the majority being able to provide a substantial explanation in support of the measure.

76 Robert A Kahn, 'Are Muslims the New Catholics? Europe's Headscarf Laws in Comparative Historical Perspective', (2011) 21 *Duke Journal of Comparative & International Law* 567.

5.2. Avoiding Segregation, Granting Gender Equality

The argument against the headscarf concealing the face claims that it contributes to social segregation in public communication and renders integration impossible. At the same time, it expresses the lack of intent to accept the rules of western civilisation.[77] Wearing the *burqa* emphasises separation and differences.[78]

Nevertheless, by prohibiting the wearing of the headscarf by women who wish to follow the rules of their religion and wear it, we increase their chances of being excluded from most customary forms of social contacts. As a result, they will stay at home, they will not take up any employment or attend school and they will become completely isolated from the majority society. On the other hand, if they relinquish obeying the requirements of their religion, and make attempts to integrate into the world dominated by the rules of the majority, we will deprive this majority of the opportunity to encounter different cultures and life philosophies, the knowledge of which might increase the power of pluralistic societies and embeddedness; we will deprive them of the opportunity for fruitful debates and discussions on a series of important issues, such as the essence of western civilisation, the societal role of religions, the equality of human beings and social groups, etc.[79] The experience of 'being different' increases tolerance and respect for liberties, and also contributes to a more in-depth understanding of our own selves. The ban of clothing curtails these opportunities.

Arguments which cite the granting of gender equality are a double-edged sword, to say the least. The ECtHR, until *SAS*, had accepted the argumentation of the states concerned, according to which wearing a headscarf covering the face violates gender equality. This approach is based on the assumption that Muslim women are forced by their male family members to wear this item of clothing. Opposing this, they claimed in every similar case that

77 Howard (n 70) 32.

78 *Ibid*, 33.

79 Clare Ovey & Robin CA White, *Jacobs and White: European Convention on Human Rights* (Oxford University Press 4th edn 2006) 310.

they were wearing a *burqa* or a similar headscarf of their own free will, following the rules of their religion voluntarily. In line with the rules of legal proceedings, the truth of such statements cannot be disputed unless the opposite is proved by evidence, and such evidence did not emerge in these cases.[80] In other words, when courts, including domestic courts and the ECtHR, protected the equal rights of the women who were applicants in these cases, they did just the opposite of the applicants' free will by displaying a paternalistic attitude towards them. Such unsolicited assistance provided by the state for women pushes those concerned right into the trap it is trying to help them avoid. Protecting gender equality contrary to women's will views them as vulnerable, helpless victims in need of assistance and guardianship, as they are unable to protect or exercise their own rights.[81] *SAS v France* was the first case where the ECtHR rejected the argument of the state, and stated that gender equality cannot be raised as an argument in the reasoning if the disputed practice is defended by the women themselves (Paragraph 119). Certainly, it is easy to imagine that there are Muslim women in Europe who are forced to wear items of clothing against their own will, but the legal protection of human rights cannot handle cases where the person concerned does not wish to exercise their human rights in the way envisaged, and does not make use of the state-legal institutional system to ask for protection. In addition, not even such cases may justify a general and complete ban, because this also violates the rights of those who make a free decision to wear certain attire, free from any pressure or force.

80 As for the opinion of women concerned, that is, living in France and wearing headscarves, see 'Unveiling the Truth. Why 32 Muslim Women Wear the Full-Face Veil in France?' (Open Society Foundations 2011), www.opensocietyfoundations.org/reports/unveiling-truth-why-32-muslim-women-wear-full-face-veil-france.

81 Lynn Roseberry, 'Religion, Ethnicity and Gender in the Danish Headscarf Debate' in Dagmar Schiek & Victoria Chege (eds), *European Union Non-Discrimination Law: Comparative Perspectives on Multidimensional Equality Law* (Routledge/Cavendish 2008) 341.

5.3. Individual Autonomy and the Freedom of Expression

The primary problem with restricting clothing that conceals the face is that it limits individual autonomy, the freedom to practice one's religion and the right to privacy without just cause and true necessity. Wearing a particular attire is a unique way of exercising the freedom of expression,[82] which is similar to other, non-verbal communication using symbols, such as a burning cross,[83] a five-pointed red star,[84] burning flags,[85] or a peace sign.[86] These may be limited under certain circumstances, as can communication by the spoken word. The Strasbourg Court did not examine the headscarf issue from the point of view of freedom of speech but regarded it as a matter relating to freedom of religion under Article 9, which is not necessarily unreasonable. However, it is difficult to justify that, while the Court's focus in relation to Article 10 (freedom of speech) is the protection of opinions which may be shocking, offending or disturbing to others,[87] when it comes to Article 9 and exercising the rights thereunder, it is considerably narrower, even if this undisputedly entails expressive elements as well, such as wearing certain attire. According to the reasoning of the *SAS* case, this means that the right to wear religious clothing (and therefore self-expression in this manner) may be restricted if it contradicts the practice of 'living together' as exercised by the majority. Such a limitation would be unimaginable in the light of the mature jurisprudence of the ECtHR in respect of freedom of speech. However, when approving the ban, the Court did not attribute any special significance to the fact that wearing a particular attire is not only a form of exercising one's freedom of religion, but also a form of exercising freedom of expression and on this the Court is not consistent with its own evolved jurisprudence related to Article 10.

82 Danchin (n 72) 9.
83 *Virginia v Black* 538 US 343 (2003).
84 *Vajnai v Hungary*, App no 33629/06, judgment of 8 July 2008.
85 *Texas v Johnson* 491 US 397 (1989).
86 *Spence v Washington* 418 US 405 (1974).
87 *Handyside v the United Kingdom*, App no 5493/72, judgment of 7 December 1976.

Having made an overview of the headscarf-related cases, we might be left with the impression that the protection of human rights at the European level cannot handle powerful manifestations of religiousness, which are alien to European societies. It seems that the liberal way of thinking, concerned as it is with respecting human rights, has difficulties accommodating the idea that someone can fulfil their religious obligations out of free will. It is difficult to raise human rights-related arguments in order to recognise a *right* with reference to a religion-based *obligation*.[88] The aforementioned decision of the Belgian Constitutional Court, approving the complete and general ban, is also confused when wishing to impose individualisation on Muslim members of society, who find this type of European approach alien. Nevertheless, when they wish to avail themselves of the human rights protection system based on the recognition of a broad spectrum of the rights of the individual, it will not accommodate them, and as such, it essentially does not fulfil its function in this respect. This makes it difficult to argue in favour of respect to be paid to the individual, that is, to apply the customary human rights-related argumentation, when in reality we encounter the paternalistic attitude of states.

6. Conclusion

The system of human rights is essentially secular. It aims to protect the rights of the individual against the majority, and its social practices and historical traditions, but in the headscarf-related cases, the ECtHR or domestic authorities and courts otherwise respecting human rights do not seem to wish to protect the right to be religious, even against the majority and restrictive traditions. In terms of wearing religious clothing and symbols, they intend to limit practising one's religion to the private sphere, which is in compliance with the principle of secularism, but is not acceptable from the perspective of the protection of freedom of religion as a human right. Freedom of religion is the right which was the hardest-fought, with the highest death-toll and bloodshed, and prior to its full recognition, nearly up to the recent past, devastating wars

88 Lewis & Cumper (n 28) 615–16.

were fought, even on European territory, for it to be recognised. If we, scared by a new challenge, curtail this right even in unjustified cases, we will not preserve but deny Europe's historic traditions and the achievements of the protection of human rights over more than 50 years.

Maybe, it would be a more honest gesture on the part of decision-makers to admit that the restrictions are not justified by the protection of the rights of others or the protection of abstract ideals such as gender equality or living together and the like, but by the fear of the rise of Islam in Europe; this is one of the indirect messages of the judgments delivered by the ECtHR. While on these premises the dogma and system of the protection of human rights should be significantly altered, this would, at least, be a reasonable idea, which could serve as a good basis for a discussion, and which would not be burdened by the severe internal inconsistency we also highlighted. At the same time, the identity 'disorder' or dissonance derived from wanting to simultaneously maintain the earlier schemes of the protection of human rights and prohibit people from dressing as they like might enhance those extremist endeavours which the imperfect response given to headscarves wishes to curb.

After finishing the manuscript of this book, on 14 March 2017 the ECJ upheld the banning of the visible display of any political, philosophical or religious sign in the workplace in two of its decisions. In Achbita, the ECJ found that it does not constitute 'direct discrimination' if a company has an internal rule banning the wearing of any political, philosophical or religious sign. In Bougnaoui, the ECJ noted that it was not clear, based on the reference submitted to the Court, that there had been a discriminative treatment of the applicant based either directly or indirectly on religion or other belief.

Chapter 4

Media Advertisements with Religious Content

1. Introduction

The appearance of religion in commercial communications in the media (advertisements) can cause problems in two ways. On the one hand, it is questionable to what extent the advertisement of religions and churches should be allowed to be made public and, on the other hand, whether believers should be protected against having their convictions offended by such advertisements. The two questions necessitate consideration of different aspects when assessing restrictions, but the common denominator in both is the desirability of avoiding offence to religious beliefs. Generally, in respect of opinions expressed in public and political discourses, individual grievances do not justify the limitation of freedom of expression, but legislation on advertisements (and the practice of the European Court of Human Rights (hereinafter: ECtHR)) provides for and allows unique and less stringent standards concerning limitations. Regarding advertisements with religious content, the aspect of competing religions as well as the requisite balancing out of the various churches and religious communities must also be taken into consideration. Legal means may also play a role in ensuring that believers are free to decide on the very important question of which religion they wish to follow, or, indeed, to opt not to follow any religion, without undue influence by media advertisements.

2. The Regulations on Religious Advertisements in the Media in Different States

The Media Directive of the European Union does not provide for any limitations of advertising religion in the media, but until 2007, it expressly prohibited the broadcast of television commercials offensive to religious or political convictions.[1] This explicit prohibition was no longer part of the Directive after the 2007 amendment, but the prohibition of broadcasting commercial communications (i.e., advertisements, sponsor messages and product placement) offensive to human dignity via audiovisual media services (that is, television and on-demand services) remained in the text.[2] Consequently, the restriction of commercials infringing on human dignity by offending religious convictions was left to be regulated by Member States, although the scope of activities subject to prohibition in the Directive was considerably narrowed. Both versions of the Directive prohibit commercial communication which discriminates negatively on the basis of religion.[3]

In light of the above, the Member States generally prohibit the dissemination of commercial messages which are offensive to human dignity, and do not provide separately for the protection of religious convictions. There is a unique approach in the United Kingdom. While religious advertisement is not forbidden, the self-regulation of advertisers provides the rules; more specifically, Chapter 15 of the Code of Broadcast Advertising sets out the rules and detailed limitations of religious advertisement disseminated via radio and television.[4]

The commercials must identify the sponsor of the advertisement on the basis of the above referenced rules, if it is not unequivocally

1 Article 12c of Council Directive 89/552/EEC on the coordination of certain provisions laid down by Law, Regulation or Administrative Action in Member States concerning the pursuit of television broadcasting activities (Television without Frontiers EC Directive).

2 Article 9(1)c(i) of Directive 2010/13/EU of the European Parliament and of the Council of 10 March 2010 on the coordination of certain provisions laid down by law, regulation or administrative action in Member States concerning the provision of audiovisual media services (Audiovisual Media Services Directive, AVMS Directive).

3 Currently: Article 9(1)c(ii) of the AVMS Directive.

4 UK Code of Broadcast Advertising (BCAP Code), www.cap.org.uk/Advertising-Codes/~/media/Files/CAP/Codes%20BCAP%20pdf/The%20BCAP%20Code.ashx.

possible to identify them from the content. In general, television advertisements may not communicate religious doctrines and convictions, except during the programming of special channels dedicated to religious themes, but even in these cases the advertisement may not depict the conviction as an undoubted fact, and must make it clear that the commercial reflects the opinion of the producer who ordered its dissemination. The latter rule also is applicable to radio advertising. Under the Code, advertisements may not refer to the alleged consequences of having or lacking faith, may not state that the conviction of the sponsor is the 'only' or 'true' faith or religion, and must not denigrate the conviction of others. The producers of the advertisements are only allowed to pursue fundraising activities through commercials for charities, in which case, the media service provider broadcasting such advertisements must endeavour to verify whether the money collected was actually donated to such charitable purposes. Advertisements may not take advantage of or abuse the weaknesses, hopes or fears of senior citizens or people with illnesses or in mourning, and may not claim that faith is capable of treating or healing physical or spiritual diseases. Advertisements may not be targeted at children under 18, and may not be broadcast in the proximity of programmes targeted at children under 18.

3. Assessment of Religious Advertisements in the Jurisprudence of the European Court of Human Rights

It is an axiom in the practice of the ECtHR relating to Article 9 on the freedom of religion that proselytism does not qualify as exercising the freedom of religion as protected by the ECHR. What is meant by proselytising is the activity of persuasion carried out by imposing undue pressure, especially if it takes place between people who are connected to one another in a hierarchical manner. In other words, the exchange of opinions of people of equal status regarding religion (attempt to persuade) may be subject to protection.[5] Proselytism beyond the permitted limitations can easily be imagined with regard to advertisements, as communication via the media is unilateral, and the exposure of the audience towards the media (stemming from the passivity of the audience as well as the power of persuasion of the media) does not qualify as equal status. This is one of the reasons why some states decided to forbid religious advertisements from the media.

There has only been one case to date in the jurisprudence of the ECtHR, in *Murphy v Ireland*, which directly focused on the dissemination of religious advertisements in the media.[6] The applicant was a pastor attached to the Irish Faith Centre, a Bible-based (free church) Christian community. In early 1995, the Irish Faith Centre submitted an advertisement to an independent, local commercial radio station for transmission. The text of the advertisement read as follows: 'What think ye of Christ? Would you, like Peter, only say that he is the son of the living God? Have you ever exposed yourself to the historical facts about Christ? The Irish Faith Centre are presenting for Easter week an hour-long video by Dr Jean Scott PhD on the evidence of the resurrection from Monday 10th to Saturday 15th April every night at 8.30 and Easter Sunday at 11.30am and live by satellite at 7.30pm'. The Irish media authority forbade the broadcast, pursuant to Section 10(3) of the Radio and Television Act 1988. According to the provisions of the Act, 'no advertisement shall be broadcast which is directed towards any religious or political end'. The Irish Courts did not reverse the decision.

The applicant turned to the ECtHR, where it was ruled by unanimous decision that the freedom of expression set out in Article 10 of the Convention had not been violated. According to the Court's statement, the Contracting States can avail of broader rights of discretion in drawing the limitations of the freedom of expression when resolving problems related to

5 *Kokkinakis v Greece*, App no 14307/88, judgment of 25 May 1993; *Larissis and Others v Greece*, Case no 140/1996/759/958–960, judgment of 24 February 1998.

6 *Murphy v Ireland*, App no 44179/98, judgment of 10 July 2003.

morals, and especially to religion. There is no uniform European view on handling attacks on religious convictions (Paragraph 67). In the Court's view, it must be considered that the audiovisual media have a more immediate and powerful effect than the print media (Paragraph 69).

The Court's opinion is that the concept of pluralism, tolerance and broadmindedness does not, as such, envisage that an individual is to be protected from exposure to a religious view simply because it is not their own. However, it cannot be excluded that an expression which does not appear to be offensive at first sight could have an offensive impact in certain circumstances. The question before the Court was therefore whether the prohibition of a certain type of expression (religious advertising) through a particular means (the broadcast media) can justifiably be prohibited in the particular circumstances of the case (Paragraph 72).

The Court considered it an important circumstance that the prohibition of religious commercials was only applied in broadcasts, so the applicant was free to advertise the same subject matter in the press or public meetings and other assemblies. Moreover, the prohibition related only to advertising. The applicant retained the same right as any other citizen to participate in programmes on religious matters, and to have services of his church broadcast in the audiovisual media, without an enforceable access right to do so and only if such an editorial decision is made by the specific medium (Paragraph 74).

The Court considered the government's argument that a complete or partial relaxation of the disputed prohibition would sit uneasily with the nature and level of the religious sensitivities involved in this case and with the principle of neutrality in the broadcast media (Paragraph 76). The Court tended to accept the government's argument that the exclusion of all religious groupings from broadcasting advertisements generates less discomfort than any filtering of the amount and content of such expressions by such groupings (Paragraph 77). It also had to be considered that a limited freedom to advertise would benefit a dominant religion more than those religions with significantly fewer adherents and resources (Paragraph 78). The Court considered that the state had demonstrated that there were relevant and sufficient reasons justifying the interference with the freedom of expression (Paragraph 82).[7]

4. Distinguishing Religious, Political and Commercial Advertisements

The *Mouvement Raëlien Suisse v Switzerland* case was closely linked with the matter of religious advertisements.[8] The billboard intended to be displayed by the applicant in public spaces was not exactly of a religious nature but it nonetheless reflected a certain philosophical view. It displayed extra-terrestrials and flying saucers, which was meant to draw attention to the applicant association. The association's philosophy was anti-God and anti-religion; they promoted the idea of a new world order founded on individual intelligence instead of democracy based on equality, and which would be supported by introducing cloning. The Neuchatel Police prohibited its display on the grounds of the immorality of the poster's content, and this decision was substantiated by the administrative provisions of the canton concerned. The Swiss courts agreed with the decisions of the authority.

Contrary to the *Murphy* case, the advertisement in this case was not intended to be disclosed in the media and was not proscribed because of its religious (philosophical) content. However, the critics of the decision, along with the dissenting judges, raised the question as to whether such an expression, which aimed to take part in the public debate, may be restricted on the basis of immorality. Is it wise to limit the self-expression of a community if its operation is otherwise permitted by law and its website, also

7 After the reform of media regulations in Ireland, the Broadcasting Act 2009 only banned religious commercials with the intent to proselytise (s 41(4)).

8 *Mouvement Raëlien Suisse v Switzerland*, App no 16354/06, judgment of 13 July 2012.

promoted by the banned advertisement, is also free to operate?[9] In other words, a similar question is raised as those which arise in relation to religious advertisements, and the ECtHR would face the difficulty of distinction if a different level of protection is intended to be provided to political and religious (philosophical) advertisements.

It is a fundamental principle of the Court's practice that the opinions expressed in public discussions must be given enhanced protection and the definition of 'public discussion' shall be interpreted in a broad sense.[10] Even a commercial advertisement, which serves the business goals of its producer, may be entitled to greater protection under the freedom of expression if the content of that advertisement is linked to a certain public discussion than advertisements which do not take part in such discussions. Accordingly, if an advertisement or announcement concerns a matter of public interest, it may be assessed differently, and a different legal and free speech standard may be applied.

The ECtHR has ruled on many occasions that the freedom of public discussion is a more important concern than limitations imposed on advertising. According to the *Barthold v Germany* case,[11] discussion on 24-hour veterinary care is a public matter, just like the issue of abortion, and therefore the restriction of advertisements relating to abortion is against the Convention.[12] The disclosure of the unfair market practices of a courier service is a public matter, and therefore an article published in the form of an advertisement is entitled to the protection of the freedom of expression.[13] A warning

9 'Alien Poster Campaign's Anti-Religious Message', *UK Human Rights Blog*, 22 July 2012, ukhumanrightsblog.com/2012/07/22/alien-poster-campaigns-anti-religious-message/.

10 Eric Barendt, *Freedom of Speech* (Oxford University Press 2nd edn 2005) 154–62.

11 *Barthold v Germany*, Case no 10/1983/66/101, judgment of 25 February 1985.

12 *Open Door Counselling and Dublin Woman v Ireland*, Case no 64/1991/316/387-388, judgment of 23 September 1992.

13 *Markt Intern & Beerman v Germany*, Case no 3/1988/147/201, judgment of 25 October 1989.

on a potential risk of cancer embedded in an article published on microwave ovens is the reflection of an opinion in a public discussion and therefore, despite the lack of conclusive scientific proof, its disclosure is permitted and may not be limited by provisions of competition law.[14]

Political advertisement is a separate category, a unique type of media content, and should be distinguished from commercial communication. A political advertisement is ordered by a political party, a group or a non-governmental organisation which wishes to express a political viewpoint with the purpose of promoting an issue represented by it. If the primary reason behind the restriction or limitation of religious advertisements is ensuring a level playing field for all churches, whereby the state must ensure that churches with greater financial resources do not enjoy greater publicity as a result (so that the 'competition' between churches is not decided by which of them has more money, and therefore more air time), then this should also apply to political publicity. Consequently, the dissemination of political advertisements is limited and regulated all over Europe.

The ECtHR held in the *VgT Verein gegen Tierfabriken v Switzerland* case that a general ban on political advertising is in violation of the Convention.[15] The facts of the case were that the publication of an advertisement by an animal rights group protesting at cruelty towards pigs was prohibited because it qualified as 'political' advertisement due to the circumstance that there was a public debate on the subject matter at the time. The ECtHR ruled that, although the limitation of political advertisements may be justified in some cases, and such restriction may be extended to groups other than political parties, in the case concerned the client behind the advertisement was not a powerful NGO with substantial financial resources which could be considered to be influential in politics, and so the limitation was unnecessary and disproportionate, and its freedom of expression had consequently been infringed.

14 *Hertel v Switzerland*, Case no 59/1997/843/1049, judgment of 25 August 1998.

15 *VgT Verein gegen Tierfabriken v Switzerland*, App no 24699/94, judgment of 28 June 2001.

Subsequently, the Court held in the *TV Vest AS & Rogaland Pensjonistparti v Norway* case that the general restriction in Norway applicable to political parties is also against the European Convention on Human Rights (hereinafter: ECHR).[16] In this case, a television broadcaster transmitted several advertisements from a small political party representing pensioner's interests in the midst of the campaign period. Based on the Norwegian media regulations, political advertisements on television are subject to full prohibition, and therefore the distributor was found guilty. The ECtHR stated that political opinion enjoys enhanced protection, and the argument that such restriction aims to prevent the more influential political parties from dominating, and to avoid the deformation of public debate by taking advantage of larger financial means, cannot be accepted in relation to an insignificant political party, and therefore Norway's general prohibition of political broadcasting is against the ECHR.

In light of the above, it came as shock when the Grand Chamber of the ECtHR decided in direct contradiction of the aforementioned two cases, and approved the general ban on political advertisements (by a nine to eight vote) and rejected the request submitted in the *Animal Defenders International v the United Kingdom* case.[17] Pursuant to the British ban on the publication of political advertisements outside of campaign periods, the publication of an advert by an animal rights NGO was forbidden, just like in the Swiss case. The critics of the decision were of the view that the arguments in the *Animal Defenders* case was not well substantiated compared to the *VgT* and the *TV Vest* cases.[18] According to one of the less than convincing arguments offered, it is ascertainable that the adoption of the general ban was preceded by a parliamentary debate, and the necessity of this was adequately assessed by the courts when

16 *TV Vest AS & Rogaland Pensjonistparti v Norway*, App no 21132/05, judgment of 11 December 2008.

17 *Animal Defenders International v the United Kingdom*, App no 48876/08, judgment of 22 April 2013 [GC].

18 Tom Lewis, 'From Activism to Self-restraint: The Strange Case of the European Court's Volte-face on Broadcasting Bans on Political Advertising' in András Koltay (ed), *Media Freedom and Regulation in the New Media World* (Wolters Kluwer 2014) 581–9.

reviewing the case. The state is the most suitable forum to assess the risks inherent to the regulations, and it is acceptable if the state concludes that a general ban, as opposed to evaluation on a case-by-case basis, will most effectively decrease risks related to the uncertainty of the legislation (Paragraph 108), and therefore the state is entitled to enact appropriate legislation. The *Animal Defenders* case did not expressly overrule the previous two cases, but it certainly does not contain a clear distinction from them either. According to Tom Lewis, the attempts to draw distinctions which sporadically appear in the arguments are not convincing (e.g., that VgT reacted to an existing public debate whereas the Animal Defenders would have initiated one, and that TV Vest was a political party, and not an NGO).[19]

Assessment of political advertisements in Strasbourg influences how religious advertisements are viewed. Until 2013, before the *Animal Defenders* case, the criticism of the assessment by the ECtHR of the two types of advertisements was not unfounded. After the *VgT* and *Murphy* cases, the conclusion was that those who protest cruelty to pigs enjoy firmer protection than those trying to save human souls.[20] However, if a long-term consequence of the 2013 decision is a decrease in the protection of political advertising, then this discrepancy will cease to exist, albeit to the detriment of the freedom of expression.

As mentioned earlier, the argument in favour of the restriction of political and religious advertising in the media is that it contributes to the creation of a level playing field, and therefore to balancing out the opportunity to participate in the public debate (convincing others). In addition to this, a further argument was presented in the *Murphy* case: Religious advertisements may offend the followers of another religion or conviction. The latter argument is simply not solid enough. If we accept that the freedom of expression applies even to offensive, shocking or disturbing opinions, this argument

19 *Ibid*, 586.

20 Andrew Geddis, 'You Can't Say "God" on the Radio: Freedom of Expression, Religious Advertising and the Broadcast Media after *Murphy v Ireland*', (2004) 11 *European Human Rights Law Review* 181, 192.

is completely discredited.[21] Even if we do not accept the ruling of the *Handyside* case as a general starting point (as many offensive and shocking opinions are restrained by law), the question remains as to whether the potentially similar effect of religious advertising is sufficient to substantiate a general ban. Religious advertisements are not necessarily offensive. Furthermore, it would be difficult to accept that religious content in itself is capable of offending the followers of other religions as a basis for limiting the freedom of expression (and, in fact, there could easily be some believers offended in their own religious beliefs if their *own* church decided to advertise itself). Social pluralism, the coexisting of various religions and mutual tolerance do not justify such a broad restriction of religious opinions where actual offence is merely potential.

5. Conclusion

Andrew Geddis reaches the conclusion, after comparing the decisions in the *VgT* and the *Murphy* cases, that the ECtHR weighed the circumstances, and reached different conclusions on the basis of the importance of political and religious advertising in a public debate. According to Geddis, while in the *VgT* case, the Court kept the focus on the fact that the case concerned a character of public interest (suitable conditions for animal-keeping), in the *Murphy* case, the religious advertisement dealt with matters of 'intimate personal convictions within the sphere of morals'.[22] The Court thus seemingly views religious opinions as being less useful to society than political opinions; the unlimited nature of the former does not present society with such advantages as open political debate. As another consequence of this, the limitation of religious content does not entail such risks as the regulation of political debate, because the state has no special interest in deforming that debate.[23]

Geddis argues against these conclusions, and we shall do the same. Without questioning that practicing religion is, in many ways, part

21 *Handyside v the United Kingdom*, App no 5493/72, judgment of 7 December 1976, para 49.

22 Geddis (n 20) 184.

23 *Ibid*, 192.

of the private sphere, that is, that nobody can be obliged to unveil their religious beliefs, the banishment of religion to the private sphere would be to deprive it of the very character that provides its essence. All religions deal with the questions that are the most important to mankind; it searches for answers and offers paths to follow. If we were to consider religiously motivated opinions to be less important than political views from a right to free speech perspective, we would impair the diversity of public debates. Moreover, in some cases, religious conviction may be in need of special protection against offence and so the prescription of certain special limitations in the context of media publicity in the interest of the protection of human dignity is not unjustified. This could partially substantiate the limitation of religious advertising and of advertisements which are offensive to religious convictions.

If we were to accept the above, we would also be implying that offending religious convictions is more injurious than offending political convictions, as with regard to the latter, it would be impermissible to limit the freedom of expression merely because of individual offence taken by a person with particular political views. If we accept that religion determines the entire life of a man of faith, or at least his most important decisions, then protection against the unique power of persuasion of the media does not seem unfounded when it comes to curtailing the operation of certain religious groups who are responsive to such power and intend to expand aggressively. Thus, while it may not be admissible to impose a complete ban, the prescription of certain limitations on religious advertising is indicated, even to the detriment of the freedom of expression. The general ban applicable in some countries does not seem to be a sustainable solution. On the one hand, the violation of religious beliefs can happen in all sorts of other ways in public life (for example, there is nothing forbidding the denial of the teachings of a religion) whereas on the other hand, this offence is nothing more than a hypothesis which is the basis for a general ban which certainly does not become reality, that is, real offence is taken in every case. At the same time, however, protection against aggressive proselytism, the enhanced protection of social groups who are more vulnerable than others (children, the elderly and the sick) and the need to censure advertisements that are flagrantly offensive to religious convictions may lead to the introduction of certain limitations.

Chapter 5

The Restriction of Blasphemy

1. Introduction

The relationship between blasphemy and freedom of speech law is not a new issue. The protection of religions, religious figures and religious dogmas is the most ancient barrier to freedom of speech in Western legal systems.[1] However, since these barriers were gradually dismantled in the twentieth century, prosecution on the grounds of blasphemy is rare in Europe today, and restrictions imposed on blasphemy do not count among the frequently discussed dilemmas related to freedom of speech, such as protection of reputation, privacy, hate speech or media regulation.

Although the question has been pushed into the background, it has not disappeared entirely. British lawyers have been reminded of this question by the *Lemon* case in 1977.[2] In Europe, it reappeared in connection with the scandal triggered by *The Satanic Verses* by Salman Rushdie in 1988–89.[3] In recent decades, the debate over blasphemy has flared up from time to time, most recently primarily due to the unclear relationship between radical Islam and Europe, secondly due to the clash of arguments in favour of the general protection of religions and those supporting the libertarian approach taken by secular European states. This debate gained new momentum after the instances of blasphemy which have had tragic outcomes over the past decade, firstly the Danish cartoons (in 2005-06), then the Muhammad-video posted on YouTube (in 2012), followed by the terrorist attack in 2015 against the editorial offices of *Charlie Hebdo*.

1 Leonard W Levy, *Blasphemy: Verbal Offense against the Sacred, From Moses to Salman Rushdie* (Alfred A Knopf 1993).

2 *R v Lemon* [1979] AC 617.

3 Lisa Appignanesi & Sara Maitland (eds), *The Rushdie File* (Syracuse University Press 1990).

This chapter serves three purposes: To provide an overview of the responses given by the European Court of Human Rights (hereinafter: ECtHR) to the restrictions on blasphemy by states seeking an answer to the question of whether universal European standards exist on this issue (Section 2); to overview, in a general way, the state regulation in countries belonging to Western legal systems, taking into account the cultural embeddedness and the complexity of various approaches (Section 3) and, in its most extensive part, to make an in-depth analysis of the theoretical questions relating to restrictions on blasphemy (Section 4), before some conclusions are drawn (Section 5).

2. The Protection of Human Rights in Europe and Blasphemy

2.1. The European Court of Human Rights and the Prohibition of Blasphemy

To date, the ECtHR has delivered judgments in favour of the state against which the application was filed in all cases where the debate was related to insulting a person's religious feelings. In cases of blasphemy, the Court gives an especially broad interpretation to the margin of appreciation principle, and is reluctant to establish any general, uniform European standard in this area.[4] In a specific, especially sensitive area (and blasphemy and the defamation of religions are such areas), the Court decided not to fill the gap in domains where no uniform common European standard exists, and it does not respond to questions in an activist manner instead providing a broader margin of appreciation for Contracting States. This does not mean that it avoids setting certain minimum standards in such questions. The criticism of religions and churches is also protected by the European Convention on Human Rights (hereinafter: ECHR) in order to enhance open public debate. However, regarding the defamation of religions and opinions offending believers'

4 Andrew Legg, *The Margin of Appreciation in International Human Rights Law. Deference and Proportionality* (Oxford University Press 2012).

feelings, Contracting States are free to decide on restrictions in their own competences. Many criticise the Court, saying that, by respecting the states' margin of appreciation, it has withdrawn from certain areas otherwise covered by the ECHR.[5] There have even been accusations of 'cultural relativism', since it is reluctant to establish uniform rules on these questions and, by doing so, it denies 'the universality of human rights'.[6] The jurisprudence relating to the defamation of religions has thus come in for a particularly large amount of criticism.[7] There is clearly also something to be said for the position of the Court, according to which there are certain especially sensitive free speech areas which are difficult to harmonise even in Europe, and where it is more desirable to maintain the competences of Contracting States.

According to the argument in favour of providing a margin of appreciation for states, the ECHR and the related case law must reflect the cultural diversity of Europe.[8] This especially holds true in the area of religion and morality and so, in these areas, restrictions on freedom of speech can be introduced more readily than, for example, in direct political debates, as European states are more or less homogeneous in terms of their political systems and commitment to democracy, one of the foundations of which is the freedom of public and political debate. The ECHR provides only subsidiary protection, supplementing the national systems for the legal protection of fundamental rights. By leaving the margin of appreciation, the Court identified those forms of expression which enjoy an unconditional and uniform level of protection in every Contracting State, and those which it neither restricts nor affirms, but instead steps back from, demanding only basic guarantees from states. The principle of subsidiarity therefore is not only expressed

5 Anthony Lester, *General Report. Proceedings of the 8th International Colloquy on the European ECHR on Human Rights* (Council of Europe 1995) 236–7.

6 Eyal Benvenisti, 'Margin of Appreciation, Consensus, and Universal Standards', (1998) *International Law and Politics* 844.

7 Helen Fenwick & Gavin Phillipson, *Media Freedom under the Human Rights Act* (Oxford University Press 2006) 488–97.

8 Paul Mahoney, 'Marvellous Richness of Diversity or Invidious Cultural Relativism?', (1998) 19 *Human Rights Law Journal* 1.

in the fact that the applicant can only turn to the ECtHR once it has exhausted all effective legal remedies domestically, but also in the interpretation of the freedom of speech, in which universally protected opinions receiving protection according to common standards are separated from areas which fall under the competence of states.[9]

2.2. Judgments Concerning the Restrictions of Blasphemy

2.2.1. *X Ltd and Y v the United Kingdom* and its Aftermath

X Ltd and Y v the United Kingdom was preceded by the last application of blasphemy as a common law offence in the UK. Blasphemous libel, that is, the written form of blasphemy, had existed since the seventeenth century as an offence regulated by England's common law, legal practice not enshrined in codified law.[10] However, it was applied in practice increasingly rarely by the nineteenth century. The prohibition of blasphemy, similarly to other restrictions across a broad spectrum (such as the prohibition of obscene expressions or cases of libel), was regulated in line with expectations which prevailed in an earlier system of social norms. In the seventeenth century, the interpretation of blasphemy in practice was similar to that of a revolt. The law defended the authority of the Church of England, closely intertwined with that of the state, through the punishment of blasphemy. Simple defamation or libel of the church was to be punished, but other Christian denominations did not enjoy any protection.[11] Later, by the end of the nineteenth century, the scope of punishable conduct had been narrowed down. From then on, proceedings were brought in cases of obscene or abusive attacks, but critical remarks, the denial of the existence of God

9 Paul Mahoney, 'Universality versus Subsidiarity in the Strasbourg Case Law on Free Speech: Explaining Some Recent Judgments', (1997) 4 *European Human Rights Law Review* 364.

10 *X Ltd and Y v the United Kingdom*, App no 8710/79, admissibility decision, 7 May 1982.

11 *R v Taylor* [1676] 1 Vent 293, 86 ER 189.

or the negation or denial of individual religious dogmas were not considered criminal offences.[12]

After proceedings in 1922, the criminal offence of blasphemy—in the absence of the application of rules—became dormant for decades. However, before becoming a closed chapter of legal history forever, it unexpectedly awoke from its lengthy moribund state in 1977. It was at this time that a magazine of the homosexual community entitled *Gay News* published a poem, written by a certain James Kirkup, a Professor of the English language. The poem depicts the imaginary homosexual acts of Jesus Christ, involving the Apostles, St John the Baptist, Pontius Pilate and its recounts in detail sexual acts—including fellatio and sodomy—between the Roman Centurion in the New Testament and the crucified dead body of Christ. For the first time in 55 years, proceedings were launched on charges of blasphemy. Prior to the decision by the ECtHR, *R v Lemon* was finally submitted to the supreme judicial forum, the House of Lords, and the judges approved the conviction of the editor and publisher of the magazine.[13] Earlier the publisher had been ordered to pay a fine of £1000 and the editor £500, and the latter was also sentenced to nine months of imprisonment, suspended.

According to the judges, earlier precedents concerning the criminal offence were controversial and chaotic, therefore in this case, the fundamental principles had to be laid down again. According to the majority of the largely divided panel, in cases of blasphemy, the criminal offence has to be examined on the basis of strict liability. No intentionality concerning triggering outrage is necessary, and the perpetrator does not necessarily have to be aware of the blasphemous nature of the act; the wilful publication of blasphemous expressions is sufficient by itself. There is no need for there to be a danger, arising from the blasphemy, that it might lead to the disturbance of 'social peace', the prohibition in general terms protects harmonious social relations and calm. In the absence of violence or the danger of hatred and intention to this effect, the restriction can be imposed purely on the basis of the offensive

12 *R v Ramsay and Foote* [1883] 15 Cox CC 231.

13 *R v Lemon* (n 2).

content; not even public interest or potential literary value might lead to exemption from liability. As opposed to this, according to the minority of the judges, the fact that no court proceedings had taken place for decades constitutes sufficient proof of the unjustified necessity of upholding this as a punishable offence in a modern society.

Lord Scarman, belonging to the majority of the judges, drew attention to a grave shortcoming of the facts required. Blasphemy protected the Church of England exclusively (it was suggested that perhaps other Christian denominations may also be covered by this protection, but in the judgment this was not clarified); the protection is not extended to other religions, which is unacceptable in a modern, pluralistic society. After new and lengthy debates, blasphemy as a criminal offence was abolished by the Criminal Justice and Immigration Act of 2008,[14] and so since 2008 blasphemy cannot be prosecuted, not even theoretically.[15]

However, in 1979, the publisher and editor of *Gay News* took their case to Strasbourg, and so the European Commission of Human Rights was in a position to deliver its first decision in the area of potential restrictions on blasphemy. In *X Ltd and Y v the United Kingdom*, the Commission took a position, and established that the right to the freedom of expression enshrined in Article 10 of the ECHR was not breached, and therefore it declared the application inadmissible and rejected it without a substantial examination.

According to the applicants, the reason for the restriction imposed on their freedom of expression is not included in the legitimate reasons in Article 10(2) of the ECHR (public safety, public morals and protection of the rights of others, most importantly). According to the opinion of the Commission, however, the original proceedings in the UK were initiated by a private prosecution, which shows that the justification of the restriction is to be found in the protection of the rights of the private person lodging the

14 Criminal Justice and Immigration Act of 2008, c IV, pt 5, s 79.

15 On the process of the abolition of rules and the accompanying debates, see Russell Sandberg & Norman Doe, 'The Strange Death of Blasphemy', (2008) 71 *The Modern Law Review* 971.

private prosecution. In the case in question, blasphemous libel, as it is construed under the applicable common law, in fact has as its main purpose the protection of the right of the people not to be offended in their religious feelings by publications (Paragraph 11).

According to the Commission, if it is accepted that the religious feeling of the people may deserve protection against indecent attacks on those matters held sacred by them, then it can also be considered as necessary in a democratic society to stipulate that such attacks shall constitute a criminal offence, to be tried at the request of the offended person (Paragraph 12). It is in principle left to the legislation of the state concerned as to how it wishes to define the offence, provided that the principle of proportionality, which is inherent in the exception clause of Article 10(2), is being respected. The Commission considers that the offence of blasphemous libel as laid down in the common law of England in fact satisfies this criterion. In particular, it does not seem disproportionate to the aim pursued that the offence is one of strict liability incurred irrespective of the intention to blaspheme and irrespective of the intended audience and of the possible avoidance of the publication by a certain member of the public (Paragraph 12). All in all, the Commission held the opinion that the prohibition of blasphemy under the given circumstances was necessary, and therefore the application of the complainants was inadmissible.

The next occasion when the question of blasphemy was raised in the UK was after the publication of *The Satanic Verses*, a novel by Salman Rushdie, which provoked tremendous outrage in the Muslim community all over the world. With respect to the book, members of the Muslim community in England applied for prosecution against the author, which was refused by the magistrates' court. Several translators of the book were attacked or killed, and the supreme Muslim religious leader declared a *fatwā* on the author, who afterwards had no choice but to go into hiding for many years. The applicants turned to the Queens' Bench against this decision. The court, and later the Court of Appeal in *R v Chief Metropolitan Magistrate ex parte Choudhury* rejected the application with the justification that a blasphemous offence can be committed exclusively against members of the Christian community.[16] An opposite decision would not only render previously permitted conduct punishable, but the court would also create for itself a very difficult question of interpretation. If the law were to protect all religions, then it should define the concept of 'religion'; and the lack of any definition of the concept would lead to considerable legal uncertainty.

The European Commission of Human Rights, in its decision, sided with the state, as opposed to the Muslims in the UK complaining about the blasphemous nature of the novel by Rushdie.[17] The admissibility decision rendering their application inadmissible states that Article 9 guaranteeing the freedom of religion and invoked by the applicant does not oblige the state to defend its citizens' religious sensitivities against defamatory statements and extreme opinions, and therefore the restriction of these will be left to the margin of appreciation provided for the state. With this statement, the Commission practically approved the unique, discriminatory nature of the offence of blasphemy in common law.

2.2.2. *Otto-Preminger-Institut v Austria*

The most important and most frequently cited judgment of the ECtHR was delivered in *Otto-Preminger-Institut v Austria*.[18] The applicant, Otto-Preminger-Institut (OPI), was a private association founded in Innsbruck, which announced a series of six showings to the public of a film entitled *Das Liebeskonzil* (Council in Heaven). The film was based on a play written in 1894, the author of which was prosecuted for blasphemy at that time. The film depicts God as a senile old man, and Jesus as a mentally retarded person feeling a strange attraction to his mother. In the film, God, Satan, Jesus,

16 *R v Chief Metropolitan Magistrate ex parte Choudhury* [1991] 1 QB 429; [1991] 1 All ER 306, DC.

17 *Choudhury v the United Kingdom*, App no 17349/90, admissibility decision of 5 March 1991.

18 *Otto-Preminger-Institut v Austria*, App no 13470/87, judgment of 20 September 1994.

and the Virgin Mary agree to punish the world with sexually transmitted diseases. The applicant prepared a newsletter on this event, which it forwarded to 2,700 members of the association and put on car windscreens; the newsletter contained a warning, according to which, in accordance with the Tyrolean Cinemas Act, those under 17 years of age were prohibited from seeing the film. The local newspaper also announced the date and place where the film would be screened. At the request of the Innsbruck diocese of the Roman Catholic Church, the public prosecutor instituted criminal proceedings against OPI's manager; the charge was 'disparaging religious doctrines'. After seeing the film, the prosecutor initiated the seizure of the copy under Section 36 of the Austrian Media Act. As a result of the decision of the Innsbruck Regional Court, the public showings could not take place. In accordance with the decision of the Regional Court, artistic freedom is necessarily limited by the rights and liberties of others granted in the Constitution (which include freedom of religion and conviction), and secondly by the essential form of human cohabitation based on tolerance and, in the event of outstanding and extreme infringements, the protection of the interests of others by law. The applicant turned to the ECtHR citing the violation of his right to freedom of expression enshrined in Article 10 of the ECHR and the Court held, by 6 votes to 3, that the decision of the state court was not in breach of the rights of the applicant.

The ECtHR pointed out that freedom of thought, conscience and religion, which is safeguarded under Article 9 of the ECHR, is one of the foundations of a 'democratic society' within the meaning of the ECHR (Paragraph 47). Those who choose to exercise the freedom to manifest their religion, irrespective of whether they do so as members of a religious majority or a minority, cannot reasonably expect to be exempt from all criticism. They must tolerate and accept the denial by others of their religious beliefs and even the propagation by others of doctrines hostile to their faith (Paragraph 47). In the judgment delivered in *Kokkinakis v Greece* referred to in the judgment—not with respect to the restriction on blasphemy—the ECtHR held that the state may legitimately consider it necessary to take measures aimed at repressing certain forms of conduct judged incompatible with respect for the freedom of thought, conscience and religion of others (Paragraph 47).[19]

The measures which were complained against were based on Section 188 of the Austrian Penal Code, which is intended to suppress behaviour directed against objects of religious veneration that is likely to cause 'justified indignation'. The ECtHR accepted that the offending measures pursued a legitimate aim under Article 10(2), namely 'the protection of the rights of others' (Paragraph 48).

The ECtHR referred to its own jurisprudence, in which freedom of expression constitutes one of the essential foundations of a democratic society and one of the basic conditions for progress and for the development of all its members. This is applicable not only to 'information' or 'ideas' that are favourably received or regarded as inoffensive or as a matter of indifference but also to those that 'offend, shock or disturb' the state or any group or member of the society (Paragraph 49).[20] At the same time, exercising freedom of expression carries with it duties and responsibilities. Amongst them may legitimately be included an obligation—in the context of religious opinions and beliefs—to avoid as far as possible expressions that are gratuitously offensive to others (Paragraph 49). This being so, as a matter of principle, it may be considered necessary in certain democratic societies to sanction or even prevent improper attacks on objects of religious veneration, always provided that any measures imposed are proportionate to the legitimate aim pursued (Paragraph 49).

As with 'morals', it is not possible to discern throughout Europe a uniform conception of the significance of religion in society. Indeed, such concepts may vary even within a single country. For this reason, it is not possible to arrive at a comprehensive definition of what constitutes permissible interference with the exercise of the right to freedom of expression where that expression is directed against the religious feelings of others. A certain margin of appreciation is therefore left to the national authorities in assessing the existence

19 *Kokkinakis v Greece*, App no 14307/88, judgment of 25 May 1993.

20 Citation from the reasoning of *Handyside v the United Kingdom*, App no 5493/72, judgment of 7 December 1976, para 49.

and extent of the need for such interference (Paragraph 50). The authorities' margin of appreciation, however, is not unlimited. It goes hand in hand with supervision through the ECtHR, the scope of which will vary according to the circumstances (Paragraph 50).

The ECtHR notes that, although access to the cinema to see the film itself was subject to payment of an admission fee and an age limit, the film was widely advertised and there was sufficient public knowledge of the subject-matter and basic content of the film to give a clear indication of its nature. For these reasons, the proposed screening of the film must be considered to have been an expression which was sufficiently 'public' to cause offence (Paragraph 54). The issue before the Court involved weighing up the conflicting interests of the exercise of two fundamental freedoms guaranteed under the ECHR. On the one hand, the right of the applicant association to impart to the public controversial views and, by implication, the right of interested peoples to take cognisance of such views. On the other hand, the ECtHR considered the right of others to properly respect their freedom of religion. In so doing, it is important to bear in mind the margin of appreciation left to the national authorities, whose duty it is in a democratic society to consider the interests of society as a whole (Paragraph 55).

The ECtHR could not disregard the fact that the Roman Catholic religion is the religion of the overwhelming majority of Tyroleans. In seizing the film, the Austrian authorities acted to ensure religious peace in that region and to prevent people from feeling subjected to attacks on their religious beliefs in an unwarranted and offensive manner. In all the circumstances of the present case, the Court did not consider that the Austrian authorities could be regarded as having overstepped their margin of appreciation in this respect (Paragraph 56). Regarding the proportionality of the sanction, Article 10 cannot be interpreted as prohibiting the forfeiture in the public interest of items, the use of which has lawfully been judged illicit. Although the forfeiture made it permanently impossible to show the film anywhere in Austria, the Court considers that the means employed were not disproportionate to the legitimate aim pursued, and that therefore the national authorities did not exceed their margin of appreciation in this respect (Paragraph 57).

Three judges attached a joint dissenting opinion to the majority decision, in which they declared that the ECHR does not guarantee the right to the protection of religious feelings. More particularly, such a right cannot be derived from the right to freedom of religion, which in effect includes a right to express views critical of the religious opinions of others. Consequently, it must also be accepted that it may be 'necessary in a democratic society' to set limits on the public expression of such criticism or abuse. To this extent, but no further, the authors of the joint dissenting opinion can agree with the majority (dissenting opinion, Paragraph 6).

At the same time, the film was to have been shown to a paying audience in an 'art cinema', which catered to a relatively small public. It is therefore unlikely that the audience would have included people not specifically interested in the film, and not wanting to see it on the basis of a well-informed decision. This audience, moreover, had sufficient opportunity to be warned beforehand about the nature of the film. The announcement put out by the applicant association was intended to provide information about the critical way in which the film dealt with the Roman Catholic religion; in fact, it did so sufficiently clearly to enable the religiously sensitive to make an informed decision to stay away (dissenting opinion, Paragraph 9). It was illegal under Tyrolean law for the film to be seen by people less than 17 years of age, and the announcement put out by the applicant association carried a notice to that effect. Under these circumstances, the danger of the film being seen by people for whom it was not suitable by reason of their age can be discounted (dissenting opinion, Paragraph 10). The authors of the dissenting opinion did not deny that showing the film might have offended the religious feelings of certain segments of the population in Tyrol, but the seizure and forfeiture of the film in question were not proportionate to the legitimate aim pursued (dissenting opinion, Paragraph 11).

2.2.3. *Wingrove v the United Kingdom*

In *Wingrove v the United Kingdom* the applicant was a film director who wrote and directed a 18-minute-long video work entitled *Visions of Ecstasy*, which, according to him, was inspired by the life and writings of St Teresa of Avila.[21] In the film, the action centres upon a youthful actress dressed as a nun (intended to represent St Teresa). It begins with the nun, dressed loosely, stabbing her own hand with a large nail and spreading her blood over her naked breasts and clothing, while writhing erotically. After doing this, she loses consciousness. The second part of the video shows St Teresa standing with her arms held above her head by a white cord which is suspended from above and tied around her wrists, while a second female, nearly half naked and dressed in black (intended to represent the psyche of St Teresa), slowly crawls along the ground towards her, and begins to caress and kiss her. In the meantime, St Teresa crawls to Jesus Christ lying on the ground crucified; she starts licking his wounds and then she sits astride him, all the while moving in a motion reflecting intense erotic arousal, while kissing him. Apart from the cast list, which appears on the screen for a few seconds, the viewer has no way of knowing from the film itself that the person dressed as a nun in the video is intended to be St Teresa or that the other woman who appears is intended to be her psyche. The film was submitted to the British Board of Film Classification (BBFC), which prohibited its distribution and showing. The Board made reference to the Court judgment handed down in *R v Lemon*, on which basis the *Visions of Ecstasy* is considered as blasphemous, and therefore is prohibited to be shown. Although Nigel Wingrove appealed against the decision, but the appeal committee approved the decision of the BBFC, without the possibility of judicial review against that decision.

Based on the application, the ECtHR came, by seven votes to two, to the judgment that the applicant's right to freedom of expression had not been violated. The Court recognised that the offence of blasphemy cannot by its very nature lend itself to precise legal definition. National authorities must therefore be afforded a degree of flexibility in assessing whether the facts of a particular case fall within the accepted definition of the offence (Paragraph 42). The judgment invoked the reasoning in *Otto-Preminger* and supported the prohibition on the grounds of protecting the 'rights of others' (freedom of religion). It concludes that the screening of the film was

21 *Wingrove v the United Kingdom*, App no 19/1995/525/611, judgment of 25 November 1996.

primarily prohibited to prevent the expected consequences, namely of outraging those who have an understanding of or sympathy towards and support for the story of Jesus Christ and Christian ethic because of the contemptuous, reviling, insulting, scurrilous or ludicrous tone, style and spirit in which the subject matter is presented (Paragraph 48). As the British authorities have indicated, it is the manner in which views are advocated, rather than the views themselves, which the law seeks to control. The extent of insult to religious feelings must be significant (Paragraph 60).

The Court also noted that the limited distribution of the film (i.e., exclusively in sex shops) would not have been sufficient to achieve the desired aim because it would have been in practice easy to copy, lend, rent, and sell and to be viewed in various homes, thereby easily escaping any form of control by the authorities. While it is true that the measures taken by the authorities amounted to a complete ban on the film's distribution this was an understandable consequence of the opinion of the competent authorities that the distribution of the video would infringe the law (Paragraphs 62–64).

According to Judge Pettiti, author of one of the dissenting opinions, the fact that, under the legislation on blasphemy, profanation or defamation *may* give rise to prosecution does not in itself justify a total ban or restriction on the distribution of a book or video tape (this is only justified if the court establishes that a criminal offence has been committed). Judge De Meyer called attention to the fact that the measure taken by the state in this case was already a 'prior restraint', which makes it impossible to express the opinion concerned, which is unacceptable. In line with this, Judge Lõhmus calls the interference a form of censorship.

2.2.4. *İ.A. v Turkey*

In the practice of the ECtHR, the next blasphemy case was *İ.A. v Turkey*.[22] The applicant this time was the proprietor and managing director of the Berfin publishing house, which in November 1993, published a novel entitled *Yasak Tümceler* (The Forbidden Phrases). Two thousand copies of the book were printed in a single run. The

22 *İ.A. v Turkey*, App no 42571/98, judgment of 13 September 2005.

book conveyed the author's views on philosophical and theological issues in a novelistic style. It contained, among others, the following controversial passage:

> Look at the triangle of fear, inequality and inconsistency in the Quran; it reminds me of an earthworm. God says that all the words are those of his messenger. Some of these words, moreover, were inspired in a surge of exultation, in Aisha's arms ... God's messenger broke his fast through sexual intercourse, after dinner and before prayer. Muhammad did not forbid sexual relations with a dead person or a live animal.

The Istanbul public prosecutor charged the applicant with blasphemy under the terms of the Criminal Code because, by publishing the book, the applicant insulted 'God, the Religion, the Prophet and the Holy Book'. The court of first instance convicted the applicant and sentenced him to two years' imprisonment and a fine. Later the Court of Cassation upheld the contested judgment (the amount of the fine was insignificant and it was possible to commute the prison sentence to a fine, which was also of a low amount). After this, the applicant turned to the ECtHR, which by four votes to three held that the original judgment was not in breach of the freedom of expression of the applicant.

As in previous judgments, the Court in this case also emphasised that the exercise of the freedom of expression carries with it duties and responsibilities, and therefore it is necessary to avoid publishing unwarrantedly offensive opinions affecting others. As such, in a democratic society, sanctions against offensive attacks on objects of religious veneration cannot be considered as unnecessary. In the controversial book, an offensive attack was published against the prophet of Islam, due to which believers were right to feel insulted. According to the opinion of the court, the measure may reasonably be held to have met a 'pressing social need'.

In the joint dissenting opinion of three judges, the authors debated the actual impact of the book (it was published in a low number of copies, and only a small part of the text was offensive to religious believers). An interesting point in the dissenting opinion is that the proceedings initiated by the state, and proceedings initiated by an individual whose religious feelings have been insulted should be given different consideration. According to the authors of the dissenting opinion, the latter is more acceptable as a legitimate restriction of the freedom of expression (in this case, the state authorities acted *ex officio*). Although the sanctions imposed were insignificant (taking into account the imprisonment commuted to a fine), the fact of conviction itself is troublesome because all convictions have a 'chilling effect' as they discourage publishers from issuing books which are not strictly conformist or 'politically (or religiously) correct'. According to the judges, the time has come to 'revisit' the ECtHR case law, which seems to place too much emphasis on conformism or uniformity of thought, and to reflect an overcautious and timid concept of freedom of the press.

2.3. The Legitimate Criticism of Churches

The above cases suggest that the ECtHR allows varying degrees of restriction on blasphemy, defamation of religion and the insult to religious feelings. However, it provides wide-ranging protection for the criticism of religions and churches. This is demonstrated by the judgment delivered in *Giniewski v France*.[23] In its issue of 4 January 1994, the newspaper *Le Quotidien de Paris* published an article written by the applicant, entitled 'The obscurity of error' concerning the papal encyclical 'The Splendour of Truth' (*Veritatis Splendor*). The article criticises the encyclical for inserting the doctrine of the Old Testament being fulfilled in the New into theological fundamental principles, while proclaiming the superiority of the New Testament over the Old Testament. According to the article, the doctrine of fulfilment led to anti-Semitism and prepared the ground in which the idea and implementation of Auschwitz took seed. Thus, the Catholics and Christians in general are responsible for the Nazi massacres at Auschwitz. The General Alliance against Racism and for Respect for the French and Christian Identity (Alliance générale contre le racisme et pour le respect de l'identité française et chrétienne) initiated proceedings against the publisher

23 *Giniewski v France*, App no 64016/00, judgment of 31 January 2006.

of the newspaper and the author on the grounds that, by publishing the above article, they made racially defamatory statements against the Christian community, which is punishable under the terms of the French Press Act. The Paris Criminal Court established the offence of publicly defaming a group of people on the grounds of membership of a religious community, in this case the Christian community, and ordered the director of the publishing house and the applicant to pay 6,000 francs as a fine.

The applicant appealed against the decision. The Paris Court of Appeal acquitted the applicant and dismissed the civil party's claims against him, but later the Court of Cassation quashed the judgment of the Court of Appeal, and referred the case to the Orléans Court of Appeal. The latter upheld the judgment of the court of first instance with respect to the applicant, and sentenced the applicant to pay 1 franc in damages and pay all costs related to the new proceedings and to publish a statement. The applicant, having exhausted all domestically available remedies, turned to the ECtHR. The Court unanimously established that the state had breached Article 10 of the ECHR.

The Court noted that the aim of the interference was to protect a group of people from defamation on account of their belonging to a specific religion, in this case the Catholic community (Paragraph 40). At the same time, the Court considered, in particular, that the applicant sought primarily to develop an argument about the scope of a specific doctrine and its possible links with the origins of the Holocaust. In such matters, restrictions on the freedom of expression are to be construed strictly (Paragraphs 50–51). The article does not contain attacks on religious beliefs as such (Paragraph 51). While the published text contains conclusions and phrases which may offend, shock or disturb some people, the Court has reiterated that such views do not in themselves preclude the enjoyment of freedom of expression (Paragraph 52). The article in question was not 'gratuitously offensive' or insulting and did not incite disrespect or hatred, nor did it cast doubt in any way on clearly established historical facts (Paragraph 52).

In these circumstances, the reasons given by the French courts in support of the applicant's conviction could not be regarded as sufficient to convince the Court that the interference in the exercise of the applicant's right to freedom of expression was 'necessary in a democratic society'. In particular, his conviction on a charge of public defamation of the Christian community did not meet a 'pressing social need' (Paragraph 53). The fact that defamation as a criminal offence was established undoubtedly has a deterring effect without imposing a severe sanction, and so the sanction applied was disproportionate.

A judgment with similar rationale was delivered in *Klein v Slovakia*.[24] In 1997, a weekly entitled *Domino Efekt* published an article in which the author expressed harsh criticism in a vulgar manner about Archbishop Ján Sokol, head of the Slovak Catholic Church, because of his outburst during a television appearance, publicly criticising the screening of the film *The People vs Larry Flynt* and the posters advertising the film, demanding that they be banned. On the poster, the protagonist was in front of the enlarged pubic area of a woman wearing underwear, in a position like the crucified Jesus. The article also refers to the archbishop's alleged past as an informer of the communist dictatorship, and among other things it states: 'I do not understand at all why decent Catholics do not leave an organisation which is headed by such an ogre'. Criminal proceedings were brought against Martin Klein, in which he was ordered to pay 15,000 Slovak crowns in damages for violating the section of the Slovak Penal Code according to which 'a person who publicly defames others due to their faith or because they have no religion shall be punished by up to one year's imprisonment (or by a fine)'. The appeal against the decision was rejected by the Kosice Regional Court. After this, the applicant turned to the ECtHR, which unanimously held that the judgment of the state court was in breach of Article 10 of the ECHR.

In his article, the applicant sharply criticised the person of Archbishop Sokol following the latter's appearance in a TV broadcast. The applicant's strongly worded pejorative opinion related exclusively to the Archbishop. Contrary to the domestic courts' findings, the Court was not persuaded that by his statements, the applicant discredited and disparaged a sector of

24 *Klein v Slovakia*, App no 72208/01, judgment of 31 October 2006.

the population on account of their Catholic faith (Paragraph 51). The fact that some members of the Catholic Church could have been offended by the applicant's criticism of the Archbishop and by his statement that he did not understand why decent Catholics did not leave that Church since it was headed by Archbishop Sokol cannot affect this position. However, the Court accepted the applicant's argument that the article neither unduly interfered with the right of believers to express and exercise their religion, nor did it denigrate the content of their religious faith (Paragraph 52). For the above reasons, and despite the tone of the article referred to above, it could not be concluded that, by its publication, the applicant interfered with the right to freedom of religion of others in a manner justifying the sanction imposed on him. The interference with his right to freedom of expression therefore neither corresponded to a pressing social need, nor was it proportionate to the legitimate aim pursued.

Two 'Polish' judgments are also worth mentioning, in which the applicants complained about their state not defending their right to the freedom of religion enshrined in Article 9 of the ECHR.[25] The applicants lodged a complaint after a Polish weekly published the Częstochowa Black Madonna and Child on its cover page, with gas masks covering their faces. According to the applicants, this constituted the criminal offence of 'publicly insulting religious feelings' (see the 'Facts' section of the decisions). The Polish investigating authorities closed the case without bringing charges, after which the complainants turned to the ECtHR. The Court established the inadmissibility of the application because it held that the in-depth investigation by the national authorities had provided a guarantee of the protection of the right of applicants to the freedom of religion and the Polish court's decision, which, in this case, gives preference to the freedom of expression, is not in breach of the ECHR, and as such, falls under the competence of the Contracting State.

25 *Dubowska v Poland*, App no 33490/96; *Skup v Poland*, App no 34055/96, judgment of 18 April 1997, and *Kubalska & Kubalska-Holuj v Poland*, App no 35579/97, judgment of 22 October 1997.

2.4. Short summary of the European Court of Human Rights' Jurisprudence

Based on the case law of the ECtHR, the following conclusions can be drawn.

- In cases of blasphemy, the Court gives a broad interpretation to the principle of the margin of appreciation and does not endeavour to establish a universal European standard on this issue, that is, within certain broad limits defined by the Strasbourg jurisprudence, Contracting States can freely decide upon the prohibition or permissibility of blasphemy.
- Followers of certain churches cannot expect their religious views to be free from all criticism; they must tolerate the expression of views that might be hostile to those. The freedom of public debate is to be protected in a broad domain.
- The above-mentioned obligation of tolerance is not unlimited; states can legitimately decide to restrict opinions which are considered to be incompatible with the respect for others' rights to freedom of thought, conscience and religion.
- The exercise of freedom of expression carries with it duties and responsibilities, one of which is to avoid the publication of defamatory, unwarrantedly offensive opinions relating to religions and those which defame religions outside the scope of a 'debate'.
- Only the manner/style/tone of the communication can be interfered with, not the content of the statement or opinion.

3. An Overview of Regulations Effective in Individual States

Several European legal systems restrict blasphemy in different ways determined by the various facts of a given case. If we wish to categorise these restrictions, we can divide them into two major groups:

- regulations prohibiting blasphemy (religious defamation) itself;
- regulations prohibiting blasphemy due to insulting the religious feelings of believers.

In the latter case, offending one's religious feelings is the precondition for applying the prohibition, according to the codified law, whereas in the former case, the publication of the blasphemous opinion itself is already unlawful.

This chapter does not set out to discuss the rules relating to the prohibition of hate speech, which is restricted or prohibited in some form or another in every Member State of the European Union. The following part of the chapter will outline the regulations of states which still have rules explicitly restricting blasphemy or defamation of religions. The existence of these regulations does not mean that they are applied in practice; on the contrary, the increasingly rare application of these regulations in practice has become a general tendency.

3.1. The General Prohibition of Blasphemy

In Denmark, somebody who ridicules or offends the dogmas of a religion or objects of religious veneration in public can be prosecuted. Local Muslim groups based their charges on this provision in the case of the Muhammad cartoons, but the court brought a verdict of not guilty.[26]

In Finland, a more than one-hundred-year-old provision of Article 10 of the Penal Code holds that a person committing public blasphemy or who despises or desecrates what is considered sacred by a given religion or religious community commits an offence and shall be liable to sanctions.

Article 125 of the Penal Code of Iceland imposes pecuniary sanctions and a maximum of three months' imprisonment on those who publicly ridicule or offend the dogmas of religious communities active in accordance with the law in the country, or the object of their worship.

26 Ministry of Foreign Affairs of Denmark, 'Official Response by the Danish Government to the UN Special Rapporteurs', 24 January 2006.

Section 163 of the Penal Code of Malta protects the Roman Catholic religion as the official religion of Malta. A person who through words, movements, images or in any other visible manner, whether in print or not, publicly defames the Catholic Church, its adherents, representatives or objects of religious veneration can be sentenced to imprisonment for one to six months. This act is applied exceptionally frequently by European standards.[27]

In Greece, pursuant to Section 198 of the Penal Code, a person who publicly and in bad faith defames God or shows disrespect for the objects of religious veneration shall be considered the perpetrator of a criminal act. Section 199 explicitly protects the Greek Orthodox Church, and other lawfully functioning churches in the country (without naming them), against blasphemy.

In Italy, according to Section 403 of the Penal Code, offending religions in public by expressing contempt for their adherents or representatives shall be considered a criminal act. Although previously the act only punished blasphemy against the 'state' (Catholic) church in 2000, the Constitutional Court, with reference to equality between religions, repealed this restriction.[28]

Pertaining to Section 261 of the Swiss Penal Code, a person who in public or in a vulgar manner offends or ridicules others' religious conviction, especially their belief in God, or defames objects of religious veneration commits a criminal act.

In France, the currently effective Constitution of 1958 stipulates that France is a secular state, and the state guarantees freedom of religion and the equality of religions. The Act on the Separation of the State and the Church was adopted in 1905, pursuant to which French public life is determined or dominated by secularism. Despite this, in the regions of Alsace and Lorraine, the specific facts determining the criminal act of blasphemy remain in effect up to the present date. Section 166 of the local Penal Code stipulates the

27 '99 convicted for public blasphemy in 2012', *Maltatoday.com.mt*, 20 April 2013, www.maltatoday.com.mt/news/court_and_police/26215/99-convicted-for-public-blasphemy-in-2012-20130420#.VQBbg05mrXc.

28 Silvia Angeletti, 'Blasphemy Laws and Incitement to Religious Hatred: Italian Legal Standards and Social Developments', (2014) 9 *Religion and Human Rights* 200.

penalty of imprisonment to be imposed on one who 'defames God in public with defamatory words or defames in public a Christian denomination and/or a recognised religious community'.

3.2. The Restriction of Blasphemy with Respect to the Insulting of Religious Feelings or Disturbing Public Order

In Ireland, the prohibition of blasphemy is enshrined in the Constitution, which refers blasphemy to the sphere of criminal law: 'The publication or utterance of blasphemous, seditious, or indecent matter is an offence which shall be punishable in accordance with law' (Article 40(6)).

Pursuant to regulations in compliance with the Constitution, it shall be considered blasphemy to publish or utter strongly offensive or defamatory statements relating to the sacred matters of any religion, which relate to issues considered sacred by any religion and cause outrage among a significant number of followers concerned, *if* the outrage was caused intentionally by the publication or the opinion expressed (Defamation Act 2009, Article 36). The Act adopted in 2009 was received with heated protests and strong criticism and Ireland, which had performed well up to that point, immediately dropped in various rankings of freedom of the press indices, and was reprimanded by various human rights organisations due to the adoption of the act, even if it was not applied in practice.[29] This question came into the limelight as a result of the adoption of the new act, as a consequence of which a constitutional convention was summoned in 2013, where the majority, in agreement with the Irish Council of Churches,[30] decided to repeal the currently effective constitutional provision and the act adopted in line with it, and

29 In 2010, Ireland immediately dropped nine places in the annual freedom of the press ranking of Reporters without Borders, an international non-governmental organisation, http://en.rsf.org/press-freedom-index-2010,1034.html.

30 'A Programme for a Partnership Government' Government of Ireland (11 May 2016) 153, www.merrionstreet.ie/MerrionStreet/en/ImageLibrary/Programme_for_Partnership_Government.pdf.

to replace it with a rule prohibiting the manifestation of religious hatred.[31] The Irish government decided to call for a referendum on this issue, but its possible date is still uncertain.[32]

In Germany, blasphemy (*Gotteslästerung*) has been a punishable offence since 1871. Originally, Section 166 of the *Strafgesetzbuch* read as follows: 'Whoever, by defaming God with publicly insulting statements, gives rise to outrage or who publicly disparages a Christian church or another religious denomination recognised by the State, or the institution or habits thereof, is liable to punishment by imprisonment for up to three years'.[33] This provision was amended later; since 1 January 1975, the following regulation has been in effect (Section 166):

> (1) Whoever publicly or through dissemination of writings insults the content of others' religious faith or faith related to a philosophy of life in a manner that is capable of disturbing the public peace shall be punished with imprisonment for not more than three years or a fine.
>
> (2) Whoever publicly or through the dissemination of writings in Germany insults a church, another religious society, or an organisation dedicated to a philosophy of life, or their

31 'Blasphemy offence should be replaced in the Constitution, says ECHR', *thejournal.ie*, 3 November 2013, www.thejournal.ie/constitutional-ECHR-blasphemy-1158623-Nov2013.

32 'Taoiseach rules out blasphemy referendum', *RTÉ.ie*, 12 January 2015, www.rte.ie/news/2015/0112/671900-news-in-brief. On the analysis of the Irish regulation, see Katherine AE Jacob, 'Defending Blasphemy: Exploring Religious Expression Under Ireland's Blasphemy Law', (2011) 44 *Case Western Reserve Journal of International Law* 803; Katherine A Rollinson, 'An Analysis of Blasphemy Legislation in Contemporary Ireland and its Effects upon Freedom of Expression in Literary and Artistic Works', (2011) 39 *Syracuse Journal of International Law and Commerce* 189.

33 Thomas Fuchs (ed), *StGB Strafgesetzbuch für das Deutsche Reich vom 15. Mai 1871 – Historisch-synoptische Edition 1871–2009* (lexetius.com 2010) 792, http://lexetius.com/leges/StGB/Inhalt;jsessionid=1j9iabjrw9qe91q3p2aemd9md6?0.

institutions or customs in a manner that is capable of disturbing the public peace, shall be similarly punished.

The separate act of blasphemy was removed from Section 166, although, in addition to defamation, the potential for disturbing public peace was included as a necessary condition of the restriction.

The Austrian Penal Code protects the religious sphere of citizens. Section 188 of the Penal Code renders it punishable to disparage and defame religious dogmas (*Herabwürdigung religiöser Lehren*), and Section 189 makes disturbing the exercise of one's religion punishable (*Störung einer Religionsübung*). Pursuant to the Penal Code, anyone who gives rise to rightful indignation by publicly defaming and/or ridiculing a person or object respected by the church or a religious community registered in the country and/or the dogma, the lawfully conducted ceremony or functioning institution of such a church or religious community shall be considered the perpetrator of a criminal act. Pursuant to this provision, in December 2014, the provincial tribunal of Linz imposed sanctions amounting to imprisonment for three months' and a fine of 5,300€ on a woman who had shot pornographic scenes on two occasions in a church.[34]

The Penal Code of Liechtenstein (Article 188) prohibits the public abuse or ridicule of a person, object, ceremony or lawfully functioning religious institution if it is committed in a manner which gives rise to rightful indignation.

In Spain, Section 525 of the Penal Code prohibits the insult of religious feelings, the defamation of religious dogmas and public ceremonies and the defamation of believers. The provision—the only one of such a character in Europe—also protects the absence of religious conviction, and the defamation of others due to the absence of religious conviction is also prohibited.[35]

Section 138 of the Penal Code of Cyprus prohibits the destruction, demolition and defamation of subjects of religious veneration if it

34 'Pornodreh in Kirche bei Linz: Drei Monate bedingt als Strafe', *Kath.net*, 11 December 2014, www.kath.net/news/48660.

35 Santiago C Arribas, 'Religious Freedom and Freedom of Expression in Spain', (2014) 9 *Religion and Human Rights* 217–18.

is done with the intention of insulting the followers of the religion, or in acquiescence of the likely injury. Pursuant to Section 141, words and sounds uttered with the intention of insulting religious feelings, movements serving this purpose or the display of objects offending believers shall also be punishable. Section 142 prohibits the publication of books, pamphlets, articles and letters containing the public insult of religious conviction, if it is done with the intention of carrying out religious defamation or of outraging and insulting the adherents of a religion.

In Czech Republic, Section 198 of the Penal Code prohibits the defamation of groups of citizens due to their religion or lack of religion, among other reasons.

In Poland, Section 196 of the Penal Code protects religious feelings and therefore it stipulates that the public defamation of an object of religious veneration or the place of worship shall be punishable.

In England, as noted above, the common law crime of blasphemy was abolished in 2008. In the Netherlands, it was only recently that the prohibition of blasphemy was eliminated from the Penal Code (Section 147) in December 2013. In Norway, until very recently, the Penal Code (Article 142) prescribed penalty to be imposed on someone who verbally or through committing an act publicly offends the dogmas of a religion exercised freely and lawfully in the country, or who desecrates an object of religious veneration, or expresses their contempt of these in an offensive manner. This ban was abolished in 2015.

3.3. The Prohibition of Blasphemy in Western States outside Europe

The freedom of speech law of the US does not prohibit blasphemy in general. As Harry Kalven, one of the first to systematically structure the jurisprudence of the First Amendment put it, blasphemy and the freedom of 'heretic' views are part of the 'untouchable consensus'.[36] The *Cantwell v Connecticut* decision of 1940 sealed this consensus.[37]

36 Harry Kalven, Jr, *A Worthy Tradition: Freedom of Speech in America* (Harper and Row 1988) 6–7.

37 *Cantwell v Connecticut* 310 US 296 (1940).

The accused person, a Jehovah's Witness, played a recording out in the street in a neighbourhood of the city with a predominantly Catholic majority. The recording attacked the Catholic Church. The judgment brought against this person on charges of inciting a breach of the peace was repealed by the Supreme Court, which ruled that in the absence of the threat of physical violence, the pure defamation offence should not be punishable, neither if it offends a religious conviction, nor if it is expressed in a public debate. The Supreme Court, in another important decision, handed down a ruling on a film banned due to blasphemy, noting that it is not the task of the state to avert real or perceived attacks against certain religious doctrines.[38]

Nonetheless, in six states of the USA, blasphemy-related prohibitions are still in effect (at least in theory as the prohibition is still in the books, but never applied in practice). These are old criminal law provisions, which—with the clear purpose of protecting Christian denominations—typically prohibit defamation, cursing in relation to God, the Holy Spirit and the Bible or the denial of the existence of God or the Creation.[39]

In Canada, a criminal prohibition (Criminal Code, Article 296) covers blasphemy (blasphemous libel), but it is very rare for such a case to be tried before a court. Over the past few years, several campaigns have been launched to amend the regulations, but none of them has been successful.[40]

In New Zealand, according to the Criminal Code of 1961, blasphemous libel is prohibited, but this prohibition is not applied in practice, either.

In Australia, there is no general, federal blasphemy law but a prohibition has been upheld which prohibits blasphemous names

38 *Joseph Burstyn, Inc. v Wilson* 343 US 495, 505 (1952).

39 Massachusetts General Laws, Art 36; Michigan Penal Code (1931), 750.102, 750.103; Oklahoma Statutes, §21.901, 21.902; South Carolina Code of Laws, §16-17-520; Wyoming Statutes, §1-29-106; Pennsylvania Code, §17.5.

40 Jeremy Patrick, 'Canadian Blasphemy Law in Context: Press, Legislative, and Public Reactions', (2010) XVI *Annual Survey of International and Comparative Law* 129.

being given to ships.[41] Of Australia's states, in Tasmania, the Criminal Code (Section 119) still prohibits religious defamation.

4. Restriction or Freedom of Blasphemy? Some Theoretical Considerations

4.1. The Reappearance of Blasphemy in the Western World: Arising Questions

After the case of the 'Danish cartoons', significantly more attention has been paid to blasphemy. On 30 September 2005, *Jyllands-Posten,* a Danish daily, published twelve cartoons of the Prophet Muhammad. Previously, Flemming Rose, the editor of the cultural section of the paper, came into possession of the information that a Danish author had been unable to find an artist to illustrate his book on the Prophet Muhammad intended for children. Rose gave his support to the cause and asked 40 artists to produce some drawings. About a week later, the Danish Islamic Society, at its demonstration in Copenhagen, demanded a public apology and the intervention of the government, and some days later, two caricaturists received death threats. After the further escalation of the case, in January 2006, Muslim countries started to boycott Danish products. On 31 January, the *Jyllands-Posten* apologised—however, this was already too little to calm down sentiments. In Gaza, armed people attacked one of the offices of the EU, and a bomb threat was received by editorial offices in Copenhagen and Aarhus. At the beginning of February, 150 demonstrators attacked the Danish Embassy in Jakarta, while in Damascus, the capital of Syria, the Embassies of Denmark and Norway were set on fire, and the Embassy of Denmark in Beirut was also consumed by fire. At the same time, the Embassy of Austria in Tehran was attacked by demonstrators, and in Pakistan Muslim physicians boycotted pharmaceutical products from Denmark, Norway, France, Germany and Switzerland. In several Islamic states, the flags of European countries were burned. On 8 February, four demonstrators were shot dead in Afghanistan, and the following day in Lebanon, 250,000 mostly peaceful demonstrators marched

41 Reg 21, s 2(d) of the Shipping Registration Regulations 1981.

in the streets. On 10 February, the French Embassy in Tehran was attacked, and the staff working at the Danish Embassy were called home from Syria. One week later, eleven people died in the riots which broke out during a demonstration in front of the Italian embassy in Libya.

In another incident, the trailer for a film entitled *Innocence of Muslims* was put on the YouTube online video sharing portal in July 2012. The text of the 13-minute video was translated into Arabic, and several scenes of it were also presented on television in Egypt. The film ridiculed the Prophet Muhammad and the Muslim religion by depicting the prophet as a womaniser and a murderer greedy for power, who kidnapped women and children in the name of the Quran. This was followed by demonstrations in Cairo, and subsequently in other Muslim countries. In Libya, the US Embassy was set on fire, and in the clashes, four embassy staff members, including the ambassador, lost their lives. In Baghdad, a suicide bomber exploded a car in the proximity of the embassies of Western states; the death toll was seven. Although access to the video was blocked in Pakistan, in Karachi, the largest city in the country, demonstrations were organised, during which the embassy of the US was mobbed. In Yemen, demonstrators demanded the expulsion of the ambassador, while in Baku, Azerbaijan, demonstrations were organised in front of the embassy. In Kabul, the capital of Afghanistan, flags were burnt; cars were set on fire and demonstrators called for death to the US. In Tunisia and Sudan, protests were similarly violent, and the German Embassy was set on fire.

Charlie Hebdo, the French magazine, attained world fame in 2006, when the cartoons published first by *Jyllands-Posten* were republished in it supplemented with its own cartoons. After the repeated publications of cartoons offending the Muslim religion in November 2011, the offices and the website of the magazine were attacked. Molotov cocktails were thrown at the building, and its website was blackout by hackers. On 19 September 2012, the magazine again published cartoons depicting the Prophet Muhammad, which again resulted in a hacker attack affecting the website of the magazine. Members of the editorial board worked under constant threats, and yet they were not willing to give an inch from the provocative style of the magazine. On 7 January 2015, two

Muslim men equipped with machine guns attacked the editorial offices of the magazine, killing twelve people (including two policemen guarding the editorial offices) and injuring several others. After the tragedy, debates flared up all over Europe on questions of immigration, the cohabitation of cultures, social integration and freedom of speech.

The brutal attack against the offices of *Charlie Hebdo* cannot be regarded as the beginning of a new world from the perspective of freedom of speech. Nevertheless, the tragedy might seem to be the point of departure of a new approach if European states draw conclusions from the so far unprecedented case of Europeans being massacred in Europe for exercising their right to freedom of speech, which will lead to them changing their policies.

From the first, instinctive reactions of the press, one interpretation seems to have emerged, that being that the attack on *Charlie Hebdo* was not only aimed at the journalists and caricaturists murdered but it was an act against European culture as such. This was the view reflected in the article by the editorial board of the *New York Times* published on the day of the massacre.[42] The discussion of the issue of the war of cultures or the clash of civilisations related to the cartoon cases is not a new phenomenon either, as in the aftermath of the Danish cartoons case similar positions and opinions were broadly published, according to which any allowance made to terrorism and curtailing European values might bring the end of freedom in Europe.[43]

The situation in Europe faces an exceptional risk: If there is a war between cultures in which the radicalised Muslims who have been admitted into Europe 'have to be restrained' (not only from carrying out terrorist attacks but also from following certain rules of their religious culture, see, for example, the debates around the public wearing of the traditional *burqa* or *niqab*), then how can we ensure

42 'The *Charlie Hebdo* Massacre in Paris (by the Editorial Board)', *New York Times*, 7 January 2015.

43 For example, András Sajó, 'Countervailing Duties as Applied to Danish Cheese and Danish Cartoons' in András Sajó (ed), *Censorial Sensitivities. Free Speech and Religion in a Fundamentalist World* (Eleven International 2006).

equal human rights, one of the fundaments of European culture, for Muslims in Europe? If we take steps against radical Islam (putting aside the dogma on the equality of human rights, for example by banning the wearing of the *burqa*), this may entail that we do not ensure, for example, freedom of religion and speech fully for Muslims. Do we not curtail or damage 'European values' by making such a strong exception? Do we expose ourselves to risks, leaving everything that is important to us unguarded, by not making such strong exceptions? And, if we retreat as Islamic terrorists want us to do (and let us say, we prohibit the publication of the *Charlie Hebdo* type cartoons), then can we buy safety at such a price and preserve the remains of our freedom?

The range of questions which might be raised with respect to blasphemy is even broader and more complex. Contrary to all appearances, the debate primarily is not exclusively, and in most European countries, not necessarily, about the clash between 'Muslim radicalism' and 'European values' but equally about Christianity vs secularism (the neutrality of the state). The emphasis on this aspect is especially marked in the home country of secularism, France and so, although the terrorist attack against *Charlie Hebdo* has great symbolic resonance, the magazine as a phenomenon, its assessment by French society and its handling by the French authorities is not suitable to base general conclusions on at a European level.

The Committee of Ministers of the Council of Europe, adopted a declaration, a week after the *Charlie Hebdo* massacre, condemning the 'horrendous act', calling it a 'direct attack' on democracy.[44] At the same time, on the very day of the killings, 7 January, the Parliamentary Assembly, the other organ of the aforementioned international organisation, called upon European states to combat intolerance and discrimination against Christians.[45] The Resolution makes an appeal to states asking them to resort to 'reasonable

44 Declaration by the Committee of Ministers on the recent attacks in Paris (Adopted by the Committee of Ministers on 14 January 2015 at the 1216th meeting of the Ministers' Deputies).

45 Tackling intolerance and discrimination in Europe with a special focus on Christians. Resolution 2036 (2015) of the Parliamentary Assembly.

accommodation' to protect people's religious beliefs. As the two documents issued simultaneously by the Council of Europe prove, the issue of religions in the public discourse in Europe cannot be limited to tackling the difficulties posed by Islam.

Robert Kahn concludes that Europe's fear of conservative Islam is partly rooted in 'Europe's uneasiness about its secular identity'.[46] From this, it follows that the strongest or the most adamant European defenders of Islam will be Christian religious conservatives,—as, not only in the *Charlie Hebdo* case but with regard to cartoons which attack any religion, all religions share the 'same fate'.[47] Neville Cox also concludes that, in the debate surrounding the restriction of blasphemy, it is ultimately the resentment of secular Western societies of religions that comes to light, because religious morality is no longer an indispensable element of public morality.[48] Ross Douthat, the publicist of the *New York Times,* also emphasises that attacks on Christianity are part and parcel of popular culture and media, just as those on Islam.[49] He raises this to demonstrate that the followers of Islam are not put at a disadvantage, nor are they discriminated against, compared to the adherents of other religions.

From this angle, the followers of all religions are opposed to a secular Europe, even if, naturally, the degree and intensity of this opposition varies considerably according to religions and communities. The decisive majority of Christians would not wish to have secular Europe eradicated and for the walls between the state and churches to be dismantled but would welcome more respect for their religions. In contrast, certain followers of radical Islam presumably would have no objection to the transformation of Europe as it is now.

46 Robert A Kahn, 'The Danish Cartoon Controversy and the Rhetoric of Libertarian Regret', (2009) 16 *University of Miami International & Comparative Law Review* 151, 178.

47 *Ibid.*

48 Neville Cox, 'Blasphemy, Holocaust Denial, and the Control of Profoundly Unacceptable Speech', (2014) 62 *The American Journal of Comparative Law* 739, 756–9.

49 Ross Douthat, 'Blasphemy Revisited', *New York Times*, opinion pages, 14 January 2015.

In addition to the social role of religions and their treatment by society, there is the question of freedom of speech, which is important in itself. As András Sajó puts it, freedom of speech 'is part of democratic identity and European (Western) culture ... no Western identity can exist without freedom of speech'.[50] At the same time, we can add, respect for dignity, tolerance and mutual appreciation are also foundation stones of European culture. Individual states, in the event of a clash between these values and freedom of speech, strike the balance in various ways and with various results. There is no absolute consensus on the freedom of speech, and thus France, pursuing revolutionary ideas, is not a model for Europe to follow.

The interpretation in which freedom of speech embodies the protection of *any* opinion against restriction, does not correspond to reality, because (1) there are reasonable, justified and slowly evolving legislative restrictions on freedom of speech everywhere, and (2) the protection of religions against opinions is not *per se* in opposition to the fundamental principles or key ideas of 'European culture', which also attach great importance to human dignity. These fundamental concepts, moreover, are complex, because European culture is multifaceted and originates from the balance and mutual recognition of conflicting values which then differs from country to country despite the common foundations and commonly shared values.

Might there be a grain of truth in the dire warnings, according to which, if we give in to radical Muslims, European culture will perish? Raising this question in this way is rhetorical and sensationalist. Obviously, if Europe significantly lessens the protection of freedom of speech as a result of terror, the terrorists can rightly take it as a victory, and might start thinking about which of the European values they should aim to erase next. However, if we disregard this topical political consideration, take a step back and concentrate solely on the question, it would be hard to claim that the protection of religious convictions against freedom of speech (in principle and not in response to the *Charlie Hebdo* murders) would be identical to

50 András Sajó, 'Szólásszabadság a lelki finomság korában' in Tamás Nótári (ed), *Ünnepi tanulmányok Sárközy Tamás 70. születésnapjára* (Lectum 2010) 356.

the unthinkable loss of European culture. Because Christianity and religious pluralism, in general, protected by a potential restriction on the freedom of speech (and, let us reiterate, the protection of human dignity), are also inseparable parts thereof.

A discussion of possible limitations on blasphemy in a democratic society covers a wide range of issues. In addition to freedom of speech, the relationship between the state and churches, immigration, multiculturalism and the cohabitation of different cultures, all of which are crucial to the future of Europe. It is difficult to select one and be silent on the others, and yet is necessary to focus the analysis here on questions of freedom of speech—how the permissibility or prohibition of blasphemy fits into the European system and philosophy of the freedom of speech? Taking such a narrow perspective risks omitting discussion of the most important questions, but if, beyond the permissibility of blasphemy, we were to examine the war between cultures or the necessary degree of immigration to Europe, then the overview would necessarily become so broad in perspective that the result would be extremely superficial. However, we must not underestimate the value of focusing exclusively on freedom of speech, since freedom of speech is a European symbol, the symbol of enlightenment and of free, liberal, western societies. Consequently, the analysis of issues related to the law of freedom of speech *per se* is a necessary and important contribution to the discourse on the future of Europe.

4.2. The Legal Notion of Blasphemy: Some Definitional Attempts

In a debate about questions relating to restrictions of blasphemy, it would seem sensible to start by providing a precise definition of blasphemy. However, this is not really possible, due both to the diversity of European legal systems and to the declining significance of blasphemy as a barrier to freedom of speech. Moreover, the concept has undergone considerable transformation over the past centuries, and its modern content has not been able to adapt to the presence of Islam in Europe; as such, blasphemy at present seems to have whatever meaning is attributed to it by the user.

To some extent, this is an exaggeration, and we can select and describe some of the possible concepts of blasphemy. One of the greatest theorists of English law, William Blackstone, defined blasphemy in the eighteenth century as follows: 'Blasphemy against the Almighty is denying his being or providence, or uttering contumelious reproaches on our Saviour Christ'.[51] This strict approach, which essentially did not even leave any room for criticising Christianity, has become considerably milder over the past centuries. According to *Stephen's Digest of the Criminal Law* (written in the late nineteenth century, but still an authoritative source much later, up until in the middle of the twentieth century in this regard):

> Every publication is said to be blasphemous which contains any contemptuous, reviling, scurrilous or ludicrous matter relating to God, Jesus Christ, or the Bible, or the formularies of the Church of England as by law established. It is not blasphemous to speak or publish opinions hostile to the Christian religion, or to deny the existence of God, if the publication is couched in decent and temperate language. The test to be applied is as to the manner in which the doctrines are advocated and not as to the substance of the doctrines themselves.[52]

The earlier English perception of law, even in the twentieth century, provided protection against blasphemy only for Christianity (more precisely, primarily for the Church of England). It is true that it substantially narrowed down the spectrum of opinions which had been previously prohibited, allowing for the criticism of religion, as long if that criticism is in decent and tempered language, in a proper manner.

The relatively recent 2009 Irish Defamation Act already takes into account the equality of religions when defining blasphemy in the following way: 'Matter that is grossly abusive or insulting in relation

51 William Blackstone, *Commentaries on the Laws of England* (1st edn 1765–9; Cavendish 2001) vol 4, ch 4, 46.

52 Art 214 of *Stephen's Digest of the Criminal Law* (9th edn 1950).

to matters held sacred by any religion, thereby causing outrage among a substantial number of the adherents of that religion'.[53] The Irish law, therefore, considers the impact of the opinion as part of the concept, that is, an expression is not blasphemy if no outrage is caused by it. It is thus important to note that the blasphemous nature of an opinion itself is not sufficient for the legal offence to be committed, and a further necessary condition is the intentional nature of causing outrage (see Section 36(2)(b)).

We can conclude, even without a uniform and permanent concept of blasphemy that, as the concept is used in Western law today (in the few European states which kept the ban of blasphemy in their books), opinions criticising religions cannot be considered blasphemous, nor does blasphemy include the act of denying the truth of religious dogmas or the existence of God, nor is it permitted to make any difference between individual religions and churches. A blasphemous expression shall be, therefore, one which defames or insults a religion (its dogmas, its respected personalities, etc.), and unwarrantedly offends or insults the adherents of that religion; that is, when judging blasphemy, the manner, the style and the tone of expressing an opinion is of utmost importance, whereas the content of the criticism is less immediately relevant.

4.3. Is there any such Thing as 'Free Speech'?

Before analysing the possible criteria for restricting blasphemy, it is reasonable to make a brief detour and go back to the origins of freedom of speech. When analysing freedom of speech, the basic consideration serving as our point of departure is the robust protection of public debate and criticism. No matter what we think of blasphemy in general, we cannot dispute that important questions of public interest and individual opinions must be provided with a high level of protection. In the absence of this, democracy cannot function, those exercising power cannot be subjected to criticism and their activities cannot be subjected to any scrutiny, and as such, transparency will

53 'Matter that is grossly abusive or insulting in relation to matters held sacred by any religion, thereby causing outrage among a substantial number of the adherents of that religion'. Irish Defamation Act 2009, s 36(2)(a).

be lacking. Whichever justification for the freedom of speech we accept, its aim is to find the truth,[54] and thereby contribute to the functioning of democratic society,[55] or, if we consider this right to be protected from the perspective of the individual's autonomy and self-fulfilment,[56] the protection guaranteed to the expression of opinions relating to public debate is in all events indispensable. In other words, by disproportionately restricting public debate, we essentially eliminate freedom of speech. The social role of religions is to seek the overriding guiding principles of the universe, and thus debates on religious issues must be of the highest public interest. From this, it follows that restricting blasphemy can only happen exceptionally; the balance is in favour of protecting opinions relating to religion.

We may question, for example, of the extent to which the depiction of a nun having fantasies of sexual intercourse with Christ (*Wingrove*) is important from the perspective of public debate and democratic public sphere. For the time being, avoiding contemplating the question of whether the ECtHR delivered the right judgment or not, we may conclude that the protection of opinions insulting religious people is also derived from the general equality of human beings (and their dignity). One of the basic premises for freedom of speech is that everybody should be granted the same rights to participate in public debates and to influence joint decisions.[57] Nobody can be excluded from the public forum on the grounds that others (maybe many, or even the majority) disagree with what they say.[58] According to Robert

54 John Milton, 'Areopagitica' in John Milton, *Areopagitica and Other Political Writings* (Liberty Fund 1999) 2–51; John Stuart Mill, *On Liberty* (JW Parker and Son 2nd edn 1859).

55 Alexander Meiklejohn, *Free Speech and its Relation to Self-Government* (Harper 1948).

56 Edwin C Baker, *Human Liberty and Freedom of Speech* (Oxford University Press 1989).

57 John Hart Ely, *Democracy and Distrust: A Theory of Judicial Review* (Harvard University Press 1981) 105–25; Ronald Dworkin, *Freedom's Law: The Moral Reading of the American Constitution* (Oxford University Press 1996) 199–202.

58 Ilias Trispiotis, 'The Duty to Respect Religious Feelings: Insights from European Human Rights Law', (2013) 19 *Columbia Journal of European Law* 499, 512.

Post, not only the recognition of equal dignity but the functioning of the state is at stake when responding to his question: 'If the state prevents citizens from participating in public discourse ... the state loses democratic legitimacy with respect to those citizens, for it prevents them from attempting to make public opinion responsive to their views'.[59]

This does not mean that every insulting and offensive opinion is protected, since there are more than few exceptions to the previous principle, the most tangible example of which is hate speech insulting communities or granting personality rights protecting the individual's autonomy, integrity and social status. These exceptions cannot, however, be arbitrarily and randomly extended; any further restrictions on freedom of speech must be justified and proportionate. The application of the above principle must not result in an act benefiting from the same protection as 'speech'. In several European countries, for example, the defamation of communities (without incitement to and instigation of hatred) is not prohibited, but of course, making any attempt to deprive the members of the same communities of the actual opportunity to exercise their rights (a verbal or written opinion which leads to an act) is.

A precursor, extremely relevant in the light of the *Charlie Hebdo* massacre and affecting the freedom of public debate, is the now almost three-decade-old *Hustler Magazine v Falwell* case from America.[60] A caricature was published in the erotic magazine *Hustler*, which distorted the then popular Campari adverts with a specific content. These advertisements in their original form told the public about the first 'experience' (i.e., the experience of drinking Campari liqueur for the first time in one's life). In *Hustler*'s parody, Jerry Falwell, a Protestant preacher, a television personality and the leading figure of the Moral Majority movement, was depicted in a fake interview as having occurred with his own mother in the garden toilet, blind-drunk. A notice printed in small type at the bottom of the page informed the reader that this was a parody.

59 Robert Post, 'Religion and Freedom of Speech: Portraits of Muhammad' in Sajó (n 43) 336.

60 *Hustler Magazine v Falwell* 485 US 46 (1988).

The reverend unsuccessfully launched a civil suit on charges of defamation, but the district court of appeal awarded a significant amount of damages to him as restitution for 'intentional infliction of emotional distress'. However, the decision of the Federal Supreme Court altered the ruling. According to the argumentation of the court, it would be erroneous and at the same time in breach of the First Amendment granting freedom of speech to establish legal liability for statements on public figures only because the disclosure intended to insult the person concerned or because the statement was disclosed with any other harmful intent. The insult and the outrage themselves do not provide sufficient foundation for the restriction of freedom of speech, because this standard is too subjective, and the freedom of speech takes priority. As long as the plaintiff cannot prove that the published opinion contains covert, false statement of facts, and the imparting of the false information was done in bad faith—i.e., knowing that the statement is false or as a result of gross negligence—freedom of speech cannot be restricted.[61] In the case of a parody, there's usually no 'fact' published.

This inspired Robert Post to elaborate a concept concerning the potential restrictions imposed on public discourse.[62] According to Post, the freedom of public discourse cannot be restricted on the grounds of pure insult and outrage, which would entail imposing certain norms of 'courtesy', which is alien to the essence of freedom. Hence, in a debate, even the strongest expressions are allowed. Eric Barendt disagrees with Post. As he puts it, the public discourse considered so important by Post can only take place under rational, reasonable circumstances and respecting certain norms. His other argument, which questions the correctness of Post's position, is that the argument in favour of freedom of speech, which would protect this right in the first place due to the dignity and autonomy of the individual, does not consider the dignity of

61 The Washington judges applied the same standard as in the famous *New York Times v Sullivan* ruling (376 US 254 (1964)) in cases relating to the protection of the reputation of public figures.

62 Robert C Post, 'The Constitutional Concept of Public Discourse: Outrageous Opinion, Democratic Deliberation and *Hustler Magazine v Falwell*', (1990) 103 *Harvard Law Review* 601.

those insulted by the opinion, who enjoys a similarly broad scope of protection.[63]

Stanley Fish also criticises the ruling for its lack of balance.[64] In this case, as he sees it, no 'idea' worthy of broad constitutional protection can be identified. Criticism and parody should be based on some realistic foundation; caricaturists usually emphasise and enlarge one of the real features of their subjects. However, in this case, the publication was not based on a real event, not even if the reference to Falwell's hypocritical conduct is obvious. Fish, in closing, states that should anybody question whether the disputed parody offended anybody, they should not hesitate to ask Jerry Falwell's mother.

To what extent is the statement of facts of *Hustler v Falwell* analogous with the Danish cartoons or the drawings of *Charlie Hebdo*? In the former case, a religious leader was attacked in person, which can provide grounds for the protection of personality rights (although he eventually lost the case in the US, in Europe, he certainly would have won it), but an analogy is difficult to find because the European drawings did not attack a specific person, but the representatives and followers of a given religion. Nevertheless, according to Guy Haarscher, there is no reason to afford different treatment to religious and political cartoons.[65] This statement, however, would seem to be too general in scope to be useful, because obviously, the restriction cannot be based on the subject matter of a caricature, only on the degree of the insult it caused. Discussing the Muhammad cartoons, Post is also more careful and does not completely rule out a restriction on blasphemy.

Let us return to the frequently heard opinion, according to which 'if we give in to the terrorists (i.e., restrict freedom of speech), they will win'. As we have mentioned, of course, we have to be careful when responding to terrorism and, even if we inserted Muhammad

63 Eric Barendt, *Freedom of Speech* (Oxford University Press 2nd edn 2005) 228.

64 Stanley Fish, *There's No Such Thing as Free Speech and It's a Good Thing, Too* (Oxford University Press 1994) 120–38.

65 Guy Haarscher, 'Free Speech, Religion, and the Right to Caricature' in Sajó (n 43) 328.

as a value to be protected into criminal codes, this would hardly be enough to win the favour of the followers of radical Islam. Hence, in the very tense situation after the *Charlie Hebdo* tragedy, raising the necessity for new restrictions on freedom of speech—in states where currently blasphemy is not punishable—is likely to be premature for a long time. However, we cannot ignore the fact that freedom of speech is not a uniform, universal right which is granted the same degree of protection in the same manner in every situation. Its restriction is subject to various rules, which, in an ideal case, can be interpreted in the same conceptual framework and system. There is no general European approach, nor does a common legal response to certain questions of freedom of speech exist. Rules on protecting religions or religious people, then—if and where such a requirement exists in Europe—do not automatically entail the absence of the freedom of speech or its termination. Nevertheless, there are already a large number of instruments for restricting free speech in the various European legal systems. Every such instrument must have rules of application with proper consideration behind them, and the exact degree of restriction that can be imposed should also be defined; we cannot pretend that freedom of speech as such is illimitable. Especially relevant examples can be found for the restriction of freedom of speech in France, where the denial and belittling of several historical events is prohibited.[66] Furthermore, there is a very strong right of reply *vis-à-vis* the media.[67] As such,

66 Holocaust denial became sanctionable in France in 1990 through the amended French press law, which has been in effect since 1881 and known as the *loi Gayssot* after its proposer. In 2001 a law recognising the Armenian genocide as genocide was adopted and by doing so, raises it to the level of undisputable fact. The so-called *loi Taubira* was also adopted in 2001. The law stipulates that slavery and trading black people were crimes against humanity committed in the course of history. The law also prescribed that these historical events should be properly taught at schools and researched in the context of historical and social science programmes. Finally, in 2005, a law commemorating the positive impacts of French presence on former French colonies—primarily in North Africa—was adopted. In 2005, there was an attempt to render the denial of the Armenian genocide a criminal offence but finally this attempt failed.

67 See art 13 of the Press Act of 1881 and art 6 of the Media Act of 29 July 1982.

not even in France is freedom of speech considered as a value that it is (nearly) impossible to restrict.

Freedom of speech can also be restricted in a broad spectrum of ways on the basis of the prohibition of promoting terrorism, and this is indeed a common point of departure in European states.[68] In principle, it is difficult to disagree with the fact that combating terrorism is a legitimate basis for restricting freedom of speech. And yet, this might give rise to questionable results, which is demonstrated by an event that took place immediately after the *Charlie Hebdo* massacre, when a 16-year-old boy was prosecuted in France for ridiculing the magazine by using exactly the same instrument as *Charlie Hebdo* had. The boy used computer-aided graphics to ridicule one of the previous covers of the magazine. In the original drawing, a Muslim held the Quran in front of him; it was pierced by a bullet ('faith does not protect you from a bullet); in the boy's drawing, one of the murdered members of the editorial board held in front of him an issue of *Charlie Hebdo*, which was pierced by a bullet in the same way. Crowds were mobilised in Europe to defend the previous drawing, whereas the boy was prosecuted because of the second drawing.[69]

Contrary to the first impression, this is not the direct application of legal 'double standards', since one opinion amounted to the defamation of religion, which is not prohibited by French law, whereas the other, amounted to promoting terrorism, which is prohibited by French law. It is clear, however, from this case that the standards applied to different cases of restricting free speech might vary greatly, even within the same legal system, and ultimately similar situations might lead to different consequences if different legal provisions are applied to them from the perspective of restricting free speech—which, in the aforementioned case,

68 Clive Walker, 'Terrorism Speech and Militant Democracy' in András Koltay (ed), *Media Freedom and Regulation in the New Media World* (Wolters Kluwer 2014).

69 'We are Hypocrites on *Charlie Hebdo* and Freedom of Speech' (Adrian Weckler), *Independent* (Irish), 22 January 2015, www.independent.ie/opinion/we-are-hypocrites-on-charlie-hebdo-and-freedom-of-speech-30926352.html.

was rather striking. However, we could as well refer to the case of Dieudonné M'bala M'bala, a comedian who was arrested for a joke (according to the authorities, in a Facebook post, he took the side of Amédy Coulibaly, who had taken hostages in a shop on 7 January 2015, and had supported the murderers committing the *Charlie Hebdo* massacre).[70] The two cases were in sharp contrast with the demonstrations in support of freedom of speech, also supported by the government.

The image of freedom of speech obtaining in European countries is different, but they have one thing in common; they all differ from the American concept. Whereas the legal system of the US permits (it does not prohibit but tolerates) insulting communities and incitement to hatred, several instruments prohibiting this are known within Europe. At the same time, religious fundamentalism and religion-based hatred in the US should not be prohibited, but patiently tolerated if we want to give an adequate response to these phenomena. In other words, tolerance is a two-way process; taking into account the lessons learned from the *Charlie Hebdo* case, tolerance should not only be shown towards drawings defaming religions but also towards religions themselves.

According to the legal system of the US, opinions against religious fundamentalism (such as, for example, *Charlie Hebdo*) must, of course, not be curtailed but, from the social culture of the US, it also follows that neither is it necessary to respond immediately to apparently grave threats (e.g., from religions) through exercising the right to freedom of speech (i.e., through publishing abusive cartoons).[71] This means that *Charlie Hebdo* is not welcome in the US either—not because its activities should be legally curtailed but because the American idea of freedom of speech is built on mutual tolerance, patience for each other, and handling problems at the level of community and not legally.[72] The absence of an immediate,

70 'Paris Attacks: Dieudonné Held as France Tackles Hate Speech', *BBC News*, 14 January 2015, www.bbc.com/news/world-europe-30811401.

71 Kahn (n 46) 163–66; Robert A Kahn, 'Flemming Rose, the Danish Cartoon Controversy, and the New European Freedom of Speech', (2010) 40 *California Western International Law Journal* 253, 275–6.

72 See Lee C Bollinger, *The Tolerant Society* (Clarendon 1986).

powerful reaction to religious radicalism is not a sign of weakness, but a sign of power.

We restrict freedom of speech in order to protect individual integrity, reputation, visual image, privacy, personal data, etc. We protect individual communities from hate speech or Holocaust denial, and we restrict opinions which promote terrorism or ridicule state symbols, in a similar manner to restrictions on pornography, nudity, vulgarity, etc. Freedom of speech is therefore not monolithic. In the area of freedom of speech, we find responses given to certain extremely complex problems that, in a fortunate scenario, can be interpreted in an identical conceptual framework and integrated into a system. In a properly functioning constitutional system, rules on the democratic public sphere constitute a structure which consistently determines the criteria and possibilities for restricting freedom of speech. Of course, this is not an overly rigid structure but one which is constantly shaped by new judicial and constitutional court rulings and legislative amendments.

As such, it does not provide automatic responses in advance to problems which may arise, and which are not fully consistent and coherent with it, even in states with the most refined and longest traditions of freedom of speech. Even so, an approach that respects freedom of speech should aim to arrive at such a system. This systemic freedom of speech, at the same time, implies very sophisticated issues of demarcation and appreciation. Therefore, when discussing 'the' freedom of speech, we have to specify exactly which question we have in mind. The recognition of the importance of freedom of speech and the general criteria for its protection do not necessarily determine whether a legal system can restrict blasphemy or not; the structure for freedom of speech established in a given legal system might include its restriction, as well as its permission, and the presence of such restriction cannot be used as a point of departure when drawing conclusions on the quality of the given legal system and the quality of the public sphere regulated thereby.

4.4. Is Religion Really Different?

Before analysing certain specific considerations surrounding the restrictions on blasphemy, we still need to raise one question: Is it possible to grant specific protection to religious convictions, which is different from and stronger than the protection of other interests or values (lifestyle, political conviction etc.), and which implies a more powerful restriction on freedom of speech? If we can confidently answer 'no' to this question, the theoretical foundations for restricting blasphemy (that is, protecting religious conviction only) will be more difficult to accept, because in this case, the criteria for restriction should be subjected to the stricter standards applicable to restricting public discourse. If, however, the answer is 'yes', the criteria for restriction might even be less stringent.

Is it possible to acknowledge the exceptional character of religious conviction in a legal sense, as compared to other convictions, or other forces and values shaping human personality? Is religious conviction in any way special by nature? Is it something that can be protected more strongly than other convictions and features which shape one's personality? If so, what is religion, and how can it be defined and distinguished from the freedom of one's philosophy of life and conscience, and protected by the same fundamental right? These are questions which clearly should not be left primarily to lawyers. However, historical experience shows that religious conviction lies in the most intimate and inmost sphere of the individual; it fundamentally determines an individual's personality and actions and, influencing the whole personality, it is present in every moment of an individual's existence. At the level of individuals, other types of convictions certainly exist, which have a similar, very powerful influence on the life of the individual, such as political orientation, patriotism and non-religious philosophies of life. However, turning to another level, above the individual, i.e. at the level of society, it is difficult to find a historically rooted conviction with a similarly powerful influence to that of religion (though in the case of individual members of the society, patriotism or political conviction can be as strong as others' religious feelings).

Anthony Ellis is of the opinion that religious conviction is no different from any other spiritual conviction,[73] whereas Neville Cox argues that Europe's difficulties in engaging with Islam are rooted in European's lack of comprehension of religious conviction.[74] Most modern Western societies have largely lost their links to religions and so there are many who do not understand the role religious conviction plays in the life of an individual.[75] We can add that, in Europe, this situation is the result of a long, centuries-old process that is still ongoing. In European societies, it is exactly this incompleteness that might cause the unease: People living at present were born in states where the significance of religion has dropped considerably, a decline to which conscious and deliberate state policy has contributed much (this holds true of the former Communist countries and secular Western societies alike). The number of people actively exercising their religion has also significantly dropped, and churches and members of religious communities have tolerated this peacefully.

On the other hand, and despite this, there are still people, either non-Europeans and/or the second and third generations of immigrants who were already born in Europe, who attach such importance to religion that they could, or even want to kill and die, for it. And, obviously, there are still places or regions in Europe, where a religious world-view is still not unusual. There are also related debates, which will not be addressed here, on the compatibility of terrorism with religion and the extent to which killing people over cartoons is in accordance with the religious prescriptions of Islam. We cannot take any position on these matters, and for the time being, they are not even important for us since, irrespective of the answer, to the European observer, people who commit such horrible crimes seem to be fanatical adherents of a religion, a phenomenon that a European person brought up in and used to a secular state finds very difficult to grasp.

Plenty of arguments can be raised against treating religious convictions differently to others. According to some opinions,

73 Anthony Ellis, 'What is Special about Religion?' (2006) 25 *Law and Philosophy* 219.

74 Cox (n 48) 756–9.

75 *Ibid.*

it is not permissible to ridicule somebody due to their origins or physical characteristics because they are beyond human control. A human being is not able to change these features through their own volition. In contrast, religious convictions and beliefs are essentially different, they are chosen by the religious person; that is, religious conviction exists as a result of one's conscious decision to be permanently reconfirmed; it is a choice as opposed to an accident of birth.[76]

Does such a distinction between innate and freely chosen personal characteristics hold true? Does the 'power' or 'importance' of a personality trait depend on how consciously we admit it? A further question: Are we sure that, in general terms, the above argumentation concerning free choice is applicable to religion? Many receive 'a ready-made' religious conviction when they are born, and never have occasion to doubt its truthfulness, or at least are never placed a situation where they should take a decision on leaving the church. Here I do not have the baptism of new born babies in mind, but the type of religiousness which is still characteristic of a broad spectrum of society, which is based on the customs of a smaller local community (or a family), and which is less conscious than taken as natural and as a given, and pursued as customary. The value of such religiousness, how deep and well-founded it is, and the extent to which individual churches approve of this type of religiousness are different questions and have no impact on this line of argumentation. I would disagree with the statement that religious conviction is in all cases the result of a conscious decision while holding that the decision on the need to protect it does not depend on whether it is received as 'ready-made' or it is the result of a conscious decision. Whether to protect a person's religious sensibilities depends rather on how powerfully they determine his/her personality and the extent to which we take this aspect of a religious person's personality as something to be protected.

Neither is it certain that following one's religious conviction is a matter of free choice beyond such cases. A believer does not necessarily think that they could have any 'option' other than following a given religion. I am not referring here to the social

76 For this reasoning, see Haarscher (n 65) 324.

pressure in certain communities to exercise one's religion or to bigotry, which is not worthy of protection. If somebody firmly believes that the dogmas of their religion are true and beneficial, what is more they are the only true and beneficial dogmas,—even if they found this truth as a result of conscious search and choice—it does not seem to be extremely reasonable or realistic to expect them to look for other choices or other convictions, to doubt the truth they have already found, or even to try and break free from such a belief. Religious conviction might mould the personality of a believer so powerfully that it does not help them to comprehend the assumption or idea that they have to choose their belief constantly, again and again—perhaps to confess or to affirm it, but why select it again if that has already been done once?

For a religious believer, faith is not a question of choice.[77] Of course, this does not rule out the possibility of healthy scepticism or uncertainty, to which a believer is exposed from time to time, or the necessity to reinforce the dogmas thought to contain the truth, which John Stuart Mill notably referred to. As Mill puts it, if one view, in the absence of a permanent debate, becomes a customary, unquestioned truth, people will soon accept it only out of habit, and it will fossilise and become a dead dogma. Before it is recognised, truth has to undergo persecution more than once and, although it is a white lie that truth will triumph in spite of all persecution 'in the course of ages there will generally be found persons to rediscover it ... until it has made such head as to withstand all subsequent attempts to suppress it'.[78] Therefore, even recognised truth benefits from free dispute.

The differentiation between personality traits 'consciously undertaken' and those 'granted by birth' in order to provide a stronger protection of the latter (because they exist not as a result of our decision, so they are not 'our fault') does not seem to be incontestable on a theoretical basis. Anybody can use offensive remarks when criticising the colour of my hair, how good I am at ballgames or my vocal range, and it would not cause me any severe distress. Obviously, the situation would be different with respect

77 On this in more detail, see Cox (n 74) 761–3.

78 Mill (n 377) 54.

to characteristics which essentially determine personality, such as nationality, mother tongue and sexual orientation. It must, however, be a 'given' personality trait (the colour of my eyes), the offensive criticism of which causes less severe pain and injury than the offensive criticism of a 'chosen' personality trait (insulting my religion). Hence, drawing a sharp line consistently between these is not possible from the perspective of the restriction of blasphemy.[79]

Another possible counterargument concerning the different treatment given to religious conviction holds that those social groups which are usually protected today (national and ethnic minorities, communities organised on the basis of sexual identity, etc.), have not, in the course of history—in contrast with, say, the members of Christian denominations—committed severe atrocities, or murdered other people *en masse*, and yet do not have the degree of powerful social influence (wealth, institutions of education, health care, social care, political embeddedness) as some of the churches still do. As such, according to this view, it is not surprising or illogical that the followers of these churches—in Europe they are primarily Christians—receive sharp or even offensive criticism.

A frequently used argument is that 'Jesus Christ was also sentenced to death for blasphemy', that is, if blasphemy had been restricted—were the judiciary and law enforcement authorities to have had the measures of the present day at their disposal—he would have had to fight the impossible if he had wanted to spread his teachings. However, this consideration, which sounds very potent and effective, conceals that what Jesus Christ said about the Jewish religion 2000 years ago—using rather powerful expressions—would be, in all events, permissible criticism of religions and churches according to the current concept of freedom of speech in Europe. That is, the kind of 'defamation' Jesus used when talking to the Pharisees is considered today in Europe as a generally permitted expression of opinion and would not fall under the effective restrictions on blasphemy. This means that, as the necessity of protecting Christian believers today should not be examined in the context of history, remembering the sins of others, the concept of blasphemy and

79 Cox (n 48) 760–1.

options for its restriction should not be considered on the basis of a 2000-year-old approach but in the current system and framework of freedom of speech.

From the philosophy of freedom of speech, it follows that the strong have to tolerate more, and stronger individuals can be offended more sharply, because the exercise of freedom of speech by nature tends to protect the weaker party through its balancing role; it provides an opportunity for the weaker party to participate in public debate as an equal member of society.[80] However, according to the argumentation to oppose that counterargument, present-day regulations should not be adjusted to the state of affairs four hundred years ago. Present day churches should not be judged for the actions of the henchmen of Tomás de Torquemada or the cruelties committed by Protestants against Catholics, for the historical sins of the past or even for the strength of state churches in the 19th century. Instead, the arguments for and against the restriction of freedom of speech should be analysed in the context of present-day needs and after identifying the groups requiring protection today.

Some of the Christian denominations in certain European countries are still strong and influential and have considerable wealth, but the question of restricting blasphemy does not concern the necessity to protect these churches and denominations from criticism. The church is not identical to its followers—while the occasional or potential restriction of freedom of speech protects the latter, this protection does not restrict the debate on the potential sins of churches, past or present. This being said, whatever we think of the restriction of blasphemy, one thing is for sure: We cannot afford not to have the opportunity under all circumstances, to write and express opinions on paedophile priests, corrupt Vatican bankers or alcoholic pastors. The criticism of churches and the protection of believers do not mutually exclude each other.

Another argument against attaching priority to religious conviction is that religions, religious conviction and churches

80 See, for example, Baker (n 56) and Dworkin (n 57).

ought to be confined to the private sphere.[81] Essentially, freedom of religion is the freedom to exercise one's religion within four walls (at home or in a closed community), as part of one's private life.

> What makes the accepted mutual respect for religions possible today is that these religions, when entering the public sphere, do not pose a serious threat to social order or to each other. Believers and nonbelievers live in a modernized, secular world, where religious doctrines do not have the power to totally define life; at the most, on the basis of individual choice, they operate in the private sphere—and the borders of the private sphere are defined by public opinion and the constitutional order. Until now, the secularized constitutional state did not have to concern itself with the content of religion—assuming the acceptance of certain preconditions.[82]

This means that if the believer has the courage to venture out to the street and appear in public life, and a church has ambitions of wielding secular influence, they must also tolerate blasphemy. Adherents of religions had better not even go outside if they wish to avoid it, and/or if the believer still goes out to the street, they violate the rules of the secular state.

As opposed to this, I am of the opinion that, for most religions, religious conviction and churches as communities uniting individuals (legal entities) can only exist and only have meaning if they are active in public life; Article 9 of the ECHR specifically mentions the right to manifest religion *in public*. One of their essential characteristics is that they wish to exert influence on the workings of society, attract believers and change the world, an ambition they pursue in several ways, such as by practising their religion publicly, by using religion-based arguments in public life and through television programmes. The state grants this right to each religious and non-religious group and opportunities to make

81 See for example the heated debate, 'Should religion be a private matter?', *debate.org,* http://www.debate.org/opinions/should-religion-be-a-private-matter.

82 Sajó (n 43) 285.

an attempt at the above. There are, of course, private aspects to exercising one's religion, which are no business of anybody else, but it necessarily has a public element, that is, it is not a fully private matter, and interpreting religion as such would deprive it of its essential, vital element, and thereby, would curtail or weaken the content and substance of the freedom of religion as a fundamental right.

4.5. Restriction of Free Expression with Regard to Blasphemous Opinions

4.5.1. Protection of Religion and Churches

The protection of religions and churches against disparaging, offensive or abusive opinions cannot provide grounds for restricting the free flow of opinions, according to the common understanding of freedom of speech, if they cannot be considered as hate speech or otherwise limitable discriminatory speech. Religions and their historical figures (founders, saints, prophets, etc.) themselves cannot be protected or be holders of fundamental rights. By contrast, churches as legal entities are subjects of law, but, if they are subject to defamatory, hateful or abusive expressions, only the protection of them (as legal entities) against defamatory speech might be applied. An attack against a religion is not an attack against the churches as legal entities. Under the law, then, a legal entity, despite being recognised by law and being an autonomous legal subject, has no feelings, specific sensitivities, human dignity, etc.

Hence, while the church as a legal entity is affected in the event of a direct attack prohibited by law in the course of exercising freedom of speech (violation of personality right, e.g., damage to reputation), in general terms the defamation of religion does not injure the church as a legal entity. As such, the past UN resolutions adopted under the pressure of Islamic states against the defamation of religion are very difficult to interpret from the perspective of the dogmas of freedom of speech, and can be considered much more as documents with political rather than effective legal consequences.[83] The protection of religions has no legal basis in the legislation on freedom of speech or in the various national and international systems of protecting fundamental rights; the law grants protection to individuals, and in given cases, to adherents of religions.[84] This has not always been so, and was not taken for granted previously because, as Robert Post notes, the state was formerly interested in suppressing blasphemy.[85] Nowadays, however, this interest has ceased to exist, and in any case, it would not provide sufficient grounds for restricting freedom of speech.

An entirely separate question is whether or to what extent attacking or offending a religion or a church harms individual believers, and if so, to what extent it can serve as grounds for restricting freedom of speech (details of this will be discussed later).

4.5.2. Protection of Freedom of Religion

The ECtHR, in its judgments concerning blasphemy, permanently confirms its position that the expression of defamatory opinions of religion may in certain cases violate the right of the believers of the religion concerned to the freedom of religion. In other words, exercising the right to freedom of speech granted by Article 10 of the ECHR may clash with the right to freedom of religion granted by Article 9, and the right to freedom of religion might occasionally emerge as the winner from this conflict. The reason is that the exercise of freedom of speech cannot in itself offend 'the rights of

83 Jeroen Temperman, 'Freedom of Expression and Religious Sensitivities in Pluralist Societies: Facing the Challenge of Extreme Speech', (2011) *Brigham Young University Law Review* 729; Aurel Sari, 'The Danish Cartoons Row: Re-Drawing the Limits of the Right to Freedom of Expression?', (2005) XVI *Finnish Yearbook of International Law* 365, 392–7.

84 Jeroen Temperman, 'Blasphemy, Defamation of Religions and Human Rights Law', (2008) *Netherlands Quarterly of Human Rights* 517; Jeroen Temperman, 'Prohibitions of Incitement under International Law: The Case of Religion' in Koltay (n 68).

85 Post (n 59) 337.

others' according to Article 10(2), and therefore it cannot violate one's freedom of religion. The Court agrees that instances when this situation might arise should be defined very restrictively; in the conflict of rights no automatically applicable prioritisation or hierarchy exists. Freedom of speech can only be restricted in extreme cases; the expression of an unwarrantedly offensive opinion of an insulting character can be restricted in order to grant the right to freedom of religion.

Bernát Török concludes that ECtHR judgments have only been partly based on this consideration, and that the court has based its justifications of restrictions on freedom of speech by the states much more on hurt to an individual's feelings than on restrictions imposed on exercising the fundamental right to the freedom of religion.[86] Nevertheless, whether the right to freedom of religion is affected at all by the publication of a blasphemous opinion remains an open question.

According to a statement made by Jeroen Temperman, it is not; consequently, the jurisprudence of the ECtHR and the Human Rights Commission of the UN, which are partly based on this, are inappropriate.

> Criticism or ridicule aimed at religion does not automatically affect a person's right to freedom of religion or belief. A person expressing to be insulted or hurt in his/her feelings on account of a critical publication or a defamatory act is not, therefore, denied in his/her fundamental right to freedom of religion or belief.[87]

The state, according to Temperman, with regard to freedom of religion, grants identical rights to those who practise a religion, irrespective of the publication of blasphemous opinions, and therefore, protecting religions from external criticism or attacks is not part of the right to freedom of religion.

86 Bernát Török, 'Can Religions or Religious People Be Protected against Blasphemy? Comments on the Case Law of the European Court of Human Rights' in Koltay (n 68) 519–21.

87 Temperman (n 84) 545.

We have to accept the approach taken by Török and Temperman, because obviously the expression of opinions offensive to religious adherents does not directly affect any element of the right to freedom of religion (the freedom to choose a conviction, to change one's conviction, to exercise one's religion, to administer or participate in religious ceremonies or to express religion-based opinions in public as well as the distancing of the state from any one conviction). Although arguments could be found to support the idea that the public criticism of a religion discourages believers and, out of fear of retaliation, they refrain from exercising their religion this does not change the fact that the state grants this right to the believer. Since the negative repercussions of hateful opinions can be treated and prevented by provisions relating to inciting hatred against a community and to the instigation of hatred as criminal offences, there is no need for a specific restriction on blasphemy.

Defamatory opinions of religion would seem to contribute much more to the violation of the rights of the individual than to the restriction of exercising the fundamental right to freedom of religion. The publication of a few cartoons ridiculing either Jesus or the Prophet Muhammad will make nobody either doubt or restrict the right of Christians or Muslims to freely exercise their religions and rights relating to freedom of religion.

I can imagine a concrete case when the disclosure of an opinion practically impacts on exercising one's freedom of religion. However, from the perspective of freedom of speech, we usually do not treat and protect such expressions as 'opinions'. I am talking about cases when the 'opinion' becomes an act. If, for example, somebody sets a church on fire, or drives a car into a religious procession, such an act shall be considered as preventing the exercise of religion, and can in no way be protected. But granting the right to freedom of religion shall not necessarily mean obliging others to show unqualified patience, understanding and acceptance for the one exercising the right.

4.5.3. Protection of Religious Feelings

To quote a classic adage: 'Every idea is an incitement'.[88] Special care should be taken when restricting freedom of speech, because there is no idea worth disclosing which would not offend or injure somebody. Harold Laski, a member of the Liberal Pantheon, wrote that 'I have no sort of sympathy with that attitude of mind which finds satisfaction in wanton insult to the religious conviction of others. But I am not prepared for its suppression. For I note that, historically, there are no limits to the ideas which religious persons will denounce as blasphemous'.[89] We have already referred to the view of Mill, who held that if a view, in the absence of a permanent debate, becomes a customary, undisputed truth, it will soon fossilise into a dogma. Therefore, free discussion and free debate will be beneficial even for the recognised 'truth' or religions, which spread their versions of the truth, wishing to make the definition of truth their own monopoly, even if to them they are indeed 'right', that is, their adherents, in theory, should stop searching for the truth.[90]

Relating to the *Charlie Hebdo* tragedy, the popular statement attributed to Voltaire was quoted very frequently: 'I disapprove of what you say, but I will defend to the death your right to say it'.[91] Should this really be the 'golden rule' of freedom of speech? For present day legal systems, the invention of Evelyn B Hall is likely to be impossible to interpret because, when judging the necessity for the restriction of freedom of speech, the criterion to be analysed is not the permissibility or unacceptability of the consequences necessitating restriction derived from 'disapproval', but the so-called 'harm principle' of Mill, on the basis of which the necessary

88 Holmes J in *Gitlow v New York* 268 US 652 (1925), dissenting opinion.

89 Harold J Laski, 'Freedom of the Mind' in Harold J Laski, *Liberty in the Modern State* (Harper 1930) 93.

90 Mill (n 54) 51–54.

91 Voltaire never said this; this popular quotation comes from a book published in 1906 about him and his friends. The original source of the quotation is Evelyn B Hall (writing under the pseudonym of SG Tallentyre), *The Friends of Voltaire* (Smith/Elder 1906), 198–9.

restriction of freedom of speech starts when the disclosure of an opinion injures others.[92]

Should protection be granted to intentionally insulting or offensive speech, intentional provocation or defamatory acts which do not participate or do not wish to participate substantially in public debate? It is worth noting that neither threat, incitement, instigation, the incitement to hatred, nor the permissibility of restricting any of these can be derived from the general principles of freedom of speech, or more specifically, from the harm-principle. According to the frequently cited rule of *Handyside v the United Kingdom*, the shocking, offending, disturbing character of the speech itself does not provide grounds for restricting freedom of speech.[93] From this, it can be concluded that opinions which offend or upset the believers of a religion cannot be restricted.

Two objections can be raised to this axiomatic principle. First, sources equivalent to the judgment (other judgments of the ECtHR, e.g., *Otto-Preminger-Institut* and successive decisions in similar cases) clearly and unambiguously reject the notion that offensive speech is protected in general—because such judgments protect the rights of believers to be unaffected by harm generated by offensive opinions—no matter how much we are inclined to draw this conclusion from this part of the statement of reasons in *Handyside*. Neither *Handyside*, nor *Otto-Preminger* are higher-level sources of law than the other. Beyond blasphemy, the restriction of offences is also allowed in other areas important for freedom of speech, such as defamation law[94] and various restrictions on hate speech.[95]

92 Frederick Schauer, 'On the Relation between Chapters One and Two of John Stuart Mill's On Liberty', (2011) *Capital University Law Review* 571.

93 *Handyside* (n 20).

94 *Lingens v Austria*, App no 12/1984/84/131, judgment of 24 June 1986; *Oberschlick v Austria (No 1)*, App no 11662/85, judgment of 23 May 1991; *Castells v Spain*, App no 11798/85, judgment of 23 April 1992.

95 *Jersild v Denmark*, App no 15890/89, judgment of 23 September 1994; *Incal v Turkey*, App no 22678/93, judgment of 9 June 1998; *Karataş v Turkey*, App no 23168/94, judgment of 8 July 1999; *Vejdeland and Others v Sweden*, App no 1813/07, judgment of 9 February 2012.

Second, *Handyside* itself partly contradicts the aforementioned axiom because, in this case, the ECtHR ultimately ruled against the offensive content (more precisely, it gave no protection to it according to the 'margin of appreciation' principle).[96]

According to some arguments, *Charlie Hebdo* ridiculed only bigoted religious fanatics, therefore it is absolutely meaningless to refer to the violation of the religious sensitivities of 'Muslims', 'Jews' or 'Christians' (i.e., attacking fundamentalists may simply bring about collateral damage, in the present case, it is the sensitivity of 'non-fundamentalist' believers). However, the question arises whether it is possible to differentiate between the 'targets' of the offence by attacking the founders and heroes of the religion, who are held in high esteem by extreme 'fundamentalists' and fair and moderate religious believers alike. Is it realistic to expect everybody to understand the offensive opinion properly and not to be offended by it?

According to another argument, which appeared after the *Charlie Hebdo* killings, keeping a distance from offensive opinions is the appropriate response to the offence and a suitable means of avoiding it. In more simple terms, 'if you do not read it, you will not be disturbed or offended'. However, the power of this argument can be contested—in the world of online communication, offences cannot really be avoided, and sooner or later one will learn about the defamatory statement, except if one completely cuts oneself off from the external world. It is not possible to turn a fully blind eye to

96 The publisher of a book for children had a lawsuit brought against him in the UK because the book violated the Obscene Publications Act of 1959. The available copies of the *Little Red Schoolbook* were confiscated by English authorities. In chapters discussing certain issues of pornography, abortion, homosexuality, obscene expressions were also found; in addition, the book did not consider the consumption of hashish as unlawful, the same applied to sexual intercourse with girls younger than 16 years of age, which forms of conduct were otherwise prohibited by English law. It discussed sexual activities pursued with animals without condemning it, it was capable of worsening the relationship between teachers and students, and considered the self-fulfilment of children as a supreme value (that is, beyond the law).

offensive online content, the possibility of which was the classical argument to support the differences concerning the regulation of television, radio and press (in the case of the latter, the readers themselves choose what to read or what to look at, whereas the viewer may unintentionally or against their will encounter content offensive to them or to their under-age children).[97]

We learn about offensive content in the form of detailed descriptions and copies, even if we explicitly and deliberately want to avoid it. Printed press is immediately scanned or photographed and then digitally distributed, so that it takes only a click on the smart gadgets in our pockets to learn about them, even if we refrain from browsing through an actual printed product at the newsstand. We could say that those who have the courage to go out to the free world, have an internet connection and access to new information and communications technology, and do not hesitate to use them, should bear the possibility or risk of personal offences. According to Török, the possible and proportionate solution is to ensure the avoidance of blasphemous opinions through legislation, that is, the prescription of an opportunity for believers not to have to face these offensive opinions.

> [N]o person can reasonably expect to live their life and not to know that his or her religion is being subject to derogatory expressions somewhere. At this point, it becomes justifiable to design a regulatory scheme that allows religious persons to avoid such opinions and expressions if they wish. In most cases, such regulations would not take the form of prohibition or content-related restriction but rather as formal requirements applying to the form and means of exercising freedom of expression in various means of mass communication.[98]

It is unquestionable, however, that believers do not have the right to be spared the mere information that somebody somewhere offended and harmed their religion. While not disputing the success of this approach in establishing a balance between the protection

97 Eric Barendt, *Broadcasting Law. A Comparative Study* (Clarendon 2nd edn 1995).

98 Török (n 86) 529.

of religious feelings and freedom of speech, which balance is coherent with the general principles of freedom of speech and has a reasonable and theoretical basis, I do not find it feasible in practice for the above-mentioned reasons, that it does not grant a chance to hide. In the age of internet, the avoidance of harm or offence is close to impossible because a blasphemous opinion published widely will be available from an indefinite number of sources; simply by not buying a printed magazine, the information contained in the magazine will not be 'avoided'. The other counterargument is that if believers avoid offensive content, ultimately they will also make open public debates difficult because the dispute will not take place, either. It is true—as counterargument to that counterargument—that this is still better than a complete prohibition, which makes the publication or disclosure of the opinion itself impossible, and it is also true that believers, depending on their individual sensitivities, might opt for avoidance, that is, there can always remain some believers who opt for participation in the public debate instead.

The question of restricting blasphemy is not only complicated because it is difficult to define the exact right and lawful interest offended by blasphemous opinions. If we were to accept that freedom of speech may be restricted to avoid offending religious feelings, we would encounter the problem of the impossibility of generally defining the standard or measure of degree of this offence, because religion is so close to the innermost core of an individual personality. Religion can be such a powerful element in shaping an individual's personality, and the approaches of believers to religion might be so varied and diverse that it is extremely difficult to establish a broadly acceptable, general legal standard concerning the protection of religious feelings (as opposed to the protection of reputation or privacy for example, where, except for certain erratic, easily offended politicians or celebrities, a more or less general standard can be established and in theory approved by legal subjects).

It means that a very powerful argument against recognising the protection of religious sensitivity as grounds for restricting freedom of speech is formed, as the general standard of restriction cannot be established on the basis of religious sensitivity, neither with respect to the believers of a single religion, who think along different lines on this question, and certainly not when it comes to the believers of differing religions for whom even the point of departure might be different when discussing offences. As Sajó puts it:

> If the government sides with religious sensitivities ... in the name of religious sensitivity even those believers who in terms of religion are less sensitive, or express their sensitivities in a different way, will be restricted. The new balance gives preference to those religions (and groups of believers), who are "more emotional".[99]

According to Sajó, religious sensitivity is mostly 'construed by society', that is, the outrage about offensive opinions is artificially generated by those who are interested to do that (e.g., with regard to the Danish cartoons, riots broke out long months after the original publication of the drawings).[100]

Is it possible at all to take a general, broadly acceptable stand on the issue of the permissibility of blasphemy as a necessary accompaniment/by-product of legal regulation? Is it not the case that individual sensitivity, frequently experienced and sometimes exploding in various and possibly violent acts, or the heated arguments protecting the secular state, is the living proof that religious conviction is 'different' and that it differs from other convictions? That is, we respect religions differently and we hate or criticise them differently—maybe more intensely? The Christian believer generally does not murder journalists, but other than that, the spiritual injury they may suffer due to blasphemy might be significant. The legal question related to freedom of speech must not be answered differently depending on whether the person asking the question holds a Kalashnikov in their hands or not, that is, when it is not the different sensitivity of followers of different religions that decides the question of restricting the freedom of speech (but the existence or non-existence of a violent minority amongst the believers, and ultimately the intensity of their readiness to use instruments of terrorism).

In attempting to analyse options for restricting freedom of speech due to the protection of religious sensitivity, we come to

99 Sajó (n 50) 349.
100 *Ibid*, 351.

the conclusion that should we want to protect democratic public debate on public affairs, we can in no way limit the content of the blasphemous opinion in general. At most, we can consider the manner of expressing the opinion as something to be subjected to restriction. Even Robert Post, who powerfully protects the freedom of public debate, concludes that in a democracy, there may be certain prescriptions on norms of civility, on the basis of which (using the terminology of the ECtHR) the 'gratuitously offensive' defamation of religion can be restricted, though he adds that in the US, such a prescription restricting public debate cannot exist due to the First Amendment.[101]

> The question is how the law should distinguish between styles of speech that are intrinsically offensive and styles of speech that are inherently protected. If freedom of speech is to serve its function of democratic legitimation, any such distinction must be drawn in such a way as to minimize damage to public debate. This suggests that the distinction cannot be drawn simply on the basis of the beliefs of discrete religious groups.[102]

This was the most essential point of the judgment in *Otto-Preminger*, and its consequences—an unwarrantedly offensive, insulting opinion which contributes in no way to public debate can be restricted.[103] 'Gratuitous offence' as an element in the statement of facts providing grounds for the restriction of freedom of speech is not alien to other areas of freedom of speech. There are parallels in defamation law, for example. However, beyond the protection of individual rights, freedom of speech might be restricted on the basis of the form, manner and tone of the opinion.

Restricting Holocaust denial is another question related to freedom of speech law, which is maybe closer to blasphemy than

101 Post (n 59) 345–6.

102 *Ibid* (footnote omitted).

103 Robert A Kahn, 'A Margin of Appreciation for Muslims? Viewing the Defamation of Religions Debate through *Otto-Preminger-Institut v Austria*', (2011) 5 *Charleston Law Review* 401, 435–40.

one would think. The prohibition of the denial of the Holocaust also handles a specific sensitivity, and the restriction on freedom of speech is more stringent because it completely and categorically prohibits the expression of certain opinions, irrespective of their style, tone and terminology. Restricting Holocaust denial has become a generally, broadly accepted rule in Europe[104] (even at the level of the European Union, a legal norm was adopted, on the basis of which Member States are more or less obliged to introduce the prohibition in their own legal systems—granting a certain degree of leeway which ostensibly derived from the constitutional norms of freedom of speech).[105]

In spite of this, the basis of the restriction is uncertain in terms of constitutional law, and its compatibility with the general principles of the protection of freedom of speech is questionable. Sanctioning handpicks certain tragedies from the context of history, and treats them as a special state of facts in the context of opinions relating thereto. Although in most countries the legislation does not explicitly name the Holocaust, the so-called 'denial laws' were obviously adopted in the protection thereof in the first place. However, from a free speech perspective, this is not easy to substantiate properly. The late German professor Winfried Brugger had the following to say about it:

> [I]n other cases related to the freedom of opinion, the Constitutional Court generally cautions the lower courts to interpret expressions in as free-speech-friendly way as possible. As regards the Holocaust this tendency is not visible. [...] Perhaps sincerity would be advisable ... or at least to admit that there is one doctrine of freedom of speech for 'normal' cases and another for 'exceptional' cases.[106]

104 András Koltay, *Freedom of Speech: The Unreachable Mirage* (Wolters Kluwer 2013) 151–68.

105 Framework decision on Racism and Xenophobia 2008/913/JHA. See John C Knechtle, 'Holocaust Denial and the Concept of Dignity in the European Union', (2008) 36 *Florida State University Law Review* 41; JHH Weiler, *The Law of Holocaust Denial in Europe: Towards a (Qualified) EU-Wide Criminal Prohibition*. The Jean Monnet Working Paper Series (NYU School of Law 2009).

106 Winfried Brugger & Gábor Halmai, '"A német a méltóság, az amerikai a szabadság alkotmánya": Winfried Bruggerrel, a Heidelbergi Egyetem professzorával Halmai Gábor beszélget', (2008) 2 *Fundamentum* 23.

As regards the prohibition of Holocaust denial, an issue has to be raised: What is it that justifies the restriction of freedom of speech? What is damaged by Holocaust denial? The right of the dead to be remembered respectfully? The human dignity and honour of those who are alive? Their personal safety, which might be threatened by violent acts motivated by incitement to hatred? Public interest? Democratic debate?

The German Constitutional Court, when it declared a similar restriction on freedom of speech in Germany as constitutional, founded its decision on the damage done to human dignity (with respect to the dignity of all persons of Jewish ethnic origin).[107]

The ECtHR has delivered several judgments in cases of applicants prosecuted for Holocaust denial, but these are less significant from the perspective of the restriction of blasphemy as a perceived analogy. In these cases, the ECtHR rejected the applications without discussing them, and by doing so confirms the fact that statements denying the Holocaust do not benefit from the protection of freedom of speech, and therefore the question of the adequacy or proportionality of the degree of restriction does not arise.[108]

On a theoretical basis, is the prohibition of Holocaust denial analogous with the restriction of blasphemy? According to Lawrence Douglas, the primary objective of sanctioning Holocaust denial is not to protect survivors' rights and feelings, but to protect

107 90 BVerfGE 241, 13 April 1994.

108 Prosecuting perpetrators pursuant to legal provisions on the prohibition of Holocaust denial was not considered by the ECtHR as the violation of freedom of speech. In *Witzsch v Germany*, (App no 41448/98, admissibility decision of 20 April 1999) the Court considered the application inadmissible because the opinion of the applicant was excluded from the protection of freedom of speech by art 17 of the ECHR (prohibition of abuse of rights). This position of the Court was confirmed by another decision, in which the application of the complainant prosecuted for Holocaust denial was again considered by the court as inadmissible (*Garaudy v France*, App no 65831/01, admissibility decision of 24 June 2003). In *Lehideaux and Isorni v France*, App no 55/1997/839/1045, judgment of 23 September 1998, it became obvious that the Court excludes only the denial of the facts of the Holocaust from the protection of freedom of speech; other historical facts do not benefit from this preferential treatment.

the facts of the Holocaust (keeping it in the collective memory) from collective oblivion.[109] The prohibition of Holocaust denial is not for a definite period of time, this act will be punishable even when none of those concerned is alive any longer and there is no sign indicating the risk of the Holocaust being repeated. Knowing that the Holocaust is one of the most substantially documented events of the recent past, why is it necessary to provide protection by law of its memories? In addition to sanctioning, an argument to consider might be the unlikely terrors of the Holocaust; its tragedy, which is nearly incomprehensible for the human mind, the understanding, perception and plausibility of the irrational human viciousness leading to these events is possible only with difficulty or ultimately impossible for the new generations brought up in peace.

According to Cox, the arguments supporting the prohibition of Holocaust denial are similar to arguments wishing to restrict the defamation of religions. He argues that the prohibition of Holocaust denial is a prohibition protecting the community (society at large, that is, not only the Jewish community), introduced in order to promote the interests of the community rather than to protect individual rights. Expressions denying the Holocaust are morally unacceptable at the level of society, and this is what is ultimately reflected in penal codes.[110] Cox argues

109 Lawrence R Douglas, 'Policing the Past: Holocaust Denial and the Law' in Robert Post (ed), *Censorship and Silencing: Practices of Cultural Regulation* (Getty Research Institute 1998) 69–71.

110 This means that the standards of general hate speech laws can be lowered in the case of holocaust denial. According to the argument of the Grand Chamber of the ECtHR in the *Perinçek* case, the denial of the holocaust can be punishable without the fulfilling the 'incitement' or 'stirring up' element, based on its generally racist and anti-Semitic nature: 'For the Court, the justification for making its [the holocaust's] denial a criminal offence lies not so much in that it is a clearly established historical fact but in that, in view of the historical context in the States concerned, ... its denial, even if dressed up as impartial historical research, must invariably be seen as connoting an antidemocratic ideology and anti-Semitism'. According to the Grand Chamber, the denial of the Armenian genocide generally (on a European level) does not have this effect. *Perinçek v Switzerland*, App no 27510/08, judgment of 15 October 2015 [GC].

that the legal recognition of specific sensitivities and the restrictions of immoral opinions which do not contribute to public debate make the restriction of Holocaust denial similar to restrictions on blasphemy.[111] The same principles which underpin the restriction of blasphemy are used to ground other, generally accepted speech restrictions in Western states. This means that it is acceptable in Europe to restrict speech which is profoundly offensive or immoral, such as holocaust denial or racist speech. But the reach of these principles are somehow limited, and they are rarely applied to underpin the restriction on blasphemy.[112]

But, if we want to envisage the right to free expression in a coherent framework, then the situation is as follows. If we take the sanctioning of Holocaust denial to be an acceptable restriction of freedom of speech, three possible, mutually exclusive conclusions may be drawn on the restriction of blasphemy, presuming that we wish to preserve the integrity and internal coherence of the complex structure of freedom of speech.

(1) We declare that the prohibition of the Holocaust denial does not serve the protection of the sensitivity and human dignity of survivors, the living members of social groups persecuted during World War II or the protection of the right to pay respect to the memories of victims, but it serves the purpose of keeping the event alive in collective memory in a form recognised by canonised history (this is the position of Douglas mentioned above). By declaring this, the analogy with the restriction on blasphemy or the protection of religious feelings no longer holds; the two types of restriction have nothing to do with one another because of the differences in the aim of the two types of restriction.

(2) We accept the unique nature of the Holocaust as a historical event and grave tragedy giving reason for specific sensitivities, and say that the prohibition of Holocaust denial is a rather strong, but at the same time, sole exception to the principle which says 'freedom

111 Cox (n 74) 751–5.

112 Neville Cox, 'Pourquoi Suis-Je Charlie? Blasphemy, Defamation of Religion, and the Nature of "Offensive" Cartoons', (2015) *Oxford Journal of Law and Religion*, 1; Neville Cox, 'The Freedom to Publish "Irreligious" Cartoons', (2016) *Human Rights Law Review*, 1.

of speech shall not be restricted on the grounds of the sensitivities and injuries of the members of a group against offensive and defamatory opinions targeted at some social group'. In this case, again, no conclusion can be drawn from the Holocaust denial ban regarding the prohibition of blasphemy.

(3) We say that the prohibition of Holocaust denial is a restriction whose preconditions, being present together (special sensitivity, the lack of participation in public debate of the opinions thereby restricted), in theory, and under certain circumstances, might be suitable for restricting other types of speech, including the prohibition of blasphemous opinions.

4.5.4. Protection from Hateful and Racist Speech

The examination of the general restriction of hate speech can serve as an aspect to consider in two ways when assessing the restriction of blasphemy: Hate speech *vis-à-vis* the adherents of religions is prohibited, but at the same time, it is also a barrier to expressing opinions based on religion (freedom of speech of believers). The question is what we should consider as 'hate speech'. Can we consider only the instigation or incitement to hatred against communities as hate speech? Or does defamation of groups and communities, which is an undoubtedly lighter offence, qualify as hate speech? The approaches taken by European legal systems also differ in this regard, and the ECtHR has yet to define a single direction to be followed in this matter, for reasons of respect for the principle of the margin of appreciation.

Regarding religion-based hate speech, the most frequent point of departure is that if somebody attacks the religion itself and not the religious community (i.e., the believers of the religion) then hate speech is not committed. The person of Jesus Christ or Muhammad cannot be subjected to protection; however, the expression of hatred for their followers can be restricted.[113] The question is whether this is a well-founded criterion and whether attacking the religion, the founders of the religion or the objects of religious veneration will not

113 Jeremy Waldron, *The Harm in Hate Speech* (Harvard University Press 2012) 123–4.

(or cannot) bring about offence to believers as well. Can the expression of hatred against Muhammad and the verbal injury of the historical personality be capable of inciting hatred against Muslim believers? If so, committing the act of hate speech, and its possible subsequent restriction, already arises as a possibility, but what cannot be judged with full objectivity is the point at which an opinion becomes 'capable' of inciting to hatred, when the balance 'tilts' and the opinion falls into the category of 'possible to restrict' or the point where it remains a powerful, offensive, and yet protected opinion.

According to Jeremy Waldron, 'offence' is not an adequate ground for restricting freedom of speech, but the protection of dignity is.[114] His main argument in favour of the restriction of hate speech is that hate speech violates the right to human dignity. Whereas an 'offence' is necessarily subjective, dignity (similarly to the protection of reputation) affects the individual's social position and their recognition as being equal. His argument rejects the approach (which I did not entirely dismiss in the preceding part) in which religious sensitivities and the feeling of being insulted might serve as grounds for restricting freedom of speech. Waldron would provide respect only 'to citizens, not to convictions' by restricting freedom of speech.[115]

The analogy with political criticism referred to by Waldron (according to which a strong and harsh attack on the objectives and positions of the Tea Party, the American Conservative political movement should not be judged the same way as attacks on the actual people participating in the movement) is not exactly accurate in the context of blasphemy, because political conviction is not necessarily to be provided the same degree of protection as religious conviction, if we assume that one's political conviction is less likely to be the main feature determining a human personality. From the individuals' point of view, the criticism of political groupings does not affect those belonging to the group as much as the criticism of a religion or church might insult even the weakest follower of the given religion, who has no self-assertive abilities at all, and who otherwise does not wish to participate in public life or in public debates, in contrast with a party and its followers who conceptually *cannot* stay out of these. Previously, we argued in favour of the statement that the

114 *Ibid*, 105–43.
115 *Ibid*, 120–3.

freedom of religion necessarily implies the right to appear in public; we still maintain this with the proviso that this does not lead to the recognition of the obligation for a religious person to appear in public, but at the same time, an insult to his/her religion might offend even a more reserved individual.

Ronald Dworkin also took a stand opposing Waldron, but from the opposite direction, that is, he even rejected the restrictions on the freedom of speech accepted by Waldron. According to Dworkin, the recognition of freedom of speech also forms part of human dignity and the right of freedom of expression is granted to human beings because, in a fair political regime, the state should treat every grown-up citizen as a 'responsible moral being'.[116] If we deprive somebody of the opportunity to participate in the public discourse with equal chances, and thereby influence the joint decision-making process, by doing so, we claim that the human dignity of this individual is not identical to that of the others, and we belittle the representatives of certain opinions. On this basis, the restriction of hate speech is not allowed. All this means that the argument in favour of protecting human dignity might serve to draw two completely opposite conclusions. In fact, Waldron finds this natural, given the obscure lines of the legal category of human dignity. He asserts that societies have to decide on a case-by-case basis whose right to dignity they may give preference to.[117]

If, as a result of the difficulties discussed above, we have to exclude from the broad category of 'hate speech' defamatory statements targeted at communities and which might insult the religious feelings and sensitivities of the members of a religious community, we will be left with a narrower category of hate speech containing a) intent to stir up, b) incitement to or c) instigation of hatred only.[118] Even if we accept

116 Dworkin (n 57), 199–202, and Ronald Dworkin: *Taking Rights Seriously* (Harvard University Press 1977) 266–78, 364–8.

117 Waldron (n 113) 139–41.

118 Legislation in Europe against free speech usually use these terms, see for example Directive 2010/13/EU of the European Parliament and of the Council of 10 March 2010 on the coordination of certain provisions laid down by law, regulation or administrative action in Member States concerning the provision of audiovisual media services (AVMS Directive), art 6, or the Public Order Act 1986, s 18 in the UK.

that this narrower hate speech category might serve as a legitimate barrier to freedom of speech, as is the case in more or less every European legal system,[119] we will encounter the problem of the impossibility of defining when the offence/defamation becomes incitement to or instigation of hatred. As long as we approach the question of restricting freedom of speech from the direction of religious believers' feelings, it is reasonable to assert that insulting individual feelings cannot serve as the basis for restricting somebody else's freedom.

However, in more serious cases of hate speech, not only an emotional shock but also the violation of individual rights arises. Incitement to hatred is not (or is not primarily) punished because that opinion insults the members of the community which has been attacked, but because it endangers the exercise of their rights, whether that be the right to life, physical integrity, freedom from discrimination or the right to human dignity. At this point, when assessing the restriction, it is not only the content of the opinion that counts but also the impact generated by the speech.[120] That is, there might be blasphemous opinions which for many, even for the majority, are 'only' insulting or offensive, but, if as a result of these opinions, a realistic danger of offending the members of the attacked community arises, the opinion may become immediately subject to restriction. Indeed, due to the similar nature of rules, this might hold true in any Member State of the European Union, and it is considered as a kind of common European minimum standard of restricting hate speech.[121]

How shall we consider, for example, the drawings of *Charlie Hebdo*? Can we not find it justified to think that those cartoons

119 See *Blasphemy, insult and hatred: finding answers in a democratic society* (Council of Europe 2010), http://www.venice.coe.int/webforms/documents/?pdf=CDL-STD(2010)047-e.

120 *Güzel v Turkey (No 1)*, App no. 54479/00, judgment of 4 April 2006, *Erbakan v Turkey*, App no 59405/00, judgment of 6 July 2006, para 68.

121 The legal basis for this standard in the EU is the Framework decision on Racism and Xenophobia 2008/913/JHA, which requires from the Member States to ban incitement to violence or hatred, Article1 (1)a).

incited to hatred against certain religious communities? If we base the necessity for restricting freedom of speech on the possible consequences generated by a communication, which is a very frequent approach in legal systems, then it is easy to think that the *Charlie Hebdo* drawings were considered not only insulting or defamatory but also inciting hatred. This is not because ultimately the followers of one religion targeted by the drawings struck back, but because, due to the drawings, hatred might have evolved even in the members of the majority against the followers of Islam, which may thus have had an impact on speech generating, confirming and supporting such hatred in a way accepted broadly by legal systems, and which makes it liable to restriction. According to common belief, those drawings 'only' defamed and insulted the religions they lampooned, and thereby their followers. Yet it is possible to imagine a situation, and this is not especially difficult in European countries coping with the integration of ethnic minorities, wherein the drawings might have provoked the hatred of (some members of) the majority society. But to judge the degree of hatred that necessitates the restriction of freedom of speech is the task of individual legal systems.

4.5.5. Protection of the Public Order and Public Peace

Török concludes that the risk of violating public order arose in none of the cases deliberated by the ECtHR, not even if the statements of reasons of the judgments make significant references to it.[122] That is, it is not very likely that Tyrolean Catholics would have attacked the screening by the Otto-Preminger-Institut *en masse*, nor is it likely regarding the British Christians that the film on St Theresa (*Wingrove*), if marketed, would have led to street riots. Although one might tend to agree with Török on this, this does not mean, and neither does he claim it, that in theory blasphemy would not or could not endanger public order.

After the *Charlie Hebdo* drawings there would have been a stronger chance of a situation endangering public order (let us not forget about the fact that even turning a waste bin upside down or publicly

122 Török (n 86) 518–19.

slapping somebody in the face may breach the public order, and even less is sufficient to endanger it). In the tense situation after the *Charlie Hebdo* attack, it is easy to imagine a situation wherein Muslims living in France or communities hostile to them endangered *ordre public*. In the future, a repeat occurrence of such tense situations in Europe is not at all unlikely. It is sufficient for a demonstration to get out of hand, and new blasphemous cartoons to be published at an unfortunate moment. In such a situation, basically different from situations analysed by the ECtHR, what would be the response to the question of whether the risk of endangering public order is a sufficient reason for restricting freedom of speech?

At the same time, if we take the impact of the opinion expressed as the point of departure, as the consideration which provides grounds for a restriction, and assert that opinions potentially triggering violent acts can be restricted in order to prevent the risk of disturbing public order and, beyond that, endangering individual rights (since the protection of public order does not mean the protection of waste bins from being turned upside down, but the protection of individuals wishing to benefit from public order and so, if public order is exposed to a grave danger, the rights of the individual—their dignity, physical integrity, and safety—will also be at risk), then finally we will arrive at a point where the specific sensitivity of the followers of the given religion might determine the degree of restriction. If some of the radicalised Muslims are willing to pick up a Kalashnikov because of a caricature while many others peacefully tolerate it, then, irrespective of this, the degree of the restriction should be adjusted to the former in order to protect public order. We are sure that this is not acceptable as such, at least at the level of principles relating to freedom of speech; at the same time, it is also clear that the protection of public order might provide grounds for various restrictions of liberties.

4.6. Free Expression and Ethical Standards

'Freedom of speech is not a license to be stupid', reads the motto on a fridge magnet I bought in Washington DC in Newseum, an impressive museum of journalism. Is it true? If we grant the right to freedom of speech, is it possible to demand that it be used in a morally appropriate manner? Or does freedom of speech belong to everybody, including idiots, those full of hatred and the blasphemous? Also, is it exercised independently from morality? The ideal of ethical freedom of speech would expect mutual tolerance from the holder of the right, it would expect self-restriction and, from the one offended, it would expect rising above the offence. This would be nice, but what if it does not work in practice?

Dworkin was an adamant promoter of freedom of speech and enemy even of those laws restricting hate speech, but this is what he said concerning the Danish cartoons:

> The British and most of the American press have been right, on balance, not to republish the Danish cartoons that millions of furious Muslims protested against in violent and terrible destruction around the world. Reprinting would very likely have meant—and could still mean—more people killed and more property destroyed. It would have caused many British and American Muslims great pain because they would have been told by other Muslims that the publication was intended to show contempt for their religion, and though that perception would in most cases have been inaccurate and unjustified, the pain would nevertheless have been genuine.[123]

Kahn takes a similar standpoint in his articles, analysing the American legal approach to extreme, inciting, incendiary speech from a historical perspective. As he puts it, there is a difference between the coverage of the protection under the First Amendment and the responsibility of a newspaper.[124]

The decisive majority of American and British papers refused to publish the Danish cartoons in 2005–06, and likewise the drawings of *Charlie Hebdo* in 2015, and due to this alleged 'cowardice', sharp criticism was targeted at the American press and European

123 Ronald Dworkin, 'The Right to Ridicule', *New York Review of Books*, 23 March 2006.

124 Kahn (n 46) 163.

press taking a similar approach.[125] For the editors, it was not self-censorship but an editorial decision. The argument in support of this was sometimes the safety of the staff working for the papers, but in most cases, they explained this attitude as wanting to avoid offending religious communities.[126] Many are of the opinion that not publishing the drawings is a cowardly and unethical decision (according to this, there is a moral obligation to express an opinion in such a situation), which would not have expressed agreement with the content of the opinion but solidarity with the staff of the magazine.[127] The debate, in this case, is no longer about the permissibility of blasphemy.

According to Kahn, in the American legal culture, the publishers of extreme opinions are not the 'heroes' of freedom of speech but its by-products to be tolerated. Justice Holmes did not write a dissenting opinion in *Abrams v US*[128] because he celebrated the Communist distributing flyers in 1919, but because 'the puny anonymities' do not pose any danger to society.[129] If we apply a somewhat artificial analogy, the only reason that the caricaturists of *Charlie Hebdo* might deserve an increased respect is their unwillingness to give up their freedom of speech, even in the shadow of a deadly threat, but this does not make their opinion, which gravely offended several religious communities, worthy of celebration.

In contrast, according to Flemming Rose, who was the first to publish the Danish cartoons, it is no less than a moral obligation to combat Islam, that is, the responsibility is just the opposite and makes it a necessity to publish cartoons offending this community.[130]

125 'Publishing Muhammad cartoons would have been too risky, says Amol Rajan' *The Guardian*, 8 January, 2015, 'Who Did—and Didn't—Publish the Charlie Hebdo Cover Image', *The Daily Beast*, 14 January 2015.

126 Margaret Sullivan, 'A Close Call on Publication of Charlie Hebdo Cartoons', *New York Times*, opinion pages, 8 January 2015.

127 '*Charlie Hebdo* Cartoons: Press Strives to Balance Freedom and Responsibility', *The Guardian*, 11 January 2015.

128 *Abrams v US* 250 US 616 (1919).

129 Kahn (n 71) 275. See *Abrams v United States* 250 US 616 (1919) 629.

130 *Ibid*, 270–9.

The insult of religious feelings is the price Muslims have to accept and pay in return for being accepted into European societies.[131] This idea is very far from the concept of 'responsible freedom of speech'.

US President Barack Obama shared the latter view, which he expressed at the UN General Assembly in his speech after the terrorist attacks committed after the Muhammad video was published on YouTube:

> That is what we saw play out in the last two weeks, as a crude and disgusting video sparked outrage throughout the Muslim world. Now, I have made it clear that the US government had nothing to do with this video, and I believe its message must be rejected by all who respect our common humanity. It is an insult not only to Muslims, but to America as well—for as the city outside these walls makes clear, we are a country that has welcomed people of every race and every faith. We are home to Muslims who worship across our country. We not only respect the freedom of religion, we have laws that protect individuals from being harmed because of how they look or what they believe. We understand why people take offence to this video because millions of our citizens are among them. I know there are some who ask why we don't just ban such a video. And the answer is enshrined in our laws: Our Constitution protects the right to practice free speech.[132]

The position of the White House was also confirmed by the Press Secretary in a statement in 2012 which underlined the responsibility of the media:

> Well, we are aware that a French magazine published cartoons featuring a figure resembling the Prophet Muhammad, and obviously, we have questions about the judgement of publishing something like this. We know that these images will be deeply

131 Kahn (n 46) 165.

132 Remarks by the President to the UN General Assembly, 25 September 2012, www.whitehouse.gov/the-press-office/2012/09/25/remarks-president-un-general-assembly.

> offensive to many and have the potential to be inflammatory. But we've spoken repeatedly about the importance of upholding the freedom of expression that is enshrined in our Constitution. In other words, we don't question the right of something like this to be published; we just question the judgement behind the decision to publish it.[133]

The publicist of *Time* magazine expressed a view with a similar content but he formulated his ideas more unambiguously.

> Okay, so can we finally stop with the idiotic, divisive, and destructive efforts by 'majority sections' of Western nations to bait Muslim members with petulant, futile demonstrations that 'they' aren't going to tell 'us' what can and can't be done in free societies? Because not only are such Islamophobic antics futile and childish, but they also openly beg, for the very violent responses from extremists their authors claim to proudly defy in the name of common good.[134]

However, is it consistent to protect the right, but not to protect the practice, and even to condemn the editorial decision? Is it realistic that the judgement of the possibility of exercising one's right and the judgement of exercising it in actual practice are not necessarily interlinked but are separable? According to some positions 'one cannot defend the right without defending the practice'.[135] Meaning that if the legal system provides freedom of speech, including freedom of blasphemy, then it should come as no

133 Press Briefing by Press Secretary Jay Carney, 19 September 2012, www.whitehouse.gov/the-press-office/2012/09/19/press-briefing-press-secretary-jay-carney-91912.

134 Bruce Crumley, 'Firebombed French Paper Is No Free Speech Martyr', *Time*, 2 November 2011, http://world.time.com/2011/11/02/firebombed-french-paper-a-victim-of-islamistsor-its-own-obnoxious-islamophobia.

135 Jonathan Chait, '*Charlie Hebdo* and the Right to Commit Blasphemy', *Nymag.com*, 7 January 2015, http://nymag.com/daily/intelligencer/2015/01/charlie-hebdo-and-the-right-to-commit-blasphemy.html.

surprise to anybody that somebody exercises this liberty. Jonathan Chait thinks that legal prohibition and moral condemnation at the level of society will lead to a similar outcome, the failure to publish opinions. In other words, in addition to granting the right, the opportunity to exercise it should also be granted, and if somebody does exercise the right to blaspheme, then we must not condemn them for this.[136]

This approach surely does not mean that no attempts should be made to dissuade the holders of offensive and defamatory opinions from expressing them, or that it is not possible to discuss these issues with them, but that the presence of such opinions must be tolerated. This tolerance, if you like, means according some sort of fundamental, essential respect to the holder of any opinion which that person has contributed to public debate, and to the expression of which they have the right. After all, is it not a solemn, triumphal moment for somebody to exercise one of their fundamental rights, the right to freedom of speech and to express an opinion? By doing so, they attempt to participate in the debates of a community, no matter how asinine or narrow-minded it is. Returning to Chait, the question is whether there is a basic difference between legal prohibition and public naming and shaming alongside legal permission (granting the right)?

Of course, a similar question can be raised regarding the protection to be granted for religious people. As we have seen, ridiculing, offensive cartoons of Jesus Christ or the Prophet Muhammad do not prevent Christians and Muslims from exercising their rights to freedom of religion. But are we sure that this is so? We grant a right, but afterwards, even in an aggressive manner, can we attack the subject of the right (the belief held)? Does preventing somebody from exercising the right to freedom of religion mean setting a church on fire only and not more? Does granting the right not mean granting in practice tolerance, understanding and acceptance towards the one exercising this right? If there is a right to freedom of speech, is it accompanied by an obligation to tolerate differing opinions, which protects the one exercising the right to free speech and is imposed on others?

136 *Ibid.*

At the same time, we must not forget about the fact that an aggressive attack against one's opinion is also an opinion itself. In addition, it is expressed in an important issue of public interest, hence the presupposition is that it is covered by the protection of the freedom of speech. It is within the confines of freedom of speech to attack others' opinions (religious conviction or cultural war fought in the disguise of a religious conviction, or somebody's blasphemous opinion) in an aggressive and sometimes offensive and insulting manner, by expressing another opinion. However, there might be situations when the non-legal restriction of freedom of speech, or more exactly, the real opportunities to speak (naming and shaming in public, undermining one's professional reputation by otherwise legally protected opinions, etc.) might inflict more severe existential or psychological damage on someone than, let us say, a court decision at the end of a legal proceedings, which we traditionally consider as an undesirable restriction of freedom of speech. Is it the right approach not to pay respect to opinions which entered the competition in the marketplace of ideas?

Arriving at the conclusion via a different route, I would say that, for me, Chait's argumentation does seem acceptable. He argues that if we protect the right, we also should protect to some extent its practical enforcement, (the outcome of its implementation) i.e., it is not possible to allow the holders or publishers of opinions protected by law to be silenced by non-legal instruments. Ethics-based freedom of speech will remain an ethical norm urged by President Obama; it is not enforceable. Those who are unethical while exercising this right can be responded to in several ways. Some of these responses are prohibited by law; others are not. It is clearly prohibited, for example, to make a public demonstration impossible by making loud noises. However, it is not prohibited to attack in articles, essays and journalism what was said or voiced at the demonstration. Applying it to the area of blasphemous cartoons, hanging the drawings on the walls of a mosque would be prohibited, to disturb a religious meeting with them even more stringently prohibited, but it is not necessarily prohibited to publish them in magazines.

We can imagine certain borderline situations, which are very difficult to decide upon. Not reacting to those violating the requirement of ethical freedom of speech is surely not a good response, but neither is it desirable to have them silenced by the stronger forces of society. We are better off interpreting 'silencing' literally, and we prohibit this in situations where the prevention of the publication of a given opinion becomes a realistic danger. The words of President Obama were very far from this when he criticised those producing the YouTube video. He did not suggest banning the offending opinions from the public sphere (but of course, the words of the US President carry a different weight; criticism voiced by him, even if diplomatic, might sound like strong condemnation). It would be very difficult to provide a consistent definition, with respect to freedom of speech, of where the border of the mandatory minimum respect for different opinions, lifestyles and exercising liberties lies, if we wanted to handle this question legally; as such, it is more appropriate for this tolerance to remain a moral command instead of becoming a legal norm.

4.7. The Argument of the 'Slippery Slope'

According to the American constitutional doctrine of slippery slope, there might be certain barriers to liberties, which, even if declared constitutional because of their compliance with all necessary requirements of constitutionality, might cause serious damage because, after being adopted, they could be used as a basis for the introduction of new restrictions, and this is how freedom starts to slip further down the slope. Frederick Schauer offered the argumentation used in *Lynch v Donnelly* as an illustration: If we consider it constitutional and allow a small town to organise a Christmas fair on its own main square displaying Christian symbols, the next step will be to organise religious ceremonies in public places, then office holders of the local municipality will participate, and sooner or later we will reach the point where churches are being supported by state resources.[137] What is unique or specific is the fact that the principle of the slippery slope can also be used in a line of argument in the opposite direction: If we prohibit the organisation of a Christmas fair in the main square of the small town using religious

137 *Lynch v Donnelly* 465 US 668 (1984).

symbols because we wish to respect the ideological neutrality of the state, the next step might be to prohibit even mentioning religion in any state institution, to exclude the Bible from the literature curriculum, to take religious paintings off the walls of state-owned museums and finally, to withhold the protection of ecclesiastical buildings by the police and the fire brigade.[138]

Therefore, the danger persists that, in the event of accepting constitutionally permissible restrictions, it will not be possible to prevent further, anti-constitutional restrictions. This argumentation is used, for example, in disputes concerning the restriction of racist expressions, which are extremely broadly protected by American law, however, not primarily on the basis of their value or usefulness or the right of the individual to freedom of speech but on the basis of the fact that if we allow the restriction of such expressions on the basis of their content, sooner or later there will be restrictions on some genuinely important and valuable speech, or at least, on expressions which, unlike the intentionally defamatory ones, wish to actually participate in public debates.

There is no logical link between restrictions; the slippery slope does not assume the functioning of the domino principle, but it is rather based on the empirical experience that, once we allow somebody to do something, later they will have more and more new demands.[139] The same might apply to restrictions on freedom of speech adopted in order to protect religions. It is true that a Muslim terrorist is not likely to be satisfied with more moderate *Charlie Hebdo* cover pages. The logic of terrorism is that if we restrict freedom of speech 'a bit', it necessarily will be followed by new restrictions and finally, freedom of speech will be eliminated or it will suffer significant damage. This counterargument itself, however, does not seem to be an unmanageable risk because, in principle, it could be raised in every case of limiting some liberty, and, according to the European approach, among competing rights (at present, the protection of human dignity or religious

138 Frederick Schauer, 'Slippery Slopes', (1985) 99 *Harvard Law Review* 361, 381.

139 *Ibid*, 381–3.

feeling vs freedom of speech) there is no order of priority as such, but in disputed situations, there is pressure for a balancing act.

The doctrine of the slippery slope is clearly American; in Europe, the objective has always been to strike a balance between competing rights, and not to enforce the primacy of freedom of speech.[140] Regardless of this, as we have discussed earlier, the hurried restriction of liberties in response to terrorism would not seem to be a wise step but would instead encourage terrorism, even if it was acceptable from a constitutional point of view. The slippery slope can be reversed; it can also be used to argue against the broad spectrum of the freedom of speech with respect to blasphemy. It is worth noting that in Europe, on more than one occasion, people have been killed because of their origin, faith, religion and other personality traits. If we allow the defamation of religions (not only criticism of them but insult to the believers), will we eventually end up in a Communist dictatorship or the gas chambers in Auschwitz? This argument is intentionally cynical, but if we reject it, then the similar argument against the restriction of freedom of speech in the other direction (protection of religious communities) will also lose some of its power.

In theory, however, one can climb up the slippery slope whereby further strengthening of the protection of freedom of speech (which might seem desirable) might lead to surprising problems. Let us take the following point of departure now: *Charlie Hebdo*'s drawings are protected opinions. What would be the right decision in a case where somebody would like to go even further than those, and let us say, intentionally damages a cross/menorah installed in a public place, saying that by committing this act they express their negative opinion of religion, and at the same time, indicate that they are willing to reimburse/replace any damage, that is, those displaying the symbol do not suffer any material damage? Under any Western legal system, this must be a forbidden act, it is already a 'conduct' and not 'speech'.

140 On the different approaches to free speech protection in the US and in Europe, see generally: Eric Barendt, *Freedom of Speech* (Oxford University Press 2nd edn 2005).

But is it sufficient to establish 'nuisance' or 'vandalism' and violating public order to serve as the basis for restricting freedom of speech? That is, if we permit something (e.g., the defamation of religions), where do we draw the line to identify which acts we prohibit? It is clear that the argument behind our current prohibition (of misdemeanour) is to take measures, not against the content of the opinion but the manner of its expression. Even so, is it enough to base these prohibitions not on genuinely important interests (human dignity or the protection of communities) but on considerations relating to the protection of property or the maintenance of public order? The slippery slope as an intellectual exercise in the field of constitutional law can also be used in Europe, but it is not really possible to take it into account as an essential guiding principle of regulation.

5. Conclusions

The permanent, systematic insult of of any religion, or the systematic insult of the feelings of religious people before the broad public have not been typical in Europe so far. Militant secularism, which in Europe is typical primarily of the French (which, however, is not strong enough to make *Charlie Hebdo* read by the masses without a brutal advertisement, namely the massacre), disregards the multifaceted, diverse approaches to the restriction or permission of blasphemy existing in Europe. As we have seen, European legal systems settle this question in various ways. After analysing the European context, including experience from the jurisprudence of the ECtHR, we can draw the conclusion that there is no common uniform European response to blasphemy from the perspective of the freedom of speech law, neither at international, nor at state level. The legal protection of the adherents of religions is not in opposition to the European concept of freedom, as still quite a few European states kept their ancient or reformulated blasphemy laws. At the same time, the application of such provisions is usually very rare; these rules are in most cases, though not exclusively, fossilised provisions stemming from the past. However, this does not exclude the theoretical possibility that, in future, existing provisions will be applied more frequently, nor does it exclude *per se* the introduction of new provisions in countries where such provisions do not exist, even if it does not seem likely at this moment.

A question to be put prior to the decision on the restriction of blasphemy is how we can define religion in a statement of facts and/or if we are able to raise sufficiently strong arguments to justify religion deserving stronger protection than other convictions and personality traits. Regarding certain individual aspects of restriction, we can clearly declare that the protection of religions and churches against defamatory, offensive opinions cannot serve as grounds for restricting freedom of speech. Whether the protection of religious people, the adherents of religions, can provide grounds for the restriction of freedom of speech is already a more difficult issue. I would argue that, on the basis of European legal traditions and the 'general concept' of freedom of speech in Europe (a common minimum standard of freedom of speech, most eminently expressed through the case law of the ECtHR), it is not *per se* unthinkable in every single European state. It is a different question whether, from the perspective of the specific internal structure and traditions of freedom of speech in individual legal systems and the social problems of the state concerned, it is appropriate to introduce or maintain such a restriction.

If we take the protection of religious feelings not as an aspect of freedom of religion but as an aspect of human dignity, we can enlist stronger, more powerful arguments in favour of restricting freedom of speech, because religious conviction is strongly linked to human dignity. However, if we wish to protect the democratic public sphere and debate on public affairs, then in no event can we restrict in general the content of a blasphemous opinion; theoretically what we can do is to impose potential restrictions on the manner the opinion is expressed, at most.

Rules governing the restriction of hate speech are also applicable in order to protect members of religious communities. The question is what we consider to be hate speech: How do we define the statement of facts in relation to restriction? Do we consider only incitement against communities or incitement to hatred as hate speech, or can we consider group defamation, which generally causes less serious harm than incitement, as hate speech?

In decisions on the restriction of freedom of speech, we typically find maintaining public order to be a less legitimate interest. Nevertheless, if we start out from the impact of the opinion expressed, and say that opinions potentially triggering violent acts can be restricted in order to prevent the danger of harming public order and, in addition, to prevent the danger of violating individual rights then, in a tense social situation, this consideration might be given more attention.

But, as we realise that it would be extremely difficult to determine, with respect to freedom of speech, where the border of the mandatory minimum respect for different opinions, lifestyles and exercising liberties lies, perhaps we can accept that it would be more appropriate to propagate the idea of responsible free speech, and strengthening the ethical foundations of the public discourse in various ways.

Closing Remarks

The issues discussed in this book not only touch upon how to adjudicate various legal disputes but also on the past, present and future of shape of what is generally touted as 'Western civilisation', and the principles determining the coexistence of people in the countries concerned. According to Puppinck, the debate on crucifixes on the walls of Italian schools was focused on defining European identity.[1] On the other hand, Andreescu and Andreescu went so far as to project a new vision for Europe after the first *Lautsi* judgment,[2] with the removal of religious symbols from public institutions and the discontinuation of the state giving preference to churches. They would have replaced the values represented by churches with values that stabilised over the fifty years in which the European Convention on Human Rights has existed.[3] For the time being, the second *Lautsi* judgment[4] upset these calculations.

***

At the end of the book, important questions remain for further consideration. Firstly, what is the role of Christianity in Europe today? Joseph Weiler, in his book inspired by the debate surrounding the Recitals of the European Constitution, expresses his incomprehension of why Europe does not stand up for her own historical roots. According to Weiler, who is otherwise not a

1 Grégor Puppinck, 'An Alliance Against Secularism', *L'Osservatore Romano*, 28 July 2010.

2 *Lautsi v Italy*, App no 30814/06, judgment of 3 November 2009.

3 Andreescu, Gabriel & Andreescu, Liviu, 'The European Court of Human Rights' *Lautsi* Decision: Context, Contents, Consequences', (2010) 9(26) *Journal for the Study of Religions and Ideologies* 47, 66–67.

4 *Lautsi and Others v Italy*, App no 30814/06, judgment of 18 March 2011 [GC].

Christian, this is a symptom of a serious identity disorder.[5] Jürgen Habermas, who is not a Christian either, holds that equality, social solidarity, individual morality and the principles of human rights and democracy are rooted in Jewish religious ethics and the Christian ethics of love, and that there are no alternatives; this heritage is still the foundation of modern Europe. According to Habermas, anything else 'is only useless postmodern chat'.[6] Larry Siedentop, in his recent book on the Christian roots of human rights, comes to a similar conclusion.[7] In the course of the debate between Habermas and Joseph Ratzinger, later known as Pope Benedict XVI, a possible approach seemed to emerge, blending the set of values, their hierarchy and the foundations of Christianity with the Enlightenment, not clashing but supporting and supplementing one another.[8]

In any case, regarding the content of secularism and the religious neutrality of the state, a broad understanding and compromise are lacking. In actual fact, we cannot define the value system on which we base our modern European societies today. Given the above, the decision on crucifixes and religious education at schools is to be taken by each European state individually, as a result of the judgments of the European Court of Human Rights (hereinafter: ECtHR) applying the margin of appreciation principle. The states have their 'freedom of speech', but it is a different question whether the price to be paid for preserving religious symbols is their reinterpretation as cultural symbols. 'Cultural religiousness' (respecting religion without a genuine, strong belief, but with a personalised, lenient interpretation of the obligations imposed on the individual by religion) also has long-standing traditions on the continent, and it is not at all certain that it has no positive impacts, supplementary to those of genuine religiousness. Nonetheless,

5 JHH Weiler, *Un'Europa Cristiana: Un saggio esplorativo* (Milano, BUR Saggi, 2003).

6 Jürgen Habermas, *Time of Transitions* (Polity 2006) 150–1.

7 Larry Siedentop, *Inventing the Individual: The Origins of Western Liberalism* (Allen Lane 2014).

8 On the debate on this issue between Habermas and Pope Benedict XVI, see Jürgen Habermas & Joseph Ratzinger, *The Dialectics of Secularization: On Reason and Religion* (Ignatius 2005).

recognising the crucifix as a cultural symbol indicates a degree of confusion and does not bring us closer to a sincere debate on the question raised by the aforementioned decision of the state.

The second question: Is it possible to take a different legal approach to issues related to the right to freedom of religion and speech, depending on whether they are related to Christianity or Islam, and if so, why and to what extent? On the whole, both European states and the ECtHR are more permissive with Christian than with Islamic symbols, although it is true that no such difference exists when it comes to adjudicating blasphemy and hate speech. Regarding the limits on wearing headscarves, the ECtHR has always accepted the restrictions imposed, and in *Refah Partisi and Others v Turkey*,[9] the Court took a clear stance on the radical form of Islam, and declared that it is not compatible with pluralist democracy, civil liberties or the democratic ideal,[10] as wearing a headscarf covering the face violates the European standards of 'living together'.[11]

Aversion to Islam seems to be a reaction that points beyond the context of human rights protection, as if it indicated a kind of self-defence reflex of Europe reflected in the relevant decisions of individual states and the ECtHR. This might weaken the system protecting fundamental rights, in a way which goes beyond the direct consequences of concrete cases—applying different standards to different religions when ensuring the right to freedom of religion will lead to a general weakening of the protection provided for this right, not only regarding Islam. Restricting freedom of religion due to cultural considerations might also serve as a basis for restrictions on practising other religions not affected by a concrete case. Notably, although the ECtHR did not avoid evaluating certain individual manifestations of Islam, even if in an indirect way, and even compared them to some elements of European civilisation, it has mostly refrained from making references to the social role played by Christianity. It is true that, at the same time, the ECtHR has delivered several judgments related to freedom of expression

9 App nos 41340/98, 41342/98, 41343/98 and 41344/98, judgment of 13 February 2003.

10 *Ibid*, para 44.

11 *SAS v France*, App no 43855/11, judgment of 26 June 2014.

which were favourable to Christianity (the case of the crucifix at school,[12] or worn on a necklace[13]), or approving the decisions of domestic courts which ruled against those offending Christian believers (blasphemy[14]). However, the ECtHR did not make it clear whether it sees any theoretical difference between the two religions when judging the degree of protection granted for opinions rooted in Christianity or Islam. This means that whereas it provides an overall stronger protection to Christianity, its theoretical foundations are uncertain and remains at the level of enigmatic references made to the significance of Christianity in a European context, such as in the second *Lautsi* judgment. This stronger protection granted to Christianity is not applied in a consistent manner (see the *Murphy* case[15]), which further increases the uncertainty.

Furthermore, the need to combat radical Islam seems to be a useful excuse when arguing in favour of excluding Christianity from public life in the spirit of radical secularisation. In this vein, arguments can be raised to support the position that exercising freedom of religion should generally be exiled into the private sphere, and that the secular state can hardly tolerate religion in public life (not to mention giving preference to any of them on the grounds of tradition and history[16]). In several respects, this position would judge Christianity and Islam as representing nearly identical potential threats to European democracy and civil liberties. The appearance of Islam in Europe results in processes running counter to the above. Population decline has been followed by an apparently unstoppable wave of immigration, as well as the perceived difficulties of multiculturalism in practice. These devel-

12 *Lautsi and Others v Italy*, App no 30814/06, judgment of 18 March 2011 [GC].

13 *Eweida and Others v the United Kingdom*, App nos 48420/10, 59842/10, 51671/10 and 36516/10, judgment of 15 January 2013.

14 *Otto-Preminger-Institut v Austria*, App no 13470/87, judgment of 20 September 1994.

15 *Murphy v Ireland*, App no 44179/98, judgment of 10 July 2003.

16 András Sajó, 'Preliminaries to a Concept of Constitutional Secularism', (2008) 6(3–4) *International Journal of Constitutional Law* 605.

opments have led many to fear that the remaining Christian character of the continent will soon be a thing of the past.[17] Thus, arguments against Islam gaining ground and having equal status as far as fundamental rights are concerned stem from two very different sources—one is radical secularism, the other is Christianity.

The third question: In what ways should hostile attitudes towards religious communities be countered? Religion-based hatred was not imported to the continent by radical Islam, far from it. Europe has serious, long-standing historical traditions of exterminating certain religious communities or forcing them to change their identities. Racism and anti-Semitism are omnipresent in Europe regardless of Islam, and the protection granted to freedom of speech implies the possibility to defame majority communities and incite hatred against them. The issues of blasphemy and hate speech discussed in this book are inextricably linked to one another and prove extremely difficult to separate. Although we unequivocally ruled out the possibility of legitimising the protection of religions and churches against hostile attitudes, offences against the religion and the church actually offend believers as individuals, the same way as incitement to hatred against or defamation of a community might infringe upon the rights of the members, even if not targeted individually, of the given community. Under certain conditions, imposing limits on religious defamation is not disallowable, or at least, we did not find it in conflict with the European principles and recognised theories of freedom of speech, and the same applies to the full liberalisation of blasphemy. Hate speech beyond the limits of blasphemy is a different matter, with the general prohibition of 'incitement to hatred' and 'instigation of hatred' set forth in legal provisions.[18]

***

17 Kenneth L. Woodward, 'An Oxymoron: Europe without Christianity', *New York Times*, 14 June 2003.

18 *Blasphemy, Insult and Hatred: Finding Answers in a Democratic Society* (Council of Europe 2010), http://www.venice.coe.int/webforms/documents/?pdf=CDL-STD(2010)047-e.

The individual European states and the United States, which is under close scrutiny in several chapters of this book, show a wide range of approaches or attitudes to the issue of religion in public life. This diversity may actually be appreciated as a value, and it is laudable of the ECtHR that it has not made any attempt to standardise the various approaches 'on the drawing board'. At present, in Europe, there is no single, uniform legal approach to the questions pertaining to the right to freedom of religion and speech discussed in this book. The frequent reference made by the ECtHR to the margin of appreciation principle is a recognition of this fact in practice.[19] At the same time, even if it allows this margin of appreciation, the ECtHR has made efforts to define certain criteria, which are to be carefully weighed up by state authorities before they adopt decisions limiting certain rights. On some questions, such as religious education[20] or blasphemy,[21] these criteria are detailed and well-established, while on others, such as the crucifix at schools[22] and religious advertisements in the media,[23] they are vague. The ECtHR has gone furthest in standardisation with respect to hate speech, where—obviously partly due to the high number of cases—some sort of European lowest common denominator can also be identified regarding the protection of communities and the degree of protection to be granted to hateful opinions.[24] However, the decisions handed down by the ECtHR, which lets states decide on the restriction of opinions with religious content (headscarves[25] and adverts in the media), so far have not been convincing enough to justify the acceptability of limitations imposed by the state. Furthermore, they contradict other decisions of the same court protecting

19 Andrew Legg, *The Margin of Appreciation in International Human Rights Law. Deference and Proportionality* (Oxford University Press 2012).

20 *Grzelak v Poland*, App no 7710/02, judgment of 22 November 2010.

21 *Otto-Preminger-Institut v Austria*, App no 13470/87, judgment of 20 September 1994.

22 *Lautsi* (n 12).

23 *Murphy v Ireland*, App no 44179/98, judgment of 10 July 2003.

24 See Framework decision on Racism and Xenophobia 2008/913/JHA.

25 *SAS v France* (n 11).

freedom of religion and speech, rendering opinions with religious content 'inferior' to other opinions in the public sphere.[26]

***

Nowadays, Europe is in dire straits. Not only does she have difficulties finding her own identity and reconciling historical traditions with modern democracy, she also finds that this vaguely defined identity, not exactly deeply rooted in a broad spectrum of societies or identified with by them, is exposed to grave attacks from outside, some slow and moderate, others rapid and violent. European diversity is a historically rooted feature, a treasure of key importance, determining her image, which is not to be 'trimmed'. However, in order to protect the 'European character' of Europe, it would be desirable to agree upon a framework into which this diversity of values, including religious traditions and the secular state, can fit together. Protecting human rights and finding the right balance between them may prove to be such a framework.

Non-Christian immigrants arriving in Europe and being accommodated there *en masse* have to be granted the same human rights as native Europeans. This does not include cases of 'government speech', when judicial decisions attribute decisive importance to historical traditions and the cultural self-identity of a state. That is, even if the crucifix can remain fixed upon the walls of state schools, and religious education can continue to be part of school curricula, for the time being, similar arguments could hardly be raised in favour of displaying the crescent in the same way or introducing mandatory Islamic religious education (at least as long as the cultural characteristics of European states do not undergo a profound change). However, from the equal right to freedom of religion could be derived the right to wear clothes of one's own choosing, which is currently not granted everywhere in Europe to the followers of Islam. If we are concerned that *burqas* are a threat to European culture and values—and we cannot rule out the possibility that there might be some grounds to justify that—

26 On this, see Tom Lewis & Peter Cumper, 'Taking Religion Seriously? Human Rights and Hijab in Europe: Some Problems of Adjudication', (2009) 24 *Journal of Law and Religion* 599, 619–27.

we should find other ways to protect them. Imposing restrictions on the right to freedom of religion and speech cannot effectively resolve this problem. Moreover, such restrictions violate European culture and its values which need to be protected. Should we wish to preserve the current image of Europe (including Christianity and secularism contending with one another), we must do more than trimming the essence of certain human rights; this is insufficient and counter-productive. Should we wish to protect secular Europe, we should opt for an efficient way of doing so, by coming to an agreement with Christianity. If the state and its legal system are at war with Christianity, depriving Europe of the support provided by her historical traditions and further undermining her self-identity, that will make her exposed and vulnerable to external forces that may also seek to deny Christian traditions.

The sight of thousands of refugees around us, and of the powerful politicians of wealthy, developed Western European societies at a loss, desperately trying to find solutions to keep the situation under control might suggest that the meticulous scrutiny and application of refined standards of fundamental rights does not necessarily merit particular attention. However, Europe as we know her, our home, with her rich culture setting an example for the rest of the world, her economic prosperity and flourishing education and her erudition, is also present in such legal niceties as the standards of freedom of religion and speech. Appropriate responses to the questions of fundamental rights will enhance the chances of preserving Europe's power and civilisation, and changes in attitudes to them will serve as a litmus paper to indicate whether Europe is faltering, should that come to pass.

Index

Selected Bibliography

Abbott, Greg, 'Upholding the Unbroken Tradition: Constitutional Acknowledgement of the Ten Commandments in the Public Square', (2005–06) 14 *William & Mary Bill of Rights Law Journal* 51.

Adenitire, John, '*SAS v France*: Fidelity to Law and Conscience', (2015) 22 *European Human Rights Law Review* 78.

Ahdar, Rex (ed), *Law and Religion* (Ashgate 2000)

Ahdar, Rex & Leigh, Ian, *Religious Freedom in the Liberal State* (Oxford University Press 2nd edn 2013)

Andreescu, Gabriel & Andreescu, Liviu, 'The European Court of Human Rights' *Lautsi* Decision: Context, Contents, Consequences', (2010) 9(26) *Journal for the Study of Religions and Ideologies* 47.

Angeletti, Silvia, 'Blasphemy Laws and Incitement to Religious Hatred: Italian Legal Standards and Social Developments', (2014) 9(2–3) *Religion and Human Rights* 192.

Annicchino, Pasquale, 'Is the Glass Half Empty or Half Full? *Lautsi v Italy* Before the European Court of Human Rights', (2010) *Stato, Chiese e Pluralismo Confessionale* http://papers.ssrn.com/sol3/papers.cfm?abstract_id=2200063

Appignanesi, Lisa & Maitland, Sara (eds), *The Rushdie File* (Syracuse University Press 1990)

Arribas, Santiago Canamares, 'Religious Freedom and Freedom of Expression in Spain', (2014) 9(2–3) *Religion and Human Rights* 209.

Audi, Robert, *Democratic Authority and the Separation of Church and State* (Oxford University Press 2011)

Audi, Robert & Wolterstorff, Nicholas, *Religion in the Public Square: The Place of Religious Convictions in Political Debate* (Rowman & Littlefield 1997)

Baker, Edwin C, *Human Liberty and Freedom of Speech* (Oxford University Press 1989)

Barclay, Stephanie, 'Passive Acknowledgement or Active Promotion of Religion? Neutrality and the Ten Commandments in *Green v Haskell*', (2010) *Brigham Young University Law Review* 3.

Barendt, Eric, 'Teaching Evolution, Creationism, and Intelligent Design in US Schools (With Some European Comparisons)' in Myriam Hunter-Henin (ed), *Law, Religious Freedoms and Education in Europe* (Ashgate 2011) 267–81.

—— *Freedom of Speech* (Oxford University Press 2nd edn 2005)

Blackford, Russell, *Freedom of Religion and the Secular State* (John Wiley 2012)

Blackstone, William, *Commentaries on the Laws of England* (Cavendish 2001)

Bollinger, Lee C, *The Tolerant Society* (Oxford University Press 1986)

Bradley, Gerard V, *Challenges to Religious Liberty in the Twenty-First Century* (Cambridge University Press 2012)

Brettschneider, Corey, *When the State Speaks, What Should it Say? How Democracies can Protect Expression and Promote Equality* (Princeton University Press 2012)

Brugger, Winfried, 'Zum Verhältnis von Neutralitätsliberalismus und liberalem Kommunitarismus – Dargestellt am Streit über das Kreuz in der Schule' in Winfried Brugger & Stefan Huster (ed), *Der Streit um das Kreuz in der Schule* (Nomos Verlagsgesellschaft 1998) 109–54.

—— 'The Treatment of Hate Speech in German Constitutional Law', (2003) 4(1) *German Law Journal* 1.

Calo, Zachary R, 'Pluralism, Secularism and the European Court of Human Rights', (2010–2011) 26(1) *Journal of Law & Religion* 101.

Cannie, Hannes & Voorhoof, Dirk, 'The Abuse Clause and Freedom of Expression in the European Human Rights Convention: An Added Value for Democracy and Human Rights Protection?', (2011) 29(1) *Netherlands Quarterly of Human Rights* 54.

Chemerinsky, Erwin, 'A Dangerous Free Speech Ruling', (2009) 45 *Trial* 60.

Cox, Neville, 'Blasphemy, Holocaust Denial, and the Control of Profoundly Unacceptable Speech', (2014) 62 *The American Journal of Comparative Law* 739.

—— 'Pourquoi Suis-Je Charlie? Blasphemy, Defamation of Religion, and the Nature of "Offensive" Cartoons', (2015) *Oxford Journal of Law and Religion* 1.

—— 'The Freedom to Publish "Irreligious" Cartoons', (2016) *Human Rights Law Review* 1.

Cram, Ian, 'The Danish Cartoons, Offensive Expression, and Democratic Legitimacy' in Ivan Hare & James Weinstein (eds), *Extreme Speech and Democracy* (Oxford University Press 2009) 311–30.

Crawford, Allison N, 'Learning Lessons from *Multani*: Considering Canada's Response to Religious Garb Issues in Public Schools', (2007) 36 *Georgia Journal of International & Comparative Law* 159.

Croghan, Katie A, 'Lautsi and Salazar: Are Religious Symbols Legitimate in the Public Square?', (2013) 41 *Georgia Journal of International and Comparative Law* 507.

Cumper, Peter, 'Religious Education in Europe in the Twenty-First Century' in Myriam Hunter-Henin (ed), *Law, Religious Freedoms and Education in Europe* (Ashgate 2011) 207–27.

Danchin, Peter G, 'Suspect Symbols: Value Pluralism as a Theory of Religious Freedom in International Law', (2008) 33(1) *The Yale Journal of International Law* 1.

—— 'Defaming Muhammad: Dignity, Harm, and Incitement to Religious Hatred', (2010) 2 *Duke Forum for Law & Social Change* 5.

Delgado, Richard, 'Words that Wound: A Tort Action for Racial Insults, Epithets and Name-calling', (1982) 17 *Harvard Civil Right – Civil Liberties Law Review* 133.

Doe, Norman, *Law and Religion in Europe. A Comparative Introduction* (Oxford University Press 2011)

Dolan, Mary Jean, 'Government Identity Speech and Religion: Establishment Clause Limits after Summum', (2010) 19 *William & Mary Bill of Rights Law Journal* 1.

Douglas, Lawrence, 'Policing the Past: Holocaust Denial and the Law' in Robert Post (ed), *Censorship and Silencing: Practices of Cultural Regulation* (Getty Research Institute for the History of Art and the Humanities 1998) 67–88.

Dow, David R, 'The Moral Failure of the Clear and Present Danger Test', (1998) 6(3) *William and Mary Bill of Rights Journal* 733.

Dunlap, Bridgette, 'Protecting the Space to be Unveiled: Why France's Full Veil Ban does not Violate the European Convention on Human Rights', (2012) 35 *Fordham International Law Journal* 968.

Dworkin, Ronald, *Taking Rights Seriously* (Harvard University Press 1977)

—— *Freedom's Law. The Moral Reading of the American Constitution* (Oxford University Press 1996)

—— 'The Right to Ridicule', *New York Review of Books*, 23 March 2006

—— 'Foreword' in Ivan Hare & James Weinstein (eds), *Extreme Speech and Democracy* (Oxford University Press 2009) v–ix.

—— *Religion without God* (Harvard University Press 2013)

Elias, Sir Patrick & Coppel, Jason, 'Freedom of Expression and Freedom of Religion: Some Thoughts on the Glenn Hoddle Case' in Jack Beatson & Yvonne Cripps (eds), *Freedom of Expression and Freedom of Information. Essays in Honour of Sir David Williams* (Oxford University Press 2000) 51–61.

Ellis, Anthony, 'What is Special about Religion?', (2006) 25 *Law and Philosophy* 219.

Ely, John Hart, *Democracy and Distrust. A Theory of Judicial Review* (Harvard University Press 1981)

Evans, Carolyn, 'The "Islamic Scarf" in the European Court of Human Rights', (2006) 7 *Melbourne Journal of International Law* 3.

—— 'Religious Education in Public Schools: An International Human Rights Perspective', (2008) 8(3) *Human Rights Law Review* 449.

Fenwick, Helen & Phillipson, Gavin, *Media Freedom under the Human Rights Act* (Oxford University Press 2006)

Fish, Stanley, *There's No Such Thing as Free Speech and It's a Good Thing, too* (Oxford University Press 1994)

—— 'When is a Cross a Cross?' NYTimes.com, 3 May 2010, opinionator.blogs.nytimes.com/2010/05/03/when-is-a-cross-a-cross/?_r=0

Fiss, Owen M, 'The Supreme Court and the Problem of Hate Speech', (1995) 24 *Capital University Law Review* 281.

—— *The Irony of Free Speech* (Harvard University Press 1996)

Fokas, Effie, 'Directions in Religious Pluralism in Europe: Mobilizations in the Shadow of European Court of Human Rights Religious Freedom Jurisprudence', (2015) 4(1) *Oxford Journal of Law and Religion* 1.

Garnett, Richard W, 'Religion, Division, and the First Amendment', (2005–06) 94 *Georgetown Law Journal* 1667.

Geddis, Andrew, 'You can't Say "God" on the Radio: Freedom of Expression, Religious Advertising and the Broadcast Media after *Murphy v Ireland*', (2004) 11 *European Human Rights Law Review* 181.

Graber, Mark A, 'Old Wine in New Bottles: The Constitutional Status of Unconstitutional Speech', (1995) 48 *Vanderbilt Law Review* 349.

Green, Todd, 'The Resistance to Minarets in Europe', (2010) 52 *Journal of Church and State* 619.

Greenawalt, Kent, *Does God Belong to Public Schools?* (Princeton University Press 2005)

—— *Religion and the Constitution.* Vol 1, 'Free Exercise and Fairness' (Princeton University Press 2006)

—— *Religion and the Constitution.* Vol 2, 'Establishment and Fairness' (Princeton University Press 2009)

Griffin, Leslie C, 'Fighting the New Wars of Religion: The Need for a Tolerant First Amendment', (2010) 62 *Maine Law Review* 23.

Gunn, T Jeremy, 'Religious Freedom and Laicite: A Comparison of the United States and France', (2004) *Brigham Young University Law Review* 419.

Haarscher, Guy, 'Free Speech, Religion, and the Right to Caricature' in András Sajó (ed), *Censorial Sensitivities. Free Speech and Religion in a Fundamentalist World* (Eleven International Publishing 2006)

Habermas, Jürgen, *Time of Transitions* (Polity 2006)

Hambler, Andrew, *Religious Expression in the Workplace and the Contested Role of Law* (Routledge 2015)

Hare, Ivan, 'Blasphemy and Incitement to Religious Hatred: Free Speech Dogma and Doctrine' in Ivan Hare & James Weinstein (eds), *Extreme Speech and Democracy* (Oxford University Press 2009) 289–310.

Harris, DJ, O'Boyle, M, Bates, EP, Buckley, CM, *Harris, O'Boyle & Warbrick Law of the European Convention on Human Rights* (Oxford University Press 2nd edn 2009)

Heyman, Steven J, *Free Speech & Human Dignity* (Yale University Press 2008)

Hill, Daniel J & Whistler, Daniel, *The Right to Wear Religious Symbols* (Palgrave MacMillan 2013)

—— 'Religious Symbols and the European Convention on Human Rights', (2013) 171 *Law & Justice* 52.

Hill, Mark, 'Is Nothing Sacred? Clashing Symbols in a Secular world', (2007) *Public Law* 488.

—— 'Bracelets, Rings, and Veils: The Accommodation of Religious Symbols in the Uniform Policies of English Schools' in Myriam Hunter-Henin (ed), *Law, Religious Freedoms and Education in Europe* (Ashgate 2011) 307–26.

—— 'Religious Symbolism and Conscientious Objection in the Workplace: An Evaluation of Strasbourg's Judgment in *Eweida and Others v United Kingdom*', (2013) 15(2) *Ecclesiastical Law Journal* 191.

Howard, Erica, 'School Bans on the Wearing of Religious Symbols: Examining the Implications of Recent Case Law from the UK', (2009) 4 *Religion and Human Rights* 7.

—— *Law and the Wearing of Religious Symbols* (Routledge 2012)

—— 'Protecting Freedom to Manifest one's Religion or Belief: Strasbourg of Luxembourg?', (2014) 32(2) *Netherlands Quarterly of Human Rights* 159.

Hunter-Henin, Myriam (ed), *Law, Religious Freedoms and Education in Europe* (Ashgate 2011)

Huster, Stefan, 'Die religiös-weltanschauliche Neutraliät des Staates – Das Kreuz in der Schule aus liberalem Sicht' in Winfried Brugger & Stefan Huster (ed), *Der Streit um das Kreuz in der Schule* (Nomos Verlagsgesellschaft 1998) 69–108.

Jacob, Katherine AE, 'Defending Blasphemy: Exploring Religious Expression Under Ireland's Blasphemy Law', (2011) 44 *Case Western Reserve Journal of International Law* 803.

Kahn, Robert A, 'The Headscarf as Threat: A Comparison of German and US Legal Discourses', (2007) 40 *Vanderbilt Journal of Transnational Law* 417.

—— 'Why there Was No Cartoon Controversy in the US', *University of St Thomas Legal Studies Research Paper* no 07-28 (2007).

—— 'The Danish Cartoon Controversy and the Rhetoric of Libertarian Regret', (2009) 16 *University of Miami International & Comparative Law Review* 151.

—— 'Flemming Rose, the Danish Cartoon Controversy, and the New European Freedom of Speech', (2010) 40 *California Western International Law Journal* 253.

—— 'Tragedy, Farce, or Legal Mobilization? The Danish Cartoons in Court in France and Canada', *University of St Thomas Legal Studies Research Paper* no 10-21 (2010).

—— 'News Value, Islamophobia, or the First Amendment? Why and How the Philadelphia Inquirer Published the Danish Cartoons', *University of St Thomas Legal Studies Research Paper* no 10-07 (2010).

—— 'Are Muslims the New Catholics? Europe's Headscarf Laws in Comparative Historical Perspective', (2011) 21 *Duke Journal of Comparative & International Law* 567.

—— 'A Margin of Appreciation for Muslims? Viewing the Defamation of Religions Debate Through *Otto-Preminger-Institut v Austria*', (2011) 5 *Charleston Law Review* 401.

—— 'Flemming Rose's Rejection of the American Free Speech Canon and the Poverty of Comparative Constitutional Theory' (2014) 39 *Brooklyn Journal of International Law* 657.

Kalven Jr, Harry, *A Worthy Tradition: Freedom of Speech in America* (Harper and Row 1988)

Kearns, Paul, *Freedom of Artistic Expression. Essays on Culture and Legal Censure* (Oregon, Hart 2013)

Keller, Perry, *European and International Media Law. Liberal Democracy, Trade, and the New Media* (Oxford University Press 2011)

Knechtle, John C, 'Holocaust Denial and the Concept of Dignity in the European Union', (2008) 36 *Florida State University Law Review* 41.

Kommers, Donald P & Miller, Russell A, *The Constitutional Jurisprudence of the Federal Republic of Germany* (Duke University Press 3rd edn 2012)

Kosse, Susan Hanley, 'A Missed Opportunity to Abandon the Reasonable Observer Framework in Sacred Text Cases: *McCreary County v ACLU* of Kentucky and *Van Orden v Perry*', (2005–2006) 4 *First Amendment Law Review* 139.

Kurland, Seth, 'The Religion Clauses and the Burger Court', (1984) 34 *Catholic University Law Review* 1.

Lamb, Rob, 'When Human Rights Have Gone too Far: Religious Tradition and Equality in *Lautsi v Italy*', (2011) 36 *North Carolina Journal of International Law and Commercial Regulation* 751.

Lasson, Kenneth, 'Group Libel Versus Free Speech: When Big Brother Should Butt In', (1984–1985) 23 *Duquesne Law Review* 77.

Laycock, Douglas, 'Theology Scholarships, the Pledge of Allegiance, and Religious Liberty: Avoiding the Extremes but Missing the Liberty', (2004) 118 *Harvard Law Review* 155.

—— 'Government-Sponsored Religious Displays: Transparent Rationalizations and Expedient Post-Modernism', (2011) 61 *Case Western Reserve Law Review* 1211.

Legg, Andrew, *The Margin of Appreciation in International Human Rights Law. Deference and Proportionality* (Oxford University Press 2012)

Leigh, Ian, 'Objective, Critical and Pluralistic? Religious Education and Human Rights in the European Public Sphere' in Lorenzo Zucca & Camil Ungureanu (eds), *Law, State, and Religion in the New Europe. Debates and Dilemmas* (Cambridge University Press 2012) 192–214.

—— 'The European Court of Human Rights and Religious Neutrality' in Gavin d'Costa & Malcolm Evans & Tariq Moodood & Julian Rivers (eds), *Religion in a Liberal State* (Cambridge University Press 2013) 38–66.

Leigh, Ian & Hambler, Andrew, 'Religious Symbols, Conscience, and the Rights of Others', (2014) 3(1) *Oxford Journal of Law and Religion* 2.

Letsas, George, 'Is there a Right not to be Offended in One's Religious Beliefs?' in Lorenzo Zucca & Camil Ungureanu (eds), *Law, State, and Religion in the New Europe. Debates and Dilemmas* (Cambridge University Press 2012) 239–60.

Levinson, Sanford, 'The Tutelary State: "Censorship", "Silencing", and the "Practices of Cultural Regulation"' in Robert Post (ed), *Censorship and Silencing: The Practices of Cultural Regulation* (Getty Research Institute for the History of Art and the Humanities 1998) 195–220.

Levy, Leonard W, *Blasphemy: Verbal Offense Against the Sacred, From Moses to Salman Rushdie* (Alfred A Knopf 1993)

Lewis, Tom, 'What Not to Wear: Religious Rights, the European Court and the Margin of Appreciation', (2007) 56 *International and Comparative Law Quarterly* 395.

—— 'From Activism to Self-restraint: The Strange Case of the European Court's Volte-face on Broadcasting Bans on Political Advertising' in András Koltay (ed), *Media Freedom and Regulation in the New Media World* (Wolters Kluwer 2014) 565–90.

Lewis, Tom & Cumper, Peter, 'Taking Religion Seriously? Human Rights and Hijab in Europe: Some Problems of Adjudication', (2009) 24(2) *Journal of Law and Religion* 599.

Linkner, Adam, 'How *Salazar v Buono* Synthesizes the Supreme Court's Establishment Clause Precedent into a Single Test', (2011) 25 *Emory International Law Review* 57.

Liu, Hin-Yan, 'The Meaning of Religious Symbols after the Grand Chamber Judgment in *Lautsi v Italy*', (2011) 6(3) *Religion & Human Rights* 253.

Lock, Tobias, 'Of Crucifixes and Headscarves: Religious Symbols in German Schools' in Myriam Hunter-Henin (ed), *Law, Religious Freedoms and Education in Europe* (Ashgate 2011) 347–69.

Mahoney, Paul, 'Universality Versus Subsidiarity in the Strasbourg Case Law on Free Speech: Explaining some Recent Judgments', (1997) 4 *European Human Rights Law Review* 364.

—— 'Marvellous Richness of Diversity or Invidious Cultural Relativism?', (1998) 19 *Human Rights Law Journal* 1.

Mancini, Susanna, 'The Crucifix Rage: Supranational Constitutionalism Bumps Against the Counter-Majoritarian Difficulty', (2010) 6 *European Constitutional Law Review* 6.

Mancini, Susanna & Rosenfeld, Michel, 'Unveiling the Limits of Tolerance: Comparing the Treatment of Majority and Minority Religious Symbols in the Public Sphere' in Lorenzo Zucca & Camil Ungureanu (eds), *Law, State, and Religion in the New Europe. Debates and Dilemmas* (Cambridge University Press 2012) 160–91.

—— (eds), *Constitutional Secularism in an Age of Religious Revival* (Oxford University Press 2014)

Marshall, Jill, '*SAS v France*: Burqa Bans and the Control or Empowerment of Identities', (2015) 15(2) *Human Rights Law Review* 377.

Massaro, Toni M, 'Equality and Freedom of Expression: The Hate Speech Dilemma', (1990–1991) 32 *William and Mary Law Review* 211.

Matsuda, Mari J, 'Public Response to Racist Speech: Considering the Victim's Story', (1989) 87(8) *Michigan Law Review* 2320.

Mawhinney, Alison & Niens, Ulrike & Richardson, Norman & Chiba, Yuko, 'Religious Education and Religious Liberty: Opt-Outs and Young People's Sense of Belonging' in Myriam Hunter-Henin (ed), *Law, Religious Freedoms and Education in Europe* (Ashgate 2011) 229–49.

McCauliff, Catherine MA, 'Religion and the Secular State', (2010) 58 *American Journal of Comparative Law* 31.

McConnell, Michael, 'Five Reasons to Reject the Claim that Religious Arguments Should Be Excluded from Democratic Deliberation', (1999) *Utah Law Review* 639.

McCrudden, Christopher, 'Freedom of Speech and Racial Equality' in Peter BH Birks (ed), *Criminal Justice and Human Rights* (Oxford University Press 1995)

McGoldrick, Dominic, *Human Rights and Religion: the Islamic Headscarf Debate in Europe* (Hart 2006)

—— 'Extreme Religious Dress: Perspectives on Veiling Controversies' in Ivan Hare & James Weinstein (eds), *Extreme Speech and Democracy* (Oxford University Press 2009) 400–29.

Montgomery, John W, 'Can Blasphemy Law Be Justified?', (2002) *Law & Justice* 6.

Muehlhoff, Inke, 'Freedom of Religion in Public Schools in Germany and in the United States', (2000) 28 *Georgia Journal of International & Comparative Law* 405.

Murphy, Elizabeth A, 'Courts Mistakenly Cross-Out Memorials: Why the Establishment Clause is not Violated by Roadside Crosses', (2011) 39 *Hofstra Law Review* 723.

Noorlander, Peter, 'In Fear of Cartoons', (2015) 22 *European Human Rights Law Review* 115.

Note, 'A Communitarian Defense of Group Libel Laws', (1987–88) 101 *Harvard Law Review* 682.

Oetheimer, Mario, 'Protecting Freedom of Expression: The Challenge of Hate Speech in the European Court of Human Rights Case Law', (2009) 17 *Cardozo Journal of International & Comparative Law* 427.

Ooijen, Hana van, *Religious Symbols in Public Functions: A Comparative Analysis of Dutch, English and French Justifications for Limiting the Freedom of Public Officials to Display Religious Symbols* (Intersentia 2012)

Ovey, Claire & White, Robin, *Jacobs and White: European Convention on Human Rights* (Oxford University Press 4th edn 2006)

Park, Daniel W, 'Government Speech and the Public Forum: A Clash between Democratic and Egalitarian Values', (2009–10) 45 *Gonzaga Law Review* 113.

Patrick, Jeremy, 'Canadian Blasphemy Law in Context: Press, Legislative, and Public Reactions', (2010) 16 *Annual Survey of International and Comparative Law* 129.

Perkins, Teresa, 'Unveiling Muslim Women: The Constitutionality of Hijab Restrictions in Turkey, Tunisia, and Kosovo', (2012) 30(2) *Boston University International Law Journal* 551.

Perry, Michael J, *Toward a Theory of Human Rights: Religion, Law, Courts* (Cambridge University Press 2006)

Post, Robert C, 'Cultural Heterogeneity and Law: Pornography, Blasphemy, and the First Amendment', (1988) 76 *California Law Review* 297.

—— 'The Constitutional Concept of Public Discourse: Outrageous Opinion, Democratic Deliberation and *Hustler Magazine v Falwell*', (1990) 103 *Harvard Law Review* 601.

—— 'Racist Speech, Democracy and the First Amendment', (1990–91) 32 *William and Mary Law Review* 267.

—— 'Meiklejohn's Mistake: Individual Autonomy and the Reform of Public Discourse', (1993) 64 *University of Colorado Law Review* 1109.

—— *Constitutional Domains: Democracy, Community, Management* (Harvard University Press 1995)

—— 'Religion and Freedom of Speech: Portraits of Muhammad' in András Sajó (ed), *Censorial Sensitivities. Free Speech and Religion in a Fundamentalist World* (Eleven International Publishing 2006) 329–351.

Puppinck, Grégor, 'An Alliance Against Secularism', *L'Osservatore Romano*, 28 July 2010

Ragep Powell, Lina, 'The Constitutionality of France's Ban on the Burqa in Light of the European Convention's *Arslan v Turkey* Decision on Religious Freedom', (2013) 31(1) *Wisconsin International Law Journal* 118.

Rassbach, Eric, 'The Persistence of Memory', *The Becket Fund*, 25 March 2011 www.becketfund.org/the-persistence-of-memory/

Reichman, Amnon, 'Criminalizing Religiously Offensive Satire: Free Speech, Human Dignity, and Comparative Law' in Ivan Hare & James Weinstein (eds), *Extreme Speech and Democracy* (Oxford University Press 2009) 331–54.

Ringelheim, Julie, 'Rights, Religion, and the Public Sphere: The European Court of Human Rights in Search of a Theory?' in Lorenzo

Zucca and Camil Ungureanu (eds), *Law, State, and Religion in the New Europe. Debates and Dilemmas* (Cambridge University Press 2012) 283–306.

Rollinson, Katherine A, 'An Analysis of Blasphemy Legislation in Contemporary Ireland and its Effects upon Freedom of Expression in Literary and Artistic Works', (2011) 39 *Syracuse Journal of International Law and Commerce* 189.

Roper, Marie E, 'Secular Crosses and the Neutrality of Secularism: Reflections on the Demands of Neutrality and its Consequences for Religious Symbols. The European Court of Human Rights in *Lautsi* and the US Supreme Court in *Salazar*', (2012) 45 *Vanderbilt Journal of Transnational Law* 841.

Roseberry, Lynn, 'Religion, Ethnicity and Gender in the Danish Headscarf Debate' in Dagmar Schiek & Victoria Chege (eds), *European Union Non-Discrimination Law. Comparative Perspectives on Multidimensional Equality Law* (Routledge/Cavendish 2008) 331–38.

Sadurski, Wojciech, *Freedom of Speech and its Limits* (Kluwer Academic Publishers 1999)

Sajó, András, 'Countervailing Duties as Applied to Danish Cheese and Danish Cartoons' in András Sajó (ed), *Censorial Sensitivities. Free Speech and Religion in a Fundamentalist World* (Eleven International Publishing 2006) 273–307.

—— 'Preliminaries to a Concept of Constitutional Secularism', (2008) 6(3–4) *International Journal of Constitutional Law* 605.

—— 'The Crisis That Was Not There: Notes on a Reply', (2009) 7(3) *International Journal of Constitutional Law* 515.

Sandberg, Russell & Doe, Norman, 'The Strange Death of Blasphemy', (2008) 71 *The Modern Law Review* 971.

Sari, Ariel, 'The Danish Cartoons Row: Re-Drawing the Limits of the Right to Freedom of Expression?', (2005) 16 *Finnish Yearbook of International Law* 365.

Schauer, Frederick, 'Is Government Speech a Problem?', (1983) 35 *Stanford Law Review* 373.

—— 'Slippery Slopes', (1985) 99 *Harvard Law Review* 361.

—— 'On the Relation between Chapters One and Two of John Stuart Mill's *On Liberty*', (2011) 39 *Capital University Law Review* 571.

Sedley, Stephen, *Ashes and Sparks. Essays on Law and Justice* (Cambridge University Press 2011)

Siedentop, Larry, *Inventing the Individual: The Origins of Western Liberalism* (Allen Lane 2014)

Smet, Stijn, '*Lautsi v Italy*: The Argument from Neutrality', *Strasbourg Observers,* 22 March 2011

Smith, Steven D, 'Religious Symbols and Secular Government', (2013) 46(2) *Israel Law Review* 193.

Stone, Geoffrey R & Seidman, Louis M & Sunstein, Cass R & Tushnet, Mark V & Karlan, Pamela S, *The First Amendment* (Aspen 3rd edn 2008)

Strand, Vibeke Blaker, 'Prohibitions against Religious Clothing and Symbols in Public Schools and Universities: Narrowing the Scope by Introducing the Principle of Equal Treatment of Religious Manifestations', (2015) 10(2) *Religion & Human Rights* 160.

Taylor, Paul M, *Freedom of Religion. UN and European Human Rights Law and Practice* (Cambridge University Press 2005)

Temperman, Jeroen, 'The Neutral State: Optional or Necessary? A Triangular Analysis of State-Religion Relationships, Democratisation, and Human Rights Compliance', (2006) 1(3) *Religion & Human Rights* 269.

—— 'Blasphemy, Defamation of Religions and Human Rights Law', (2008) (26)4 *Netherlands Quarterly of Human Rights* 517.

—— *State–Religion Relationships and Human Rights Law: Towards a Right to Religiously Neutral Governance* (Brill 2010)

—— 'Freedom of Expression and Religious Sensitivities in Pluralist Societies: Facing the Challenge of Extreme Speech', (2011) *Brigham Young University Law Review* 729.

—— (ed), *The Lautsi Papers: Multidisciplinary Reflections on Religious Symbols in the Public School Classroom* (Brill/Martinus Nijhoff 2012)

—— 'Of Crosses and Homophobia', (2013) 2(12) *Arbeidsrechtelijke Annotaties* 87.

—— 'Prohibitions of Incitement under International Law: The Case of Religion' in András Koltay (ed), *Media Freedom and Regulation in the New Media World* (Wolters Kluwer 2014) 459–70.

Török, Bernát, 'Can Religions or Religious People Be Protected against Blasphemy? Comments on the Case Law of the European Court of Human Rights' in András Koltay (ed), *Media Freedom and Regulation in the New Media World* (Wolters Kluwer 2014) 509–31.

Trispiotis, Ilias, 'The Duty to Respect Religious Feelings: Insights from European Human Rights Law', (2013) 19 *Columbia Journal of European Law* 499.

Waldron, Jeremy, 'Dignity and Defamation: The Visibility of Hate', (2010) 123 *Harvard Law Review* 1596.

—— *The Harm in Hate Speech* (Harvard University Press 2012)

Walker, Clive, 'Terrorism Speech and Militant Democracy' in András Koltay (ed), *Media Freedom and Regulation in the New Media World* (Wolters Kluwer 2014) 471–508.

Wallace, E Gregory, 'When Government Speaks Religiously', (2004) 21 *Florida State University Law Review* 1183.

Weber, Anne, *Manual on Hate Speech* (Council of Europe Publishing 2009)

Weeden, Darnell, 'A First Amendment Establishment Clause Analysis of Permanent Displays on Public Property as Government Speech', (2009–10) 35 *Thurgood Marshall Law Review* 217.

Weil, Patrick, 'Headscarf Versus Burqa: Two French Bans with Different Meanings' in Susanna Mancini & Michel Rosenfeld (eds), *Constitutional Secularism in an Age of Religious Revival* (Oxford University Press 2014) 196–215.

Weiler, Joseph HH, *Un'Europa Cristiana: Un saggio esplorativo* (BUR Saggi 2003)

—— 'The Law of Holocaust Denial in Europe: Towards a (Qualified) EU-wide Criminal Prohibition', NYU School of Law, *The Jean Monnet Working Paper Series*, 2009.

—— 'State and Nation: Church, Mosque and Synagogue. The Trailer', (2010) 8 *International Journal of Constitutional Law* 157.

—— 'Crucifix in the Classroom Redux', (2010) 21 *European Journal of International Law* 1.

—— 'Freedom of Religion and Freedom from Religion: The European Model', (2013) 65(2) *Maine Law Review* 760.

Williams, Adrian Marshall & Cooper, Jonathan, 'Hate Speech, Holocaust Denial and International Human Rights Law', (1999) 6 *European Human Rights Law Review* 593.

Witte, John, 'Lift High the Cross? An American Perspective on *Lautsi v Italy*', (2011) 13(3) *Ecclesiastical Law Journal* 341.

Yudof, Mark G, *When Government Speaks: Politics, Law, and Government Expression in America* (University of California Press 1983)

Yusuf, Hakeem, '*SAS v France*: Supporting "Living Together" or Forced Assimilation?', (2014) 3 *International Human Rights Law Review* 277.

Zick, Timothy, *The Cosmopolitan First Amendment. Protecting Transborder Expressive and Religious Liberties* (Cambridge University Press 2014)

Zucca, Lorenzo, 'The Crisis of the Secular State: A Reply to Professor Sajó', (2009) 7 *International Journal of Constitutional Law* 494.

—— 'Crucifix in the Classroom: The Best Solution to the *Lautsi* Case', *Social Science Research Network*, working paper, August 2010 papers.ssrn.com/sol3/papers.cfm?abstract_id=1664796

—— '*Lautsi*: A Commentary of the Grand Chamber Decision', *Social Science Research Network*, working paper, 14 April 2011 papers.ssrn.com/sol3/papers.cfm?abstract_id=1809577

—— *A Secular Europe. Law and Religion in the European Constitutional Landscape* (Oxford University Press 2012)

Zucca, Lorenzo & Ungureanu, Camil (eds), *Law, State, and Religion in the New Europe. Debates and Dilemmas* (Cambridge University Press 2012)

www.ingramcontent.com/pod-product-compliance
Lightning Source LLC
LaVergne TN
LVHW020643300926
849161LV00004B/790